British Transport Since 1914

An economic history

Derek H. Aldcroft

DAVID & CHARLES

NEWTON ABBOT   LONDON

NORTH POMFRET (VT)   VANCOUVER

HE
243
.A87
1975

Set in 11 on 13 pt Plantin and printed in
Great Britain by John Sherratt & Sons Ltd
for David & Charles (Holdings) Limited
South Devon House   Newton Abbot   Devon

Published in the United States of America
by David & Charles Inc   North Pomfret
Vermont 05053   USA

Published in Canada by Douglas David &
Charles Limited   132 Philip Avenue
North Vancouver BC

To Judith
with gratitude and affection

Contents

7

List of tables

List of half-tone illustrations

Introductory note

by Baron Duckham, general editor

Senior Lecturer in Economic History, University of Strathclyde

Transport history, though by no means the tidiest of disciplines, has attracted enormous attention in recent years. Quite apart from the plethora of enthusiasts' books flooding the market there has also been a quickly expanding literature of more serious work. In preparing this history of British transportation since World War I the author was given a free remit but with two qualifications: that the survey should be reasonably wide-ranging over the various transport media and that the developments should be seen against the background of economic and social change generally.

It is anticipated that this volume will be of particular value to university undergraduates and college students. But it is also my personal hope that it will have a wider, non-academic readership among those who have a genuine interest in the evolution of transport within its historical context.

Dr Aldcroft has an extensive knowledge of both twentieth century economic growth and of transport history. His many works in both areas have justly established him as a recognised authority. Rightly, I believe, the weight of the book's critical comment lies in the period since 1945. These have been—and remain—years of rapid and sometimes bewildering change in all forms of transport. Students at all levels will be grateful to Dr Aldcroft for his clear narrative and forthright comment. The inter-war period has by necessity been dealt with more briefly; but the reader is given a firm outline, while the select bibliography contains ample references to the more specialised work available.

Preface

THIS SURVEY OF BRITISH TRANSPORT since 1914 deals mainly with transport developments within Great Britain, but for completeness I have added sections on aviation and shipping. Obviously in a short volume such as this it is not possible to cover every aspect of the subject, nor is it possible to delve at depth into any particular issue or problem. Thus I hope the reader will forgive the fact that some aspects of the subject, for example waterways and coastal shipping, do not receive full treatment. These are interesting branches of transport it is true, but they are rather overshadowed by more important developments and problems in the main sectors of transport which obviously must take priority.

One main difficulty was deciding on a terminal date. Transport is changing so rapidly, particularly on the governmental policy front, that one is tempted to make last minute news. As far as possible I have resisted this temptation if only for the reason that journalism has never been my forté. That apart, there is an inevitable time-lag in the publication of much official data and so one is effectively cut off a year or two from contemporary events. In any case, the Transport Act of 1968 provided a useful halting point and for the most part I have not gone much beyond this date. Occasionally, where data allowed, or when important changes seemed to merit attention—the recent structural changes in aviation for instance—I have ventured close to the contemporary scene, but apart from this I have aimed to complete the survey up to the end of the 1960s.

Several individuals and authorities have been most helpful in providing assistance in one form or another. In particular I should like to mention the Chamber of Shipping of the UK, Lloyd's Register of Shipping, the British Railways Board, the British Transport Docks Board and the International Civil Aviation Organisation, for providing masses of statistical data, far more in

13

14 PREFACE

fact than I could use. Dr C. Sharp of the Economics Department of the University of Leicester gave me access to some of his material on road transport and also acted as a stimulating debating critic, while Mrs J. Southgate of the Chartered Institute of Transport and Mr G. Ottley of Leicester University Library patiently responded to my many requests for material. To all I am indeed extremely grateful.

The following authorities also very kindly supplied the photographic illustrations: BOAC, British Railways Board, British Petroleum Company Ltd, and Leicester City Transport.

The Houblon-Norman Fund of the Bank of England made a very generous grant towards the cost of financing research on the post-1945 period. Mr P. Bemand, who acted as my research assistant for six months, provided very valuable assistance in collecting and analysing much data, and in many other ways. I should also like to thank the general editor, Baron Duckham, for helpful comments and advice, and my literary agent and good friend, Michael Shaw, for his patience and good humour when handling a demanding author. But the prize bouquet must be reserved for Miss Judith Watts. Once again she rose to the occasion and made sense of my atrocious handwriting—something which I can scarcely do myself! Moreover, pending my departure to Sydney, she managed to type the manuscript in a very short space of time despite her many other commitments. It is appropriate therefore that this volume should be dedicated to her and I sincerely hope that it provides a little compensation for the many hours which she has devoted to it.

DHA
Leicester 1973

CHAPTER ONE

Wartime control and problems of reconstruction 1914-21

GOVERNMENT CONTROL OF TRANSPORT

THE FIRST WORLD WAR affected transport in several ways though its impact on the subsequent peacetime structure of the transport system was undoubtedly less dramatic than that of the second war. Its most immediate influence was the way in which the government took control over the two major branches of transport, railways and shipping. The importance of lines of communication in terms of a national war effort had long been recognised; as far back as 1871 provision had been made, under the Regulation of the Forces Act of that year, for the government to assume control of the railways in the event of armed hostilities, while in 1912 a corporate body, the Railway Executive Committee, comprising the general managers of the various main line companies, had been set up with wartime management in mind.

Thus it came as no surprise when, on the outbreak of war, the government immediately took control of the railways. The railways remained in private hands and day-to-day management was to be exercised by the REC. The services of the railway network were to be at the disposal of the government, and the latter undertook to compensate the railways on the basis of their net income for 1913. The practice adopted was to pay them monthly instalments of compensation, including an allowance for deferred maintenance. During the course of the war additional provisions were added with regard to capital expenditure and wage increases.

In contrast, control over ocean shipping was instituted in a very piecemeal manner as and when the need arose. The pressure of rising prices and shortage of tonnage and space resulted in an ad hoc policy of requisitioning tonnage at controlled rates of freight, and by 1916 about 37 per cent of British shipping had been requisitioned. But it was not until the end of 1916, when the Ministry of Shipping was established, that universal requisitioning of ship space was implemented. Within a few months the new Ministry had requisitioned virtually the whole of the merchant fleet at fixed rates of hire, and during 1917 control was extended internationally by the formation of the Allied Maritime Transport Council which was to supervise the distribution of tonnage for the Allied powers. By the end of the war this international authority controlled the movements of the greater part of the international sea-going fleet.

As far as other forms of transport were concerned wartime control was far less extensive and elaborate. Canals belonging to the railways were controlled from the beginning, but independent waterways remained outside until March 1917. The coasting trade, because of its complexity, remained free until the last year of war when a loose form of control was instituted, while there was relatively little regulation over road transport.

Though control over transport was fairly extensive by 1918, in all cases the management of transport undertakings remained in private hands. Wartime operation was in effect a partnership between the state and private enterprise and the expectation was that after the war the undertakings would revert to their prewar position. This expectation was fulfilled except in the case of the railways.

There seems little doubt that but for the institution of government control the transport requirements of war would not have been met; or at best they might have been—but at a price. The vast task involved in the movement of freight and troops alone necessitated a much more efficient use of transport resources than was likely to occur under a free market, especially as rolling stock, equipment, tonnage and manpower became scarcer as the war progressed. Much of the shipping tonnage in the Indian, Australian and South African and Far Eastern trades was to be withdrawn and redirected to the North Atlantic to secure essential supplies, while faster turnround and full loading of ships had to be achieved.

The success of this policy can be seen from the fact that by the end of 1917 every 100 tons of shipping that entered UK ports brought in on average 150 tons of imports as against 106 tons in the first half 1914. Similarly ruthless economies in the movement of goods and passengers by rail had to be carried out since some companies were heavily involved in troop movements—the London & South Western Railway alone handled no fewer than 20 million soldiers. Efforts were made to discourage ordinary personal travel, and significant improvements were made in the efficiency of freight handling. For example, the reorganisation of coal haulage in 1917 saved about 700m ton-miles annually and thereby reduced the pressure on the existing rolling stock.

The exercise in wartime administration of Britain's transport system can be regarded as a creditable achievement. There were many difficulties and problems during the course of the war and even the occasional mishap—as in the case of a shipload of rhododendrons being imported from abroad at a time when shipping space could have been used for more essential supplies! But by and large the record was one for praise not criticism. According to Fayle the war record of British shipping was 'one of extraordinary achievement',[1] while an official committee on transport in 1918 gave a glowing account of the administration of the railways during the period.[2] Despite a severe loss of manpower, and a reduced amount of rolling stock the railways were carrying a much larger volume of traffic than they had done before the war. Even road transport made its contribution, though Lord Curzon's remark to the effect that 'the Allies floated to victory on a wave of oil' seems somewhat wide of the mark.

THE CONSEQUENCES OF WAR

Wartime administration is now largely of academic interest and the more important matter is to discover the impact of the war on the different forms of transport. In some respects it undoubtedly imparted beneficial effects. Two new forms of transport, aviation and road transport, received a significant boost both technically and commercially and ensured their place in the future pattern of transport services. The large demand for military aircraft in the

B.T.—B

latter half of the war was accompanied by a considerable improvement in the technical efficiency of flying machines so that it was only a short step before they became commercial possibilities. Secondly, wartime experience in transport services had demonstrated that unified control, especially in the case of the railways, could lead to substantial improvements in operational efficiency, a factor which was to play a significant part in the argument that the railways should be reorganised.

The other side of the balance sheet gave cause for some concern. Though British shipowners had done quite well financially, war-time losses decimated the UK mercantile marine. Altogether 7¼ million gross tons of shipping, equivalent to 38 per cent of the prewar fleet, were lost, and the net loss after replacement amounted to about 3½ million tons. Most other countries suffered less severely; only about one quarter of the world fleet was sunk or destroyed and most of this loss was made good by new construction. Thus by the end of hostilities total world tonnage was very similar to that in 1913 whereas Britain's fleet had been reduced by about 15 per cent. And the fact that the war had given an enormous boost to shipbuilding and fostered the seeds of nationalism in maritime matters, posed a threat to Britain's maritime supremacy in the future. Furthermore, by the end of the war British and international trade were very much lower than in 1913 and British shipowners had lost many services to foreign competitors, notably American, Japanese and neutral operators.

Coastal shipping and the canals suffered an even greater setback. Canal traffic fell by a third, and in the competitive climate of the inter-war period this loss was never regained. Even more dramatic was the 50 per cent reduction in the volume of coastal shipping. Here there were special short-term factors operating against the trade and coastal shipowners did show greater powers of resilience than the canals after the war. The decline was caused in part by war losses, the employment of vessels in Admiralty service, and deteriorating port facilities. But the main factor was the competition of rail transport as a result of the government's policy of freezing railway freight charges; by the end of the war coasting rates, which had once been very competitive with those of the railways, were 100 per cent, and in some cases much more, above the comparable railway rates.[3]

The railways of course had problems of their own. The physical losses had not been disastrous but they had suffered severe depreciation and run-down of rolling stock and equipment. Repair work, maintenance and investment had been restricted during the war because of shortages of materials and labour, high costs and delays in the payment of depreciation compensation by the Government. The railways lost about 30 per cent of their original labour force to the armed forces. Moreover, because of the intensive use of equipment, especially at week-ends, normal repair and maintenance work was more difficult to carry out. The result was that by the Armistice the railways were short of rolling stock, while a considerable amount of equipment and track were badly in need of repair. There was an absolute deficiency of some 80,000 wagons, and up to 20 per cent of locomotives and 10 per cent of coaches were out of commission because they were awaiting repair.

However, absolute shortages do not give a really accurate picture of the magnitudes involved since much rolling stock and track were kept in use though they were in need of repair or should have been scrapped. It seems very likely that the railways accumulated a substantial backlog of investment and repair work during the war. The Colwyn Committee reckoned that the government's outstanding liability to the railways, largely on account of arrears of maintenance and repairs and replacement of stores, amounted to some £150 million.[4] Recent estimates of capital formation suggest that railway investment during the war was only half that of the immediate pre-war period, and the total short-fall for the period at 1920 prices amounted to about £60·5 million.[5] This of course must be regarded as a minimum estimate since it does not allow for the additional depreciation incurred as a result of war. Though the resources of the railways were probably sufficient to meet this in the short-term, it is important to emphasise the point since it is from this date that investment on the railways really began to lag behind requirements, a problem which became worse as the railways' financial fortunes deteriorated in the inter-war years and beyond.

DECONTROL AND RECONSTRUCTION

Though the short-term physical impact of the war on the British transport system was severe it was not of such magnitude as to impede its operations unduly, and given a year or two of recon-struction it was anticipated that things would soon be back to normal. In any case the main concern at the time, at least as far as the government was concerned, was not the physical repair of the system, which was ultimately the responsibility of the owners, but the question of releasing the undertakings from control.

The treatment eventually accorded to shipping and railways was somewhat different. Though both were eventually decontrolled shipping was allowed to revert to its free competitive form of the nineteenth century whereas the railways ended up by receiving a large dose of regulation and rationalisation. Initially the government's transport policy was far from clear and in both cases the possibility of nationalisation was seriously considered. But eventually pressure of business opinion prevailed and it is unlikely that Parliament would have accepted any measure of nationalisation. However, the difference in the treatment of these two industries calls for examination. The structure, history and problems of the two sectors were themselves somewhat different and these in part determined the outcome. In the past shipping had been far less subject to government regulation than railways; indeed given its complex structure and the international scope of its activities it would be difficult for government to exercise control easily during peacetime. Financially shipowners were in a fairly strong position at the end of the war and the need to re-establish their trading links as quickly as possibly gave added force to their demand for speedy decontrol. The railways, on the other hand, had been subject to an increasing degree of government control and regu-lation—down to 1914 over 200 Acts of Parliament relating to rail-ways had been passed—and wartime control involved the govern-ment in financial obligations. Moreover, a process of combination had been going on steadily during the nineteenth and early twentieth centuries. The war gave force to this movement in two respects. First, the experience of unified operation had suggested to many that a further measure of concentration would be beneficial. Members of the Railways Executive Committee, especially the acting chairman,[6] were known to favour the idea, while in 1918 the Select Committee on Transport came to a similar conclusion. The committee argued that some sort of unification should take place though it was not sure whether this would best be accomplished by public or private ownership. 'From a purely technical view, it appears . . . to be desirable that there should be unification of ownership [for] so long as the companies remain as separate corporations it will be difficult to apply either method of securing economies to the fullest possible extent.'[7] Secondly, the increasingly parlous financial state of the railways after 1918 (partly as a result of wartime control) gave some urgency to the need to find a more efficient operational structure.[8] The result, as we shall see, was the Railways Act of 1921.

The way in which the shipping industry was decontrolled need not detain us long since of greater importance from a long-term point of view was the reorganisation of the railway system. The state had no financial obligations to shipping and little attention was paid to the future of the industry. In the interim the government was solely concerned with securing adequate shipping space at reasonable rates of hire for the carriage of essential supplies in the transitional period. Hence tonnage was released from control on a piecemeal basis, very much in the way it had been implemented, as and when tonnage became sufficient to match requirements. The process was accomplished fairly quickly and by the end of October 1919 only 109 vessels, excluding government-owned and prize ships, remained on full requisition, though throughout the year and into 1920 the government ensured that it retained the use of enough ship space at fixed rates of hire for its import requirements so as to avoid paying the inflated free market rates. The last vestiges of control were swept away later that year, though the Ministry of Shipping was not finally dissolved until March 1921.[9]

In some ways the timing of decontrol was unfortunate. The

general release from control coincided with a sharp upswing in the freight market and a boom of unparalleled intensity ensued between the late spring of 1919 and early 1920. Ships and shipping companies were bought up at highly inflated prices and many owners squandered their resources on vessels which were ill-suited to their future requirements. Moreover, it gave an enormous fillip to shipbuilding and much tonnage ordered in the boom only came on stream after the speculative bubble had burst. By 1921 a large volume of tonnage was laid up and there was probably enough shipping in existence to last for a decade or more without further building. The boom was a world-wide phenomenon, a reaction in part to the aftermath of war. Yet it can hardly be ascribed to a real shortage of shipping at this time; rather it was a 'paper' shortage caused by some rather unusual conditions, the chief of which was the chronic port congestion both in the UK and abroad which seriously impaired the efficiency of shipping. Decontrol did not in fact cause the boom; but had the government retained a greater degree of control over freight rates in 1919–20 and at the same time taken steps to deal with the problems in the ports the eagerness with which shipowners invested in new tonnage might have been curtailed, and the industry might not have had so much spare capacity in the inter-war years.[10]

REORGANISATION OF THE RAILWAYS

Much more serious consideration was given to the future of the railways. Indeed, it was not until the summer of 1920, when nationalisation was rejected as an unsuitable solution, that a plan for reorganising the railways finally emerged. Eventually, in a modified form, this became the Railways Act of 1921, which was to determine the course of railway history through to nationalisation.

The background to reorganisation is somewhat complex and needs reconstruction in a little detail. Though there was a wide measure of support for some form of reorganisation of the system it is probably correct to say that it was the financial difficulties of the railways which ultimately forced the government to take action. As long as the railways were under government control the companies had little to worry about on the revenue side because of the financial guarantee. But by early 1919 it was becoming clear that the railways were losing money as a result of rapidly rising costs at a time when rates and fares were still controlled. Wages and costs had risen by well over 100 per cent during the war period yet there had been only one increase in charges, a 50 per cent increase in passenger fares in 1917. Given these conditions the railway owners would not have been able to resume profitable operations had the government removed the financial guarantee. Thus to gain time to consider what should be done the government confirmed the extension of the financial guarantee made in 1916 (for a period of two years after the official end of the war) and brought in a Bill to establish a Ministry of Transport.

In effect this delayed any immediate action to deal with the problem since the new ministry, which took over responsibility for the railways from the Board of Trade, did not come into being until the summer of 1919. By then the immediate task was to get a revision of rates and charges, but again there was some delay until the Rates Advisory Committee, set up under the Transport Act of 1919, had made a thorough investigation into the system of rates and fares. Thus is was not until 1920 that charges were revised to a level of between 75 and 100 per cent above those ruling prewar. Unfortunately costs continued to escalate rapidly in the boom of 1919–20 so that by the time the revisions were made the discrepancy between costs and charges remained almost as large as before. The result was that the net revenue of the railway system declined sharply after 1918, with a loss of over £10 million being recorded in 1921 which the government had to make good under the terms of the agreement. Though conditions improved after the middle of 1921, with the fall in costs, this period marks the beginning of the maladjustment in costs and charges which has plagued the railways to the present day.

Meanwhile the government and the owners had been considering the future organisation of the railways after the removal of control. As already noted, there was a fairly wide measure of agreement regarding the desirability of creating a more unified system in place of the 120 or so companies then still in existence.

Furthermore, given the deteriorating financial position of the railways this seemed to offer an opportunity of improving profitability by cost reduction and economies of scale, though in the debate on reorganisation there was only a very hazy notion as to how economic benefits would accrue as a result of amalgamation. Again however there was considerable delay since it was not until May 1921 that the Railways Bill was presented to Parliament.

There were several reasons for this delay. First, the government was anxious to get the rates structure revised so that the railways would be financially more viable by the time the owners were ready to resume full control. Secondly, there was some doubt initially as to what form the reorganisation should take. On more than one occasion both Lloyd George and Winston Churchill had intimated that public ownership might be a possible solution, and at the end of 1918 Churchill had actually stated this to be the government's policy. This was undoubtedly a premature and unguarded announcement; and, in any case, even had the government been willing it is very unlikely that it could have forced such a measure through Parliament. Yet it should not be dismissed too lightly; the Government obviously gave the matter serious consideration since it was not until June 1920 that nationalisation was officially rejected as a solution,[11] whereupon the government published its White Paper on Reorganisation. This contained a scheme for amalgamating all companies into seven major groups and gave the Ministry of Transport fairly sweeping powers over various aspects of railway operations, including charging, capital expenditure and the provision of facilities. Not surprisingly there was considerable opposition to these proposals—many railway owners regarded them as backdoor nationalisation—and as a consequence they were considerably modified by the time the Bill was presented to Parliament. In turn the provisions of the latter were eventually modified before it finally became law on 19 August 1921.[12]

The Railways Act of 1921 was one of the most important pieces of railway legislation ever passed since it represented the first serious attempt to tackle the problem of railway organisation and planning as a whole. There were six major sections to the Act and of these the first three—covering reorganisation, regulation and charging—were the most important (the remaining sections covered wages and conditions of service, light railways and general matters). The first part made provision for the amalgamation of almost all railway companies into four large groups—the London & North Eastern, the Southern, the Great Western and the London, Midland & Scottish—all of which remained in existence until 1947. The process of concentration was effected rapidly and by the end of 1923 it was all but complete. The grouping was a logical continuation of a process which had been taking place in the nineteenth century. The principal aim behind the scheme of reorganisation was that it would eliminate, for the most part, inter-company rivalry and reduce the costs arising from duplication of facilities. It was also assumed that substantial economies would accrue from unified operation. To facilitate progress in this respect the Minister of Transport was given important regulatory powers by which he could require the railways to standardise their equipment and adopt schemes for co-operative working with respect to rolling stock, plant and equipment, etc (Part II). In return the railway companies received £60 million[13] as 'a full discharge and in satisfaction of all claims'.[14]

Probably the most important section of the Act was that dealing with rates and charges since this was to have most bearing on the future performance of the railways. The declared aims were to simplify the existing rate-making machinery and provide a more flexible and scientific rate structure than that which had existed in the nineteenth century when maximum permitted rates had been legally enforced. A Railway Rates Tribunal was set up to supervise control over rating procedures and its first task was to approve a new standard of charges submitted by the companies, (to come into force in 1928). Charges were to be fixed in the first instance so as to yield a standard net revenue equivalent to that of 1913, and though there was no guarantee that this level would be reached, the tribunal was to review charges annually and suggest any modifications which might be required in the light of this target. To simplify the rating procedure an attempt was made to reduce the number of exceptional rates, which had become so widespread before 1914 that only a small proportion of traffic was being carried at standard rates. Exceptional rates could only be granted between 5 and 40 per cent below the standard, and for all other changes in rates the consent of the tribunal had to be obtained. The third feature of the charging arrangements involved the reclassification of commodity schedules on which the new standard charges were to be based. The Act did not lay down specifications but left the Rates Advisory Committee to draw up the new classifications and, after negotiations with interested parties, a new general classification was drawn up in 1923. Merchandise and mineral traffic were divided into twenty-one separate categories compared with eight under the schedules compiled in 1894. Otherwise the principles which determined classification of a commodity for purposes of charging remained very much as before—value and bulk in relation to weight being the prime factors.

THE RAILWAYS ACT IN RETROSPECT

We have considered the legislation at some length for justifiable reasons. The Act was regarded as a landmark by contemporaries, and indeed it was so in many respects, since it bore its influence on the railways until nationalisation, and even beyond. The future pattern of railway development would no doubt have been considerably different had the legislation never been passed. The significance of its content only becomes really apparent after a study of inter-war railway history but it is perhaps pertinent to comment on its provisions in some detail at this stage since it can be argued that an opportunity was lost in framing the legislation.

First the question of amalgamation. This was largely inspired by wartime experience and hurriedly pressed into force as a result of the deteriorating profitability of the railways. It was widely believed that large-scale operation would be more efficient working and produce the economies and cost reduction which the railways so urgently needed. But wartime experience was not necessarily a good guide to peacetime conditions when the pressure to economise was relaxed. After the war there were four large groupings, which at certain points still competed with each other, but there was no guarantee that substantial economies would occur without some powerful control over their activities. In any case there was never any clear idea as to the size of the potential economies or how they could be secured. At the time no investigation had been made either by the government, owners or independent experts into the possible benefits to be derived from large-scale operations. There was almost complete ignorance regarding the optimum size of a railway unit, and only vague ideas about what sort of economies would flow from the mergers. The grouping that eventually materialised was not based on any clearly conceived economic rationale but was designed more to satisfy vested interests and to achieve a tidier railway map. Certainly economies did arise from the grouping but economic considerations were not the determining factor in the eventual outcome. The fact that the number of groups was reduced from seven, as originally proposed in the White Paper, to four, was largely the result of strong opposition from railway owners to the original plan, in particular the opposition from Scottish companies which were to be hived off separately.[15] But why four groups rather than any other number? Or if economies of scale were so important why not one autonomous corporation controlled by a semi-public board. There was certainly no logical economic explanation put forward to justify grouping by four.

This was by no means the only area to which lip-service was paid to economic considerations. Despite all the good intentions the new rate-making machinery was decidedly cumbersome and outmoded (and in the conditions of the inter-war period it became even more out-dated). It was based largely on the recommendations made by the Rates Advisory Committee which did little more than give its blessing to the time-honoured system and principles of charging which had prevailed in the past.[16] This meant that little consideration was given to the question of the costs of carrying different classes of traffic in determining rates; the value of goods was to remain the main criterion which in effect meant that many rates would still fail to reflect the true cost of carriage. This neglect was all the more unfortunate in that amalgamation had greatly increased the scope for cross-subsidisation, at a time when the emergence of a new competitor, with charges closely related to costs, made it all the more imperative that the railways should adopt a more rational pricing policy. Admittedly the problem was complex, but it had been discussed frequently by railway economists before 1914 and it is curious that the Rates Advisory Committee should fail to consider the matter.

It is doubtful too whether the rate-making machinery was any more flexible under the new legislation. Apart from the special provision for exceptional rates within the stated ranges all proposed changes in rates had to obtain the approval of the tribunal. In fact it could be argued that the new system was less flexible than previously. Under the old system statutory maxima were fixed but the companies were free to vary their charges either up or down within this limit; by the 1921 legislation they could only quote exceptional rates within the prescribed limits. On the other hand, provision was made whereby charges could be revised with reference to the prewar standard revenue, whereas previously any changes in the maximum rates involved a lengthy enquiry and it was up to the companies to prove that there had been a change in the costs of operation.

On passenger fares the legislation had little to say. The companies were, it is true, obliged to submit a schedule of standard charges but they were given much greater freedom with respect to the fares they actually charged. There was little control over exceptional fares[17] and the tribunal's power was confined to assessing the reasonableness of any fare and the effects of existing charges on passenger traffic.[18] In other words, the tribunal's power over passenger fares was very limited and hence any action to be taken with reference to the standard revenue ultimately fell on freight charges. Why freight charges should have been singled out for special treatment, given the importance of passenger traffic as a revenue earner, is not altogether clear but this much is certain: by placing emphasis on freight charges only the vexed question of joint costs and joint pricing as between passenger and freight traffic was skilfully ignored. Clearly this was hardly a policy designed to promote a more rational pricing policy for railway traffic.

The final criticism that might be made of the 1921 Act was its failure to abolish or modify the many nineteenth century legal restrictions which curtailed the railways in their freedom to discriminate, especially in matters of charging. These restrictions, relating to undue preference, reasonable facilities and the publication of all charges, were more appropriate to the time when the railways had a near monopoly of inland transport. As this monopoly was undermined in the inter-war years these regulations hampered the railways' ability to compete with road transport on a commercial basis.

It is easy of course to be critical of legislation from the vantage point of hindsight. But even if we ignore future events and place ourselves in the position of contemporary legislators it is clear that the Act suffered from serious deficiencies. In particular, it gave scant recognition to economic matters both with regard to the amalgamation and the manner of charging. And second, it drew too much on past experience rather than on future need. It certainly produced a far neater and tidier railway network but it did relatively little to ensure the financial viability of the system.

CHAPTER TWO

Inter-War trends: the changing structure of transport services

BEFORE 1914, and during the war for that matter, the transport system of this country was a relatively simple affair structurally speaking, compared with what it was to become in the inter-war years and later. The movement overseas of both passengers and freight was conducted entirely by sea and in the maritime field Britain had established a partial monopoly in the latter half of the nineteenth century. Inland transport, especially long distance, was dominated by the railways, though in the case of freight transport the canals and coastal shipping still acted as marginal suppliers, especially for the conveyance of heavy and bulky commodities. The railways were also important in the provision of short distance and urban transportation though in this field horse-drawn vehicles and street tramways also made an important contribution. But generally speaking, railways and shipping dominated the transport scene; motor transport and civil aviation were very much in the experimental stage of development and as yet there was little indication that they were destined to become an integral part of Britain's transport system.

The first world war can be seen as something of a watershed in the history of transport, since in the years that followed, the changes in the pattern of development were more rapid than before 1914. There was however a marked contrast between sectors. Most of the old established forms of transport—railways, canals, shipping and tramways—either stagnated or declined whereas previously they had been growing steadily. On the other hand, two new forms of transport, motor transport and civil aviation, whose origins lay in the prewar period, expanded rapidly though the latter only accounted for a small share of expenditure on transport by the end of the period.

The analysis of the main trends may be considered in a little more detail. It is difficult to obtain a comprehensive or very precise picture of the magnitudes involved since the statistical data are incomplete, especially for freight transport, while different indicators throw up rather conflicting results. For instance, if we examine the figures for total employment in transport and communications it appears that the sector as a whole marked time. Total employment reached a peak in 1920 at 1,482,000 and it was not until the late 1930s that this level was surpassed. However, employment statistics cannot by definition reflect the rapid growth in private motoring, while they are heavily weighted by the reduction of employment in some of the older forms of transport which was not matched by a commensurate fall in output. Output data for transport suggest that this sector grew fairly rapidly between 1913 and 1920 through to 1938—in fact more rapidly than total output of the economy—though there was some slowing up in the rate of expansion in the mid 1930s.[1] This trend is confirmed by the data relating to consumers' expenditure on transport. Private consumers' expenditure on passenger transport (at constant 1938 prices) almost doubled between 1920 and 1938 and the share of this sector (including communications) in total spending rose from 3·8 per cent before the war to 6.5 per cent in 1925–9, and to 7·5 per cent in 1935–8.

A breakdown of the figures (see table 1) shows clearly the very rapid growth in expenditure on private motoring. The percentage increase is quite phenomenal, though one has to remember that the base from which it started was very low. Nevertheless, by 1938 expenditure on the purchase and running of vehicles (including motor cycles) had risen to just over £135 million as against £179 million spent on public transport. In the latter sector it was again road transport which set the pace and by the end of the period expenditure on this branch was nearly double that on rail. Most of the increase went on bus and coach travel since all other

Table 1   Consumers' expenditure on transport, 1920–38 (at 1938
                                  prices)

	£ million			% change
	1920	1929	1938	1920–38
Private transport	25·8	78·6	135·2	+424
Public transport				
of which:	143·0	157·4	178·9	+25·1
railways	52·6	53·0	56·3	+7·0
road transport	71·8	89·1	109·4	+52·4
Sea and air travel	18·6	15·3	13·2	—29·0

(Source: R. Stone and D. A. Rowe, *The Measurement of Consumers'
Expenditure and Behaviour in the United Kingdom, 1920–1938*, Vol. 2
(1966), 59, 72, 77)

forms of road transport—tramways, taxis and horse-drawn
vehicles—declined in importance. Expenditure on rail travel
managed a modest rise through to 1938 but unlike road transport
there were some quite sharp downturns, notably between 1929 -32.
Expenditure on shipping services declined quite sharply whereas
that on air transport rose steadily, though even by 1938 it amounted
to only £0·5 million.

The expenditure data can however give a misleading impression
of the relative importance of different branches of transport; this
is especially the case with respect to road and rail since much of
the travel on public road tranport consisted of short-distance and
local journeys at a relatively high price per passenger mile. Hence
information on passenger miles travelled (table 2) perhaps gives a
better idea of the relative distribution between different modes,
though the overall trends are not altered. In 1920 passenger miles
travelled by rail accounted for about 60 per cent of the total
passenger mileage by public inland transport, while the share of
bus and coach travel was not much more than 10 per cent and
tramways and trolleybuses accounted for a quarter. By 1938 buses
and coaches accounted for almost as many passenger miles as the
railways whose share of the total had fallen to 42 per cent. No
figures are available for private car travel, but a rough estimate
for 1938 suggests that passenger miles by this mode amounted to
about 27,000 million,[2] that is over one half the total for all forms of
public transport.

Table 2   Estimated number of passenger miles travelled by final consumers on public land transport in the UK, 1920–38 (million)

	1920	1929	1938
Railways	19,214	18,912	20,009
Tramways and trolley buses	8,058	9,494	8,148
Bus and coaches	3,457	11,307	19,037
Taxis and hire cars	1,624	929	587
Horse-drawn vehicles	216	63	13
Total	32,569	40,705	47,794

(Source: Stone and Rowe, *op.cit*, Vol. 2, 71)

There is little doubt therefore that the inter-war period saw a massive penetration of the market by motor transport which, from almost negligible beginnings, had by the end of the period become a very serious rival to existing forms of inland transport. On the freight side, for which the statistical data are insufficient to carry out a similar exercise, the same process was taking place, though the extent of the penetration was almost certainly less severe since the railways retained their monopoly of the carriage of heavy bulky products. As far as aviation is concerned, although its history is spectacular, it remained very much a marginal supplier of transport services both in the passenger and freight markets. In this period it posed no serious threat to either inland transport operators or to international sea transport. The individual sectors may now be considered in turn.

THE RAILWAYS IN DECLINE

Much to the surprise of the framers of the 1921 legislation the railway companies did not, either individually or collectively, meet their standard revenue targets in the inter-war period. Apart from 1922 net receipts of the four main-line companies fell short of the 1913 level throughout the period, and in some years, especially the 1930s, the shortfall was more than one quarter. All the companies experienced a contraction in revenue though on balance the Southern Railway fared better than the other three groups.[3] The main factors working against the railways were the stagnation in traffic, the growth of road competition and the cost-price structure of the system.

B.T.—C

In contrast to the period before 1914 the volume of traffic ceased to grow steadily in this period. In fact not only was there an overall stagnation in traffic levels but quite severe contractions in both passenger and goods traffic occurred in 1920–1, 1925–6, 1929–32 and 1937–8, years characterised by sharp recessions in economic activity generally. The overall trend in freight traffic was sharply downward and in no single year did it attain the 1913 level. All classes of goods—merchandise, coal and other minerals—experienced a setback; even in the best year of the 1930s (1937) the volume of merchandise freight was only 74 per cent of pre-war and that of minerals and coal 83 per cent. Passenger traffic held up rather better though there was little sign of real growth; by the end of the period the number of passenger journeys by rail was very similar to that in 1913 but in terms of passenger miles there was a slight increase in traffic.

The check to railway expansion cannot simply be ascribed to the competition of motor transport. The latter, as we shall see, did have a serious impact but it was confined mainly to the passenger and merchandise sectors. In the case of coal and minerals the railways lost very little to road haulage since the latter was not well adapted to carry this type of traffic. Unfortunately the railways retained a monopoly in the very branches of traffic which were in secular decline—the products of the heavy staple industries, coal, iron, steel, shipbuilding and textiles—which the railway network had been designed to serve in the nineteenth century. The railways specialised in the conveyance of this type of traffic and the returns from it, especially from coal, were good. The loss recorded in coal traffic was considerable from 225·5 million tons in 1913 to 188·2 million in 1937, and in 1933 it had receded to as low as 165·4 million tons. Naturally enough the railways in regions with a high concentration of such activities, eg South Wales, South West Scotland and North East England, were affected the worst. In the last named region mineral traffic carried by the railways in 1932 was only one half that of 1924 and by the end of the 1930s it was still only 69 per cent.[4] Not surprisingly the London & North Eastern Railway barely managed to earn 60 per cent of its pre-war revenue during the 1930s. By contrast, the Southern

Railway, the bulk of whose revenue came from passengers, fared much better.

The loss of the heavy staple traffic would not have been so bad had there been compensations elsewhere. The market in merchandise freight was growing rapidly at this time but here the railways lost out to road transport, and in any case they were not very well adapted to securing the newer traffic, much of which originated in the Midlands and South of the country. And in the only branch of railway traffic which did not show a marked decline, namely passenger, the pressure of road competition checked any prospects of expansion.

COMPETITION FROM ROAD TRANSPORT

The rapid growth of motor transport undoubtedly posed a serious problem for the railways. Its development during this period was little short of dramatic given that before the war the motor vehicle was still in the stage of being technically perfected both in an engineering and production sense. Certainly considerable strides had been made within the last few years before the war to make vehicles more reliable and increase their average speeds; better lubrication and tyres and fewer breakdowns through improved maintenance were important in this respect. Nevertheless, vehicles still remained somewhat unreliable, they were produced for the most part on a costly one-off basis and only the wealthy could afford to run their own cars. At the end of the war probably less than 350,000 motor vehicles of all types were in use on Britain's roads. Yet within the matter of a few years, buses, private cars and road haulage vehicles streamed forth in profusion. There was a great burst of expansion in the years immediately following the war and by 1921 the number of vehicles in use (including motor cycles and taxis) had risen to nearly 850,000. This growth was assisted by the release of many ex-army vehicles on the market, which not only made a number of reliable vehicles available for use as lorries or conversion into small buses, but also helped to spread essential knowledge of vehicles. Many of the first civilian operators 'learnt by doing' and while many did become hauliers, others graduated into garage proprietorship, maintenance work, etc. After the early 1920s the rate of expansion slowed down somewhat though it still remained at a high level; by the end of the decade the number of vehicles in use was over two million and by 1938 just over three million, and of this total over two million represented private cars.

The reasons for this spectacular growth are not difficult to find. Rapid advances were made in the methods of producing vehicles and in their technical performance. In the former context the shift from a bespoke basis of production to the mass production of vehicles was largely accomplished during the 1920s. Changes in the design of vehicles and various technical improvements ensured greater reliability of vehicles and led to a significant reduction in operating costs. The shape and size of buses, for instance, was radically altered in the 1920s so that by the end of the decade they were very much more reliable from a technical point of view than they had been before 1914, while they resembled quite closely the vehicle we know today. During the 1930s the most notable advance was the introduction of the diesel engine to commercial road transport. Despite its higher initial cost the diesel engine burnt fuel more economically than the petrol engine, which made it attractive to operators with high annual mileages. By the middle of the 1930s the diesel engine was well established in public service vehicles and the larger road haulage vehicles, and subsequently it ousted the petrol engine. From the economic point of view the most important technical innovation was the introduction of the pneumatic tyre which made for higher speeds, lower fuel consumption and smoother running than was possible with the solid type. In the early days tyres had been an expensive item in the running costs of vehicles; for example, in 1906 it cost 4d per vehicle mile for solid tyres on a four-wheeled London bus whereas by 1932 the cost on a six-tyred London bus using pneumatics was less than 0.10d per vehicle mile. Such improvements soon enabled the bus to emerge as a rival to the tram and later the railway. Overall the effect of these advances was to reduce considerably both the capital and running costs of motor vehicles and this in turn widened the market. The price of cars fell by about one third to one half between 1923 and 1929 alone, while the operating costs of public service vehicles fell by one third to one half between 1922 and 1937. This, together with rising real incomes, suburban development and the increasing desire for greater mobility, led to a rapid extension of the market. Much of the expansion can be attributed to the increase in sales of the small family car the price of which came within the income range of many middle and lower-middle class families. By 1939 motoring was no longer a luxury confined to the idle rich.

Compared with the railways road transport had two main advantages. By the early 1930s, if not before, costs had been reduced sufficiently to allow operators to compete with the railways in terms of price, though not of course on all routes. Moreover, road operators had the advantage that their charges were based on operating costs whereas railway charges, with their high degree of cross-subsidisation, were not (see below). Secondly, it was a much more flexible and convenient form of transport, particularly suited to short-distance and cross-country journeys, for local delivery and for the conveyance of small consignments of merchandise. The advantages of the private car scarcely need emphasising.

The main difficulty is to estimate what the railways actually lost through the advent of motor transport. One problem in this respect is that there is little hard data relating to private motoring or to the freight side of operations. Secondly, motor transport generated much new traffic, often within areas with no rail connections, which would never have otherwise materialised. As Stone and Rowe observed: 'there seems little doubt ... that a large part of the increase in bus services was due not so much to direct competition with other transport as to reaching new sources of demand previously untapped'.[5]

In other words, though the railways' traffic growth was obviously checked as a result of road transport their losses cannot be equated with the latter's gains. The railways lost heavily on some short and medium distance routes where competition from road operators was often severe, but over long distances (say 100 miles or more) the railways continued to hold their own, though even here competition was becoming more intense by the later 1930s.

The majority of passenger journeys made by road were probably non-competitive with rail, in the sense that they either would not otherwise have been made or they were effected between points without rail connections. Since large numbers of road journeys were made over short distances and within towns it is plausible to argue that it was the tramways, whose traffic remained static in the inter-war years (see table 2), which were affected most seriously in this respect. It has been estimated that the number of journeys on public road service vehicles (that is buses and coaches) over distances comparable with those by rail amounted to about 108 million in 1937. For private car journeys (other than local ones) an estimate for 1931 gives a total of 150 million,[6] and grossing this up to make allowance for the increase in the number of cars in use produces a total of roughly 250–270 million car journeys for 1937. Altogether then the total competitive journeys by all forms of road transport were probably in the region of 400 million by 1937. However, not all these journeys would have been made but for the existence of motor transport. If we make allowance for this then at a rough 'guesstimate' the railways lost about 250–300 million journeys to their competitors; in other words, the railways would have had that many more passengers to the good had there been no road competition. This loss appears quite large when set against the 1,230 million or so passenger journeys travelled by rail in both 1913 and 1938.

The losses on the freight side are even more difficult to ascertain. Here most of the competition was confined to merchandise traffic and, as in the case of passenger travel, competition was most acute over short and medium distances. The break-even point was probably in the region of 75 miles, above which the railways maintained a competitive edge, though in time competition extended further afield while the railways had no answer to very low back-haul rates quoted by road operators. The only estimate for the amount of freight carried by road is that made by Walker, who gives a figure of 100 million tons for 1936 compared with 48 million tons of merchandise freight which went by rail, a drop of nearly 20 million tons on 1913. Again however not all of this can be considered as pure loss from a railway point of view since much road haulage consisted of local delivery work which was non-competitive with rail. On the other hand, merchandise traffic was a growing market in this period and it is probable that the railways would have stood to gain as much traffic as they actually lost absolutely between 1913 and 1936 had there been no outside competition. In short, the total rail loss amounted to about 40 per cent of the road hauliers' merchandise freight traffic.[7]

Overall therefore, the railways lost quite a considerable amount of traffic to their competitors, though the bulk of these losses occurred in passenger traffic and merchandise freight. In the case of heavy freight—coal and minerals—it was largely unfavourable economic circumstances that accounted for the decline. These two factors were responsible for the bulk of the railways' absolute losses of traffic, though the potential losses were of course greater than those actually sustained. Hence total traffic units carried by rail (that is passenger and freight combined) were lower on average than before the war, while fluctuations in the volume of traffic were both more severe and more frequent than previously. Such changes were bound to have an adverse effect on revenue since, given the high proportion of fixed and inescapable costs in the short term, units costs tended to vary inversely with the volume of traffic. Hence the operating ratio (that is railway expenditure as a proportion of receipts) tended to rise when traffic was falling, resulting in a reduction of profit margins, and vice versa, while the secular decline in traffic over the period resulted in a long-term deterioration in the operating ratio[8] and hence lower profit margins on average than compared with prewar. Given the fixed and rigid nature of so many costs it was difficult to effect a reduction in the short term at least. On the revenue side the railways' pricing policy did not help matters either and it is to this question that we must now turn.

PRICING POLICY AND COSTS

This is a complex subject and only the relevant essentials can be outlined here. The basic defect of railway pricing policy, and one which the Railways Act of 1921 did nothing to remedy, was its unscientific nature. Broadly speaking, railway services were priced on the basis of what the traffic would bear rather than on the actual cost of carriage and this inevitably entailed considerable cross-subsidisation between services. In practice what this meant was that railway charges were too high on the low-cost operated routes and services and, conversely, too low on the high-cost ones. Consequently road operators, whose charges were more closely aligned to costs, could attract the best (most profitable) traffic on the dense routes and leave the railways with the less profitable high-cost traffic for which their charges were too low. And moreover, the fact that the railways failed to cost and price their services correctly meant that they were never in a position to cut out the uneconomic parts of the system.

But this was not all. It is evident that the railways made little proper attempt to adapt their pricing policy to meet the changed conditions of the period. This can be explained partly through ignorance about operating costs of individual routes and services of the system and partly because of the restrictions imposed on their powers of charging by the 1921 Act, though, as we shall see later, this excuse for inaction has worn a little thin with time. Admittedly the railways did reduce their charges considerably as a result of road competition; this took the form of an increasing number of exceptional rates and fares (contrary to the intentions of the 1921 legislation) so that by the end of the 1930s, 85 per cent of passenger receipts and some 70 per cent of freight receipts were derived from exceptional charges. In several respects this exercise was counter-productive. In the first place, it meant that the rate schedules became very complex and in the process adversely affected customer relationships. There were so many variations on standard fares that passengers lost patience with the system, and the same point can be made with respect to freight rates. Secondly, the rate reductions were made in a most unscientific manner; generally they consisted of across-the-board cuts regardless of the relevant costs or the strength of external competition. For example, exceptional rates were used most extensively for that type of traffic least affected by road competition; in 1935 the largest proportion of traffic carried at such rates was found to be that in heavy commodities, whereas only 63 per cent of merchandise freight was carried at reduced rates. Similarly on the passenger side, cheap fares were granted on nearly all routes irrespective of the degree of competition or relevant cost considerations. Eventually the average fare per passenger mile was lower than that for road operators; it averaged 0·64d per mile whereas it has been estimated that to maximise revenue the railways should have charged an average fare of around 0·904d per passenger mile.[9] A far more discriminatory policy was required to take account of variations in costs and competition. Broadly speaking, the railways should have concentrated their rate reductions on that type of traffic which was profitable to carry but which was most subject to road competition. On the other hand, charges should have been raised on the traffic least susceptible to substitution and on the unprofitable traffic which could have been dispensed with in the long run.

The question is why did the railways not adopt a more rational pricing policy? One reason was that they had little knowledge about operating costs for particular routes and classes of traffic and little was done to rectify this ignorance in the inter-war period. The problem was aggravated by the increasing degree of cross-subsidisation which inevitably followed from amalgamation, and this no doubt reduced the incentive to determine the costs of specific services. Moreover, the Act of 1921 must share some of the blame for the unsatisfactory nature of the railways pricing policy. It perpetuated the old system of pricing based on the valuation of commodities and provided little incentive to modify the system. The legislation also preserved many of the nineteenth century restrictions relating to undue preference, reasonable facilities and the publication of charges, which hindered the railways' commercial freedom when competing with road transport. The hopeless profusion of exceptional rates and charges could also be attributed to the fact that the companies anticipated difficulties in securing the consent of the Railway Rates Tribunal to a general revision of charges, while the tribunal itself was a body quite incapable of producing any satisfactory solution to the railway rate structure.[10]

Having said this it can also be argued that the railways themselves could have made greater efforts in this direction and almost certainly they interpreted the provisions of the 1921 Act too rigidly. The Act did not prohibit the adoption of a more rational pricing structure though clearly it made its realisation more difficult. There was, moreover, nothing to stop the railways from applying for selected increases or a general revision of charges, but only once did they do so—in 1937 when they were granted. On the passenger side the restrictions on charging were less severe yet even here the railways did little to adapt the structure. And even price discrimination was not forbidden so long as it did not lead to undue preference for any one group of traders.

A more scientific and commercially competitive pricing policy would not of course have solved all the railways' problems. It would not have brought back traffic lost as a result of the decline in the basic industries for instance. But it would have allowed the railways to compete on a more equal footing with their competitors. And it would certainly have done more to maximise revenue than the policy actually pursued. As it was the policy of general rate reduction in this period had the effect of causing charges to fall seriously out of line with costs. Though prices and costs were tending to fall in these years labour and fixed costs remained sticky in a downward direction. The upshot of this was that by 1938 unit operating costs were around twice the 1913 level whereas the average level of charges (passenger and freight) was only about 50–60 per cent above prewar.

Hence it can be argued that competition and depressed activity in those trades on which the railways depended heavily for traffic were not the only factors making for reduced profitability. The gap between charges and costs clearly made for a lower net revenue than before the war. This gap had originated during the war when charges were frozen, and indirectly road competition intensified the problem in the inter-war years. The railways were caught in the awkward position of having rather inflexible costs at a time when prices (including their charges) were moving downwards. Since their competitors' charges were falling it was not always possible to raise rates to match costs, though as already outlined a more rational pricing policy would have alleviated the problem to some extent. Given the failure on this score the only option open to the railways was to secure cost reductions via economies in operation or through technical innovation.

ECONOMIES AND TECHNICAL PROGRESS

Cost reductions could be derived from three main sources: savings resulting from the amalgamation, improvements in methods of operation including more efficient utilisation of manpower, and technical innovation. Savings from all three sources would inevitably overlap so that it is not very easy to distinguish exactly the specific savings flowing from any one source. However, on the last of these counts relatively little was achieved. There were no new revolutionary techniques applied to rail operations in this period on a scale sufficient to generate large cost gains. The main technical advances consisted of new forms of traction, diesel and electric. The former made little headway at all, while most of the electrification was confined to the Southern Railway, and in any case it is doubtful whether a large scale programme of electrification would have produced very large gains.[11] As far as the amalgamation is concerned, it is difficult to estimate exactly what savings were derived since prices were drifting downwards in this period, and, this problem apart, some of the improvements in efficiency would no doubt have occurred in the absence of amalgamation. Broster suggested a figure of £15 million for the annual savings realised from this source,[12] most of which were derived from the more efficient use of resources, though it is far from clear whether all these savings could be directly attributable to the grouping process.

The railways do appear to have secured substantial savings on the manpower side. The total labour force was reduced from 735,870 in 1921 to 588,517 in 1939 (inclusive of ancillary staff). This, together with improvements in efficiency, produced an improvement in labour productivity (man-hours per train mile) of some 40–50 per cent between 1913–36, most of which occurred after 1923. On this reckoning, had the 1936 labour force been no more efficient than that of 1913 then the total number of employees required in 1936 would have been about 46 per cent larger than it actually was. At the then current rates of pay this would have entailed the expenditure of £40·8 million more on wages, and £1·5 million more on fuel and supplies, assuming 1913 standards of operation. The total saving of over £42 million was equivalent to one quarter of gross railway revenue in 1936, and without this the railways would have incurred a deficit of nearly £9 million as against the actual return of £33·4 million.[13]

It would seem therefore that the railways achieved considerable cost savings in one form or another as a result of the better utilisation of their resources and without these, net returns would have been very poor indeed. Moreover, the economies were not derived at the expense of their customers since standards of service, especially on main-line routes, tended to improve in these years. Even so, there was still considerable scope for further improvements in operating performance. As we have seen, the application of new forms of traction was very limited outside the Southern Railway, while the problem of reducing excess capacity by withdrawing uneconomic services was hardly tackled at all. Savings arising from the closure of branch lines amounted to a mere £1·5 million. Many of the improvements that were made had only a marginal impact in terms of operating efficiency and did little to render the railways more competitive with road transport. Perhaps the major neglect was the failure to streamline business operations in a way that got the best out of existing resources. Freight handling methods, for instance, remained grossly inefficient, and criticisms on this score have a long history. Bulk consignments of freight moving at high speed in through trains were the exception rather than the rule. Railway wagons were too small, too lightly loaded and badly marshalled. In short, the scope for further economies by rationalising services and pruning the uneconomic parts of the system was enormous, but neither course of action was seriously contemplated by the railways in this period. Perhaps the main fault of the railways was that they still placed great emphasis on capturing or retaining as much traffic as possible regardless of whether or not it was profitable.

A SOLUTION TO ROAD COMPETITION

Once the inevitable was realised the railways switched their line of attack with regard to road transport competition. First, they endeavoured to 'get on to the road' themselves, and secondly, they pressed for some restriction to be placed on the activities of road operators. This latter pressure ultimately bore fruit in the form of licensing legislation. Before examining the measures it is necessary to look briefly at the structural development of the road transport industry.

The rapid growth of motor transport in the 1920s brought forth a proliferation of operators both in the passenger and haulage sides of the industry. The ease with which one could enter the industry led to the emergence of many small firms some of which expired very quickly. The road haulage sector was especially notable for the small unit of operation. By 1930 there were nearly 350,000 goods vehicles in use, but of these about three quarters were owned and operated by manufacturers and traders for their own use. The remainder belonged to hauliers proper who operated their vehicles for hire or reward. In this sector there was almost a complete lack of organisation—there were very few large firms—compared with the passenger side, and the unit of operation was much smaller. The average number of vehicles per operator was three, as against nine in the case of passenger transport, while about one half of the concerns in the industry owned only one vehicle. Large firms, providing regular scheduled services, such as Pickford and Carter Paterson, were the exception rather than the rule. Not surprisingly therefore, road haulage was a highly competitive cut-and-thrust business. The small independent hauliers were out to get what business they could regardless of the methods they employed. Competitive rate cutting therefore became a marked feature of the industry and there was no uniformity in charging practices. Quite often hauliers would quote uneconomic rates to secure loads, especially on return journeys, and it was this sort of practice that the railways were anxious to stamp out. The only way in which many of them could keep going was by paying low wages, working drivers excessively, neglecting the maintenance of vehicles and avoiding proper asset depreciation. Not all road hauliers should be tarred with the same brush—there were respectable firms which practicised a high standard of business behaviour—but it is clear from the early reports of the licensing authorities in the 1930s that such malpractices were by no means rare occurrences.

On the passenger side development was more orderly and structurally the industry assumed a greater degree of coherence despite some unfavourable features. Even before the first world war motor bus services had been introduced on a fairly wide scale and London General's switch to motor traction had all but driven horse services from the streets of the metropolis. In the provinces progress was somewhat slower, though even here several well-known companies were running motor bus services before 1914. After the war motor traction swept all before it; the remaining horse-drawn services vanished from the streets and tramway traffic peaked out and then stagnated. In the process four distinct types of operator emerged— the municipal authorities, the territorial or associated companies, the independents and the railways. Initially local authorities were reluctant to introduce motor buses partly because they had already invested extensively in tramway networks; but soon after the war many municipalities started bus services either in areas not served by trams or in place of abandoned tramway routes. By 1928, ninety local authorities were operating bus services compared with eighteen in 1914. Most of the services were of a local nature and in many cases the operating authority held a quasimonopoly within its area, though inter-running agreements were negotiated with private operators and other municipal authorities. By the early 1930s local authorities accounted for nearly 12·8 per cent of all vehicles in the industry and 23·4 per cent of all passengers carried by bus; individual fleet size was quite large, averaging around 54 vehicles as against just over 6 for all other operators.

The private sector of the industry was dominated by the associated or territorial companies; most of these were fairly large concerns—the Midland Red had over 1200 vehicles in 1938— and many of them were grouped under the umbrella of holding companies. Three, British Electric Traction, Thomas Tilling and Scottish Motor Traction, held extensive interests in more than 50 bus companies. Ultimately they came to control about 40 per cent of the total bus and coach fleet in the country which carried some 50–60 per cent of all passengers.[14] Most of the operators within these groups concentrated on long distance stage and express services and their areas of operation were defined by a complex set of territorial agreements. It was with these conglomerates that the railways became associated. Originally the railways had been pioneers in this field, but it was not until they acquired general powers to operate buses in the late 1920s that they went into the business on a large scale. This they did mainly by investing in going concerns; eventually they acquired an interest in about 40 per cent of the vehicles operated by the associated companies though rarely did they acquire a majority holding in any one company. By contrast the railways found it less easy to buy their way into road haulage because of the lack of large firms; thus apart from the purchase of one or two firms such as Pickford and Carter Paterson, the railways confined their activities to buying motor vehicles for the provision of collection and delivery services at railheads. In 1938 they owned only 10,000 haulage vehicles out of a total of nearly half a million.

The independents, or 'pirate' operators as they were often called, formed by far the largest numerical group. About 90 per cent of all operators came under this heading, though they owned less than 40 per cent of all buses and coaches and carried only 15 per cent of all passengers outside the London area. The majority of these companies had fewer than five vehicles apiece, and though pressure of competition drove many out of business the prospects were such that there was ample opportunity for the newcomer to try his hand. The independents concentrated on excursion and contract work though they also played an important part in developing express coach services.

Thus by the early 1930s the industry consisted of a small number of large and fairly respectable operators together with a host of tiny independent firms. Large firms owned the majority of vehicles; one per cent of the operators controlled over 50 per cent of all public service vehicles, while 99 per cent of the firms, with less than 100 vehicles apiece, shared the remainder. Despite the greater degree of organisation and concentration compared with road haulage, the industry was very unstable in the 1920s, with fierce competition and poor conditions of service. Generally speaking, it was the small operators or independents which gave cause for concern. Many of them had little idea how to manage a transport undertaking; they maintained services with broken-down buses driven by incompetent drivers, until the vehicles dropped to pieces. The provision of services was poor; buses often ran to no fixed timetable and various doubtful practices were adopted in order to steal traffic from competitors, which not only led to wasteful competition but also threatened public safety. The position was worst in urban areas, especially in London where at least until 1922 the Underground Group (which had acquired control of London General in 1912) had managed to maintain a semi-monopoly of passenger services. Then came the wave of independents whose buses, literally in all shapes, sizes and colours, invaded the streets of London and created havoc. By the end of 1924 there were no fewer than 200 operators running about 500 vehicles. The position became so chaotic that the government was forced to take action in that year to restrain the activities of metropolitan omnibus operators.

Before looking at the steps taken to restrict road transport it is important to inquire whether such a policy was justified, since more recently both the need for and the desirability of control have been questioned.[15] It is true that at the time there was a considerable body of opinion in favour of restriction; in particular, the Royal Commission on Transport (1928–31) and the Salter Conference (1932) on road haulage had favoured some form of regulation, while the government had already attempted to control London's transport in 1924, though not with any great degree of success. However, one reason why the need for restriction met with approval was because most of the evidence about conditions in the industry was drawn from the larger, well organised groups of operators and from the railways, both of whom were anxious to curb the indiscriminate competition of the small scale operators. The latter were scarcely represented at the inquiries, and the consumer not at all. Moreover, much of the evidence was based

Page 49

Above: Electrification of Inter-city trunk routes in Britain is still selective and apart from the Southern Region covers only the West Coast main line between Euston, Liverpool, Manchester and Glasgow, completed in 1967/74. The principal feature is the regular service, usually at hourly intervals between main centres, even half hourly between London and Birmingham, at speeds averaging overall about 80 mph. This is the Euston-Manchester Pullman service.

Below: In the last decade BR devoted most of its freight service improvements to the expansion of company block trains, and the development of Freightliner services as part of the 'container revolution'. This container train is seen at York Way, near King's Cross, one of the pioneer Freightliner terminals.

Page 50

Above: The traditional mechanical railway signalbox has remained largely unchanged in basic operating methods for almost a century. Control areas often cover no more than a station and the block sections on each side. Mechanical signalling survives on secondary routes and on a few principal main lines but is gradually being modernised. This example was at Guildford.

Below: During the last fifteen years perfection of electronic control techniques combined with miniaturisation of relay interlocking equipment have permitted a vast expansion in power signalbox control areas to as much as 100 route miles or more. Operation is from push buttons on a track diagram on which are indicated the location and identity of every train in the area. This is the operating room at Saltley.

on opinion and subjective judgements rather than on hard established facts. Thus, according to Hart, it was difficult to prove at the time that the road haulage industry was unstable because of excessive competition and low rates and that this in turn led to neglect of maintenance, a high rate of accidents and bankruptcies. On the other hand, though conditions in the industry were certainly not as bad as the opposition made them out to be, it later became apparent, from the reports of the licensing authorities, that they were far from ideal. Their reports show that the standard of conduct of some operators was very low indeed in that many vehicles were unfit for service, and there was certainly much indiscriminate and wasteful competition; furthermore, some form of control appeared desirable in the interests of securing greater coordination of services, not only within the road transport sector but also between road and rail. Whether the type of control actually adopted was the most desirable is quite another matter.

Be that as it may, the government ceded to the requests of the pressure groups by passing the Road Traffic Act (1930) and the Road and Rail Traffic Act (1933). The first of these imposed a fairly rigid form of control over passenger transport. By means of an elaborate licensing system covering vehicles, services and employees, Traffic Commissioners were empowered to regulate conditions in and entry into the industry, the main effect of which was to give the established operator priority over the new applicant. Road haulage was dealt with in a similar manner by the legislation of 1933. All owners of goods vehicles were required to obtain a licence to carry—an A licence for those operating for hire or reward, a C licence for traders carrying their own goods, while B licences were issued for both purposes though there were limitations on the type of traffic which could be carried for hire in this case. As with the passenger side, applicants for licences had to prove that there was a need for new services, though the powers of the Licensing Authorities were more limited with respect to road haulage.

The main effect of the legislation was to freeze the pattern of development in road transport. By protecting the established operator, who also secured priority treatment when new services were in question, the scope for the entry of newcomers was limited. The growth of the industry was checked, at least in terms of the number of operators and vehicles. On the passenger side the total number of public service vehicles rose by only just over 3000 between 1931 and 1938, while the number of operators fell from 6434 to 4798. Though protection accorded to established operators meant that many small firms remained in existence, some of them were disfranchised by the commissioners because they could not satisfy the new legal requirements. Concentration in the industry also increased since the easiest way to expand was by taking over smaller concerns. By 1938 over 60 per cent of the buses and coaches were owned by firms controlling 100 vehicles or more each, as against 47 per cent in 1931, while the number of very small firms declined. Road haulage was affected in a similar manner. The growth of the industry slowed appreciably; in fact it was confined entirely to C licence vehicles since the number of A and B licence-holders and the vehicles they operated declined after 1935. Again there was a tendency towards concentration, but it was much less marked than in the case of passenger transport and by 1939 the small man still predominated.

It has been argued that protection and restriction on entry inhibited both change and enterprise in road transport and put a premium on inefficiency, and as a result the consumer was denied the benefits of competition.[16] Up to a point there may be a certain amount of truth in these allegations. But one is not readily convinced, nor has it been satisfactorily demonstrated, that the public suffered severely, if at all, from control. There is no evidence to suggest that consumers were handicapped by a real shortage of road transport capacity, and in the case of road haulage any problem in this respect could be overcome by using owner-account vehicles since there was virtually no restriction on the issue of C licences. Competition was certainly reduced, but this was not necessarily a bad thing since it meant the elimination of excess capacity in some cases, which in the long run could benefit consumers through lower unit costs. That excess capacity existed is abundantly clear from the fact that much licensed tonnage was never taken up because the licencees could not find work for it.

There is no evidence either that the larger established operators in road passenger transport abused their more privileged position under the licensing system. Indeed their services improved during the 1930s, and in any case the large operators were in a much better position to provide unremunerative services by cross-subsidisation. Moreover, the licensing bodies certainly did not interpret their powers so rigidly as to preclude the granting of licences for new capacity should there be shown a real need.

The case against restriction appears even weaker when account is taken of the net gain in terms of conditions of service which the public secured. In nearly all their reports the Traffic Commissioners were able to state that there had been a remarkable improvement in the standard of equipment used and in the comfort and cleanliness of public service vehicles. Vehicles were no longer worked to a standstill before repair and 'dirty interiors, unhealthy fumes, bad springing and noisy machinery are now a rare occurrence in public service vehicles, while the safety of the public is increased by constant supervision of the maintenance of steering, brake gear, and general improvement.' Passengers not only enjoyed the benefits of safer and more reliable services but also the advantages which followed from a much greater degree of coordination of timetables and fare schedules. In the East Midlands Area alone some 600 time and fare tables were coordinated within the first year of the licensing system. The road haulage sector also shared in these improvements, especially with respect to the condition of vehicles, and by the end of the period a more responsible body of road hauliers was emerging.

As far as other forms of transport are concerned the new laws seem to have had only a negligible impact. In assessing applications the authorities were to take into account existing services provided by non-road operators. Potentially the main beneficiaries should have been the railways, but though competition was reduced there was little noticeable response in railway revenues. In some cases, eg long distance passenger services, the railways were able to secure some relief from excessive bus and coach competition, but there is precious little evidence to suggest that they were protected unduly from their competitors. The authorities certainly did not go out of their way to favour the railways in the sense of acceding to all their demands at the public hearings, and in some cases they clearly took the side of road transport which they felt ought not to be discouraged. The allegation that, by restricting the growth of the least costly form of transport, the railways were protected and thereby became less enterprising is also something of a myth. Road competition certainly did not disappear in the 1930s and inertia did not attack the railways. If anything they became more progressive in adopting measures to combat competition, eg reduced fares and faster and more comfortable trains, than at any time since the war. Curiously enough, one relevant argument not put forward by the anti-restriction lobby is that had the competitive freedom of road transport been left unchecked the railways might have been forced to consider with greater urgency the need to abandon their loss-making services. One estimate suggests that about a third of the route mileage could have been abandoned.[17]

LONDON TRANSPORT: A SPECIAL SOLUTION

London's transport system had long been recognised as a special problem. Even by the turn of the century traffic developments in the heart of the city had become chaotic with the uncoordinated development of trams, buses, underground and suburban railways, leading to waste and duplication of services, not to mention the confusion on the streets. Several inquiries were conducted into the question between 1900 and 1919 and all stressed the seriousness of the situation and the urgent need to secure greater unification and coordination in the provision of services. Legislation to tackle the problem did not materialise however, and it was left to the initiative of the Underground Group to provide some relief by acquiring control over competing transport undertakings. By the end of 1912 this combine had secured a semi-monopoly of London's transport system, for only the Metropolitan Railway, the main-line railways, 14 local authority tramway systems and a few independent bus operators, remained outside the group's network. This stability was rudely shattered soon after the war as hoards of independent bus proprietors invaded the streets of

London. In 1924 the London Traffic Act appeared on the statute book which gave the Minister of Transport power to regulate or prohibit motor bus traffic in certain streets while the licensing authority for the area, the Metropolitan Police Commissioner, could prescribe approved routes for buses.

This only provided a temporary and rather partial solution to the problem. Initially it did serve to stabilise the number of buses in the London area, but due to loopholes in the legislation there was little control over coach services with the result that operators shifted ground and proceeded to bring more coaches on to the streets. Nor did it do much to alleviate the problem of traffic congestion. One way out was to extend the underground rail services but with indiscriminate competition at street level it was difficult for the Underground combine to attract capital for this purpose. It seemed, therefore, that the only way to ensure orderly development and a rational allocation of investment resources was by establishing unified control over the whole system of London transport. It was on these grounds that the London Passenger Transport Board was set up in 1933.

This body was the largest transport undertaking in the world. The Board acquired a monopoly of passenger transport services (by taking over the existing undertakings), except for taxis and the main-line railways, over an area of 2,000 square miles. Its primary duty was to provide an adequate and properly coordinated system of passenger transport for the London area and avoid all unnecessary and wasteful duplication of services. The Board had able leaders, notably Lord Ashfield and Frank Pick of the Underground combine, and even by the end of the decade it had achieved remarkable progress in bringing order to London's transport undertakings. Services were improved and extended, particularly the underground system, a greater degree of coordination between alternative transport modes was achieved, rolling stock and equipment were modernised and fares in many cases were reduced. Despite the degree of success the experiment was not repeated elsewhere, though the experience provided a powerful counter in the nationalisation debate after the second world war. Moreover, though the LPTB did great things it could not solve the most pressing problem, that of traffic congestion which if anything got worse during the 1930s as it did in most large urban areas. But then this problem is still with us today.

CIVIL AVIATION

Like motor transport civil aviation developed rapidly in the inter-war period. But it remained a very small sector of the transport system throughout, it was extremely unprofitable, and for the most part it had virtually no competitive impact on other forms of transport. Moreover, the main developments were concentrated on the external front.

Flying was technically possible by 1914 but it was very un-reliable, very dangerous and a costly exercise; consequently there were no regular commercial air services worth speaking of. Under the stimulus of war technical advancement was rapid so that by the end of hostilities regular flying was more feasible. Shortly after the war several companies were set up to provide regular services to the Continent, but within a short space of time all had discontinued operations since they proved to be extremely un-profitable ventures. Excessive competition, very high operating costs and the primitive nature of the early aircraft were the main factors responsible for the poor returns. In 1921 the government stepped in and offered the pioneer operators a subsidy which kept things going for another two or three years. Four companies were eventually operating services to the Continent with domestic feeder links. Nevertheless the position was still unsatisfactory and operations continued to be very unprofitable, partly because of excess capacity on the same routes including competition from French subsidised airlines. The solution to the problem appeared to be one large company, a fact recognised by the government in 1924 when it established its 'chosen instrument', Imperial Airways, which took over the four companies then in existence. This company secured a monopoly of subsidised air transport and was to receive annual payments for 10 years on a descending scale, for which it undertook to fly one million miles per annum and develop and maintain an efficient network of air services. In effect this meant that few other companies were likely to be established.

The company achieved a qualified success in its task. Within the first decade of its formation regular air links were forged with India, Africa and Australia, while Imperial Airways continued to operate services to Europe. This ambitious schedule was made possible by virtue of the rapid technical improvement in the performance of aircraft. The small (maximum seating for 4), unsafe, high cost, single-engined planes of pre-Imperial days were replaced by safer, faster, multi-engined craft. By the early 1930s, 13-ton four engined machines with accommodation for 38 passengers and cruising speeds of 105 mph were being put into service, while a few years later aircraft with cruising speeds of 140–200 mph were becoming available, a far cry from the early days when aircraft could rarely attain the speed of a fast train.[18] Without such improvements it would certainly not have been feasible to provide services over long distances. During the contract period Imperial Airways extended its route mileage from 1520 to 15,529, while passenger traffic increased from 10,321 to 66,324. The financial position of the company also improved. In 1935 subsidies, as a proportion of total revenue, amounted to less than 28 per cent as against 70 per cent in 1930, though it should be noted that the original subsidy had been considerably increased.[19] Moreover, without such payments, amounting to well over half a million pounds in 1935, Imperial Airways would have made a large loss.

The company's record was not above criticism however, and it came under heavy attack when inquiries were instituted in the middle of the 1930s. One of the main complaints was that too much attention had been paid to fostering communications with the Empire, some of which were unprofitable, at the expense of developments elsewhere, though in this respect the company was not entirely to blame since the government's original intention and its subsequent policy directives were designed to do just that. Consequently, services to Europe had been reduced to a minimum while little had been done to establish links with South America, Scandinavia and West Africa, and the first commercial survey flights across the North Atlantic were not carried out until 1937. However, it was the neglect of the European sector that created most concern especially since this had given an opportunity for several independent and unsubsidised companies to establish flights to European cities in the early 1930s, whereupon the government repeated its policy of the 1920s. In 1935 a second chosen instrument, British Airways, was set up to take over the main independent operators on the European network. The company was given a virtual monopoly of subsidised European services together with the task of developing new routes, notably the South American. Imperial Airways could then concentrate its resources on the Empire routes. Essentially therefore this produced the division of function as between short-haul and long-haul operations which was adopted in the post-war period. In the interim this distinction was not to last for long however, since the two companies were merged into one public undertaking, British Overseas Airways Corporation, at the beginning of the war.

Apart from the feeder services of Imperial Airways there were virtually no regular air services operated within Britain before the early 1930s. There were several good reasons for this absence, including a government refusal to subsidise internal routes. This apart, several other factors checked development. For most of the 1920s few decent aerodromes were available, and until 1922 Croydon was the only airport from which regular air services operated. The main retarding factor was economic however. Poor quality and high operating costs of the early aircraft provided little incentive to establish services in a country in which distances were short and the competition of surface transport severe. Given the technical limitations of aircraft, flying could not offer time and cost savings over ground transport.

By the early 1930s many of these factors had changed for the better. The number of suitable aerodromes increased rapidly from the late 1920s, largely as a result of the municipal building programme; by 1935 no fewer than 95 were in existence. Navigational aids, an important necessity in Britain's climate, underwent considerable improvement. Rapid progress in aircraft technology brought faster, safer, more reliable and more economical machines suitable for internal services. Cruising speeds well in excess of the fastest trains were by then becoming common. Thus in the early 1930s a whole host of companies came into being largely to service the domestic market. By the middle of the decade a network of regular services had been established and in all some 20 concerns operated about 76 different services. All the main cities were provided with air transport and many of the islands had been linked to the mainland. By the late 1930s 5000 route miles were being operated over which about 150,000 passengers were carried.[20]

The business was far from being profitable; in fact as far as we know no single company ever made a profit, and in the case of Railway Air Services,[21] one of the largest companies, the losses tended to increase as time went on. There are several reasons to explain this disappointing performance. Demand for internal air travel was very limited and it tended to fluctuate sharply. In part this was due to the rather erratic nature of the services offered. It was found amost impossible to maintain punctual, all-weather, day and night services because of adverse climatic conditions and inadequate facilities, both ground and navigational. In 1935 for example, less than one ninth of the scheduled services were operated without any break at all, and for much of the time aircraft were sitting idle on the ground. Load factors were exceptionally low, averaging about 35 per cent (Imperial Airways had a load factor of about 68 per cent and still could not break even), and it is doubtful whether 100 per cent load factors would have enabled the companies to make profits. Given the large number of companies the amount of traffic, when averaged throughout the year, was spread very thinly and the revenue derived from it was barely sufficient to meet direct operating costs. Passenger fares were therefore high, ranging from 3d to 10d per mile compared to just over 1d by rail, and this inevitably choked off demand. But price was not the only factor which discouraged air travel, since in many cases it was inferior in speed, comfort and frequency to that of rail. On many of the shorter routes journey times were often longer than those by surface transport on account of the time taken to get in and out of the airports. It was only on very long distance routes, and more particularly on those involving a water crossing, that air travel could offer appreciable time savings over surface transport; but on many of these routes the demand for transport of any sort was relatively limited, whereas on the dense traffic routes between major cities the quality of surface transport limited the scope for air traffic.

The situation was made worse by the large number of competing companies. Though many enjoyed only a brief existence there were always eager newcomers ready to take the place of those retiring from the business so that the number of companies in existence at any one time remained high by any standard.[22] Rationalisation of the structure was urgently required and some attempt was made in this direction eventually, the main influence behind which was Railway Air Services. This company acquired an interest in, or control of, a substantial part of the internal airline business. However, not a great deal of improvement materialised from this process partly because little attempt was made to combine the various interests into one coherent undertaking, while in 1938 several new companies were formed as a result of agreements between the railways and certain financial groups.[23] Only late in the day (1938) did the government step in with a subsidy and a licensing scheme in an effort to remedy the chaotic situation. The outbreak of war soon cut short the implementation of the scheme, but it seems very unlikely that it would have done much to make the industry financially viable since no fewer than 14 companies had their applications granted by the Licensing Authority, while the total subsidy payment to any one concern was limited to £15,000 per annum.

It would not be incorrect to say that aviation was still in the pioneer stage commercially by the end of the period. It had reached a stage similar to that of motor transport just before 1914, in that it was still a luxury form of travel enjoyed (or endured) by the rich. Motor transport, on the other hand, had already broken through the middle class barrier and was poised to break through to the lower orders in 1939. For aviation the attack on the middle class market came with the explosive growth of air travel after the second world war. Until then civil aviation acted only as a marginal supplier of transport services both in the passenger and freight markets. Thus surface operators, both on land and at sea, experienced no real competitive threat from this newcomer until after 1945.

SHIPPING

The branch of transport which suffered worst in this period was overseas shipping. After a spectacular post-war boom, when freights and ship prices rocketed, there were few really prosperous years for British shipowners. Freight rates and profits were either stagnant or declining for most of the time. The worst years were the early 1930s at the time of the world slump, and the sorrowful state of the industry was brought home sharply with the dramatic collapse of the Kylsant empire.[24] Tramp owners suffered more severely than the liner section of the industry. Some companies failed to cover even their direct running costs in the 1930s and as a result arrears of depreciation mounted to a total of nearly £11 million for the years 1930–5. A slow recovery took place in the later 1930s but even in the best year (1937–8) prosperity was still some way below the immediate pre-war years.

Even more depressing was the fact that Britain's supremacy in shipping was steadily undermined during the period. Though she remained the largest maritime power, her tonnage fell both absolutely and relatively. Between 1914 and 1938 world tonnage rose by no less than 46 per cent whereas the British fleet actually declined by nearly 6 per cent, with the result that the UK's share of total world tonnage fell from 42·8 to 26·0 per cent. A similar decline was experienced in the share of world trade carried in British bottoms.

The difficulties experienced by British shipowners were not unique to this country. Maritime concerns the world over were faced with the same problem: a surfeit of tonnage caused by the growth of foreign fleets, improvements in the technical efficiency of ships, and a slowing down in the rate of growth of world trade. In the post-war boom alone enough shipping was brought into existence to last a decade or more without any further construction; but building continued in many countries, especially in those fired with a nationalistic spirit to strengthen their maritime interests. The position became even worse in the 1930s when the growth of world trade was checked. Thus in the depth of the slump world seaborne trade was about the same as in 1913 but the volume of world tonnage was nearly 50 per cent larger than before the war. Even this tends to underestimate the seriousness of the situation since there had in the interim been a considerable improvement in the efficiency of shipping (oil-fired ships, diesel propulsion etc) which greatly increased the speed and carrying capacity of the tonnage available. Accurate estimates are difficult to make in this respect but some idea of the magnitudes involved are given by figures supplied by the League of Nations. These suggest that the freight carrying capacity of the world doubled between 1914 and 1939 (though this is possibly an excessive estimate), roughly half of which could be attributed to greater efficiency. When set against the 35–40 per cent increase in sea-borne trade over the same period one gets a clear notion of the scale of the problem. Even with the recovery in trade in the later 1930s much excess capacity in the form of idle ships or under-utilised tonnage space remained.

Yet why, one may ask, did a maritime expert such as Britain fare so badly relative to many other countries? That she had more to lose because of her semi-monopoly before 1914 is not an entirely satisfactory answer. One problem of course was that many countries subsidised their maritime activities, whereas British shipping remained virtually unaided until the 1930s and then was only marginally assisted. A variety of uneconomic expedients were used to boost shipping in other countries and British shipping certainly lost business to subsidised competitors. Too much should not be made of this factor however since some countries, notably Norway, managed to do quite well without any financial aid. Secondly, the most important source of employment, the home trades, gave less than cause for rejoicing. Though world trade was less buoyant than before the war it did at least expand in the inter-war period, whereas Britain's trade languished, especially on the export side. Both liners and tramps were affected by the stagnation in the export trade. Exports failed to regain their pre-war level and for most of the 1930s they were well below the previous peak. The dramatic collapse of coal exports—by nearly one half between 1913 and 1938—struck a severe blow to tramp shipping from which it never recovered, and the problems of this sector of the industry were later intensified by the rise of specialised carriers, the diversion of cargo to the liner trades, and competition from foreign tramp vessels. The liner trades suffered almost as badly from the sharp drop in merchandise exports and loss of emigrant traffic. The tonnage of non-coal exports fell from nearly 17 million tons in 1913 to just over 10 million in 1933, and even in the later 1930s hardly went past the 11 million mark. The emigrant traffic also dwindled—it was about 40 per cent less than pre-war on average through the 1920s, and in the following decade it disappeared almost completely when Britain for the first time became a net importer of people.

It is true that imports rose modestly during the period, but the volume increase was nowhere near commensurate with the severe losses in outward traffic and so could scarcely provide adequate compensation. In any case it is quite likely that foreign shipowners gained the best part of any increased activity in the inward trades, judging by the fall in the proportion of national (that is British) entrances to the total at British ports. Moreover, a large proportion of the increase in imports consisted of oil which provided employment for a type of ship largely neglected by British shipowners. Foreign services were often better and cheaper than our own, and in some cases subsidies gave the edge to our competitors.

If British shipping was perhaps more vulnerable than most to the unfavourable influences of the period one cannot explain everything in terms of external factors. Indeed, one student of the industry has gone as far as to argue that the malaise and stagnation in this country's maritime trades were largely self generated in that had British owners been more enterprising and dynamic they would have done much better.[25] This view possibly treats somewhat lightly the special problems facing British shipowners but there is certainly plenty of evidence to suggest that they did not grasp all the opportunities that were available. After all, the growth of shipping fleets abroad—and apart from the German the British fleet was the only one which contracted during this period—does indicate that outlets for expansion existed even though excess capacity prevailed in these years. Yet not only did British shipowners fail to exploit new trades, but on almost every route, including the main home trades, they lost ground to competitors.

No doubt subsidised competition was responsible in some cases, but one cannot ignore the fact that countries which gave little assistance to their maritime enterprises, eg Denmark, Norway, Greece and Sweden, did equally well if not better. Indeed, non-subsidised fleets expanded more rapidly than most of the subsidised ones and they managed to increase their share of world seaborne trade either by exploiting new trades or by encroaching upon British routes. In the American trade, for example, Norwegian shipowners trebled their share between 1920 and 1938 whereas British activity declined smartly.[26] Similarly in the relatively new and fast expanding oil trade Britain allowed her initial lead to be whittled away by the Norwegians. In 1913 Britain had owned one half the world tanker fleet, but neglect after the war saw this share drop to one quarter by the end of the 1930s in the face of rapid expansion elsewhere. In 1939 Norway's independently owned tanker fleet (that is owned by shipping rather than oil companies) was twice as large as the British and her tankers carried one quarter of the oil imported into this country.

Technically too the British shipping industry was falling behind. It was becoming a high cost operator relative to its main rivals partly on account of differences in manpower costs, subsidies etc, and one answer to this was cost-reduction through innovation. This meant investment in faster and more efficient vessels to reduce costs and enhance competitive power. The main development on the technological front in these years was the use of oil as a fuel. It had several advantages over coal. It was much easier and cleaner to handle, but more important it was very much more economical. It provided a 50 per cent increase in heat value for the same bunker space, and hence allowed more room for cargo, but when used in a motor ship one ton of oil did the same amount of work as two tons of oil and three tons of coal employed in conventional steam boilers. The use of oil as a source of energy made rapid headway after the first world war. Between 1918 and 1938 the proportion of world tonnage using oil as a fuel, either for steam raising or in the internal combustion engine, rose from 18 to nearly 53 per cent. In Britain on the other hand the new fuel was relatively neglected partly because of the plentiful supplies of cheap coal and partly because many British shipowners and ship-builders, as in the case of the railways, were prepared to place their faith in steam by attempting to improve the efficiency of steam installations despite the fact that diesel power offered a cheaper alternative. By 1939 only one quarter of the fleet used diesel pro-pulsion compared with around one half in the case of the Scan-dinavian and Dutch fleets. The latter, both of which were non-subsidised, took every opportunity to invest in modern and efficient vessels to enhance their competitive power, a course of action which British shipowners would have done well to emulate.

It is not sufficient to argue that the difficult economic conditions of the period were responsible for the failure of British owners to exploit new trades and innovate for then one would need to explain why some foreign shipping lines reacted differently to the same conditions. Probably, as Sturmey suggests, the problem stems from within the industry itself. The innate conservatism and complacency of British owners, reflecting both a satisfaction with past performance in the days of world supremacy and the increas-ing inflexibility of an industry dominated by family control and conference agreements, made them reluctant to explore new possibilities. After all, the criticism is not that they failed to invest but that much money went into building traditional ships unsuited to the changing conditions. 'There was an attitude of complacency, that the British industry was best by definition, had the most suitable ships and generally knew best, together with an introverted concern with serving British trades which was in marked contrast to the extrovert attitude of younger shipping enterprises in other countries.'[27]

CHAPTER THREE

Ownership, structure and control: the legislative background

INTRODUCTION

SINCE 1939 the ownership and structure of British transport, especially inland transport, has changed considerably. This is partly explicable in terms of natural evolution and development but a more important determinant has been the massive legislative programme relating to transport which has been carried out since the war. Indeed, perhaps the most impressive feature of British transport in the post-war period has been the enormous amount of legislative activity in this sector of the economy. Even before these great statutory changes legislation had been passed which affected almost every branch of transport. In the inter-war years, for instance, there were (as has been noted) some legislative changes of considerable importance, some of which, notably the Railways Act of 1921 and the London Passenger Transport Act of 1933, formed the prelude to nationalisation. Since 1945 however the volume and complexity of transport legislation has increased enormously and it is difficult to comprehend the present set-up without some knowledge of the changes wrought by legal enactments.

At present there are four distinct types of operators in British transport: the State or nationalised sector, municipal authorities, public trusts or boards and finally independent or private operators. Within each branch of transport these different forms of ownership frequently overlap, though in some cases one particular type tends to predominate. Thus practically all railway and inland waterway facilities are in public ownership, whereas most of the country's

66

Page 67

Above: Typical of urban transport in the late nineteenth and very early twentieth century was the horse tram. Most tramway systems were electrified by municipalities well before World War I, but this Leicester Corporation vehicle still depended on horse power in 1902.

Below: By 1914 the double-deck motor bus was king of London's streets. Other cities were somewhat slower to follow, but here is an interesting double-deck Guy of Leicester City Transport, photographed in 1927.

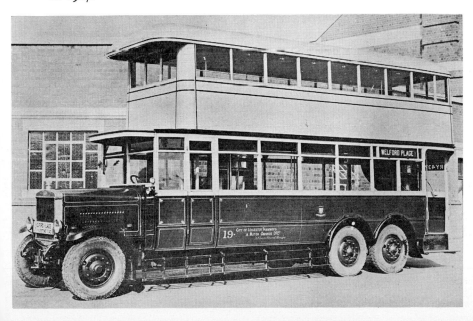

Page 68

Above: At the outbreak of World War II the best city omnibuses differed very little structurally from those of today. This is an AEC vehicle of 1938 belonging to Leicester Corporation.

Below: In an effort to reduce unit costs most local authorities now use single-man working in their transport system. This Leicester Metro-Scania of 1970 is equipped for pay-as-you-enter operation.

merchant shipping is owned by private enterprise, the main exception being short-sea or cross-channel passenger services. Apart from these two extremes, most other branches of transport are represented by more than one type of ownership. In road passenger transport, for instance, the state, local authorities and private companies all run services, while in road haulage private enterprise predominates, though alongside an important minority state holding. All forms of ownership are represented in the case of the ports and docks. The construction and maintenance of roads is shared by the state and municipal authorities and the ownership and control of aerodromes is largely in the same hands. Finally, most of Britain's civil aviation is nationalised, though there is a growing independent sector.

Changes in ownership and structure have been very much determined by legislation, though statutory control of transport as such has been much wider and has embraced all forms of transport regardless of the type of ownership. For convenience it may be classified into four categories. First, all branches of transport, whatever the form of ownership, have been subject to varying degrees of control relating to technical matters, safety requirements and terms of employment, as embodied, for example, in the Merchant Shipping Acts and the Road Traffic Acts. Second, certain branches of transport, again irrespective of whether they are publicly or privately owned, have had to conform to legislation which seeks to regulate or license their activities in one way or another. Notable in this respect are the licensing arrangements relating to road transport and civil aviation and the control over the charging policy of the railways. Third, major pieces of legislation have been passed which deal specifically with certain sectors such as aviation, docks, aerodromes and roads, some of which involved important structural changes. Finally, the main framework has been set, at least as far as inland transport is concerned, by the major Transport Acts of 1947, 1953, 1962 and 1968, which cover several branches of transport and which introduced severe upheavals in the structure and ownership of British transport. It is the latter, together with some specific pieces of legislation relating especially to civil aviation, which are relevant in this context, since for the most part they provide the background to the nationalised sector.

It would be tedious and somewhat repetitious to review all the above legislation in detail at this point since much of it can be more conveniently introduced at a later stage. Similarly, the more detailed structural format of the respective branches of transport may be deferred until we come to consider the individual transport agencies. In this chapter therefore we shall be concerned mainly with the broad structural changes which have taken place in the largest sector, that of nationalised transport, and the way in which these have been determined by the successive Transport Acts. The legislative framework within which the State sector has operated has in part conditioned the way in which the rest of the transport system has developed since the war. Moreover, it is difficult to discuss meaningfully the developments in the separate branches without some prior knowledge of the organisational changes brought about by the Transport Acts. These cover a large part of Britain's transport system, but generally speaking they exclude aviation, roads and airports. Statutory changes in these fields can be more conveniently discussed under the respective agencies.

MOTIVES FOR NATIONALISATION

That a large segment of British transport was transferred to public ownership in 1947 should occasion no surprise. The Labour Party had long advocated the nationalisation of transport as one of its major policies, partly on the grounds that transport had a natural tendency towards monopoly and could not therefore be left in private hands. It would be misleading however to argue that political ideology was the main force behind practical policy. Admittedly the Labour Party had always maintained that nationalisation was one of its main planks of policy and in this respect it kept to its word. The quality and cost of transport was bound to be a crucial factor in the Labour Party's grandiose plans for the industrial and economic revival of Britain after the war and hence could hardly be left out of account.[1] It should also be recognised that by 1945 nationalisation was largely a dead issue, at least as far as the railways and civil aviation were concerned, since some form of public ownership or control was probably inevitable whatever the political complexion of the Party in power. Nor was public control of economic activity the exclusive preserve of the Labour Party. Before the war the Conservatives had experimented with public corporations quite readily and late in the day they had even introduced a prototype nationalisation measure to deal with the airways. The railways, moreover, had been subject to increasing statutory control throughout their history and after the first world war nationalisation had been considered seriously at cabinet level at a time when such a policy was regarded as nothing short of revolutionary. Finally, the experience of two world wars had made the idea of unified ownership and control a much more acceptable proposition than it might otherwise have been.

For their part the Labour Party advanced some sound economic arguments to support their case for nationalising transport. Their main line of attack was the railways. It was claimed, and quite justifiably in many respects, that they had been neglected before the war and that the owners had failed to press forward with technical modernisation as fast as might have been expected. During the war railway assets deteriorated further through intensive use, but the experience of these years had also shown that the railways could be run more efficiently when under unified control. By the end of the war a drastic overhaul and modernisation of the railway system was urgently required and, given the cost involved and the limited financial resources of the railways, this could only be achieved by the financial backing and control of the government.[2]

On most of these points it was difficult to fault the party's claims. As in the first world war transport was tightly controlled but it was on the railways that the main burden of inland transport requirements fell. At the peak (1944–45) freight traffic was about 50 per cent greater than prewar while passenger traffic almost doubled, yet the rolling stock available for service declined as a result of an increasing amount of equipment under or awaiting repair and the relatively slow rate at which new rolling stock was constructed. The railways were therefore moving a very much larger volume of traffic without any effective increase in capacity and this was only made possible by the more intensive and efficient use of resources as a result of the careful planning of wartime transport operations. For example, the average load per passenger train in 1943 was more than twice that of before the war, while the freight train load per train mile rose from 122 to 156 tons over the same period. Considerable rationalisation of the movement of freight as between road and rail also resulted in substantial economies.[3]

The railways emerged from the ordeal in a sorry state. Labour, materials and equipment were in short supply, physical assets had been allowed to run down through lack of maintenance and investment, and a fair proportion of the rolling stock was either ready for scrapping or awaiting repair. The backlog was more serious than after the first war and in fact the position deteriorated further in the immediate post-war years as a result of a severe shortage of essential supplies. Moreover, the railways had limited cash resources with which to finance re-equipment. Under the wartime financial agreement with the government a large slice of their profits had been requisitioned, and although £151 million had been accumulated in a trust fund to meet arrears, payments into the fund had been based on historic replacement costs which meant that the sum was clearly insufficient given the subsequent sharp rise in prices. Wages and the price of many materials were approaching twice those of prewar while railway charges had been frozen. Soon after the war traffic began to fall off and the revenue position of the railways deteriorated.

The economic problems of the railways no doubt justified drastic action in the conditions prevailing at the time but Labour's policy was directed at a more comprehensive transport system. The nationalisation of the railways formed part of a plan for transferring to public ownership the entire, or at least a very large part, of the inland transport system. By so doing it was anticipated that it would be possible to provide a comprehensive and co-ordinated system of inland transport which would result in a more rational allocation of the use of resources. Indeed, this was the central feature of Labour's transport policy. 'It was the desire to "coordinate" all forms of transport throughout the country, in the manner already achieved in London, which constituted a powerful motive for the nationalization of surface transport in 1947'.[4]

On paper the arguments looked impressive, though at the time little was done to ascertain what benefits would accrue from nationalisation or just how co-ordination was to be realised. The Transport Bill introduced in November 1946 was designed to provide a once and for all solution to the internal transport problem in that it constituted the first attempt to deal with the matter as a whole.[5] However, many of the government's original intentions regarding transport failed to materialise and some indication of things to come was foreshadowed during the debate on the Bill. Despite the government's earlier emphasis on the economic merits of unified ownership and control the proceedings were heavily concentrated on minor points and the terms of compensation to the owners. Both sides neglected the central issues, namely questions relating to technical modernisation and investment, the integration of services and the criteria for charging. Even the government had little specific to say about such matters or the related question of the economic benefits to be derived from unified ownership. Reorganisation was generally agreed to be necessary but there was only a hazy notion as to the economic implications arising from such action.

THE TRANSPORT ACT OF 1947

The extent of Labour's nationalisation policy with respect to transport was wider than most people had anticipated. Nearly all branches of transport were affected apart from coastal and deep sea shipping. The railways were expropriated outright while other branches of transport were partly nationalised.[6]

The Act of 1947 set up the British Transport Commission as the authority responsible for inland transport in Great Britain. This body was charged with the general duty of providing 'an efficient, adequate, economical and properly integrated system of public inland transport and port facilities . . . for passengers and goods with due regard to the safety of operation' (sect 3 (1)). To achieve this the commission was given wide powers of control and acquisition over the carriage of goods and passengers by rail, road and inland waterways, and the provision of port facilities; in addition, the commission could provide certain amenities connected with transport services such as catering and hotels. However, the BTC did not get a monopoly of all inland transport by any means. The main line railways and London Transport were taken over in their entirety, but for the rest the commission had to be content with partial ownership. With respect to canals and waterways, ports and passenger road services, its immediate acquisitions were confined mainly to those concerns which had belonged to the railway companies, though since the latter had acquired considerable holdings in these sectors in the past the new authority became one of the largest operators of such forms of transport. Moreover, since the commission was given fairly wide powers relating to the acquisition of undertakings in the private sector its potential monopoly powers were considerable. However, these powers were not subsequently used to any great extent, though in the case of road transport the BTC did later add to its interests inherited from the railways by acquiring the road passenger holdings of the Scottish Motor Traction Group and Thomas Tilling together with a number of smaller provincial companies.[7]

Road haulage was dealt with more explicitly. Here there were few large undertakings and the inheritance from the railways was much less than in the case of passenger transport. There was also less justification for highly centralised ownership of large fleets since the optimum size of firm was fairly small. Nevertheless, the BTC was to become the largest long-distance carrier of freight by road, since the Act enjoined it to take over A and B licensed operators whose main activity involved the carriage of freight for distances of 40 miles and upwards outside a radius of 25 miles from their operating base. Owner account vehicles (C licence holders) and A and B licensed carriers operating within a 25 mile radius were left free to continue their business subject to the licensing law of the 1930s. In effect this meant the BTC had to build up a road haulage business almost from scratch. Initially the 400 largest concerns were acquired which formed the nucleus of British Road Services, the operating arm of the Road Executive.

Subsequently the fleet was enlarged by further compulsory acquisitions so that by the end of 1951 BRS owned about 44,000 vehicles[8] (with a total capacity of 310,000 tons) and had established a network of trunk services. This fell very far short of even a partial monopoly of road freight transport. The remaining A and B licence operators had more than twice as many vehicles (119,000), while the rapid growth of own account operations after 1946 gave rise to no less than three quarters of a million C licence vehicles. In fact the latter provided about 60 per cent of total capacity of all road vehicles while over 80 per cent of all capacity was owned by private operators.[9]

Thus by the time the BTC's acquisitions were complete in 1951 the authority's control over inland transport fell well short of complete monopoly. There still remained a substantial private sector, especially in road transport, while municipal transport remained outside its jurisdiction. Control over docks and inland waterways was confined mainly to those formerly owned by the railways, while it had no powers over taxis, coastal shipping and internal aviation. Nevertheless, the BTC had become, without doubt, the largest single transport agency within the country.

The internal structure and organisation of the commission, the broad details of which were laid down in the Act, are fairly straight-forward. The BTC itself was to be primarily a policy-making and directing body, responsible for the general provision and planning of transport subject of course to directives from the minister and government. One of its chief tasks on this front was to promote the main objective underlying nationalisation, namely the integration of transport facilities by planning the role of each form of transport. The commission was not an executive authority; management and executive functions were to be carried out by its agents, known as Executives, which were appointed by the minister and were responsible to the BTC. The number of executives was left to the minister's discretion, but the Act specifically designated five, one each for the Railways, Docks and Inland Waterways, Road Transport, London Transport and Hotels (see chart).[10] Each executive was to be responsible for the general management of the particular properties in question and would carry out those

ORGANISATIONAL STRUCTURE OF NATIONALISED TRANSPORT (under 1947 Act)

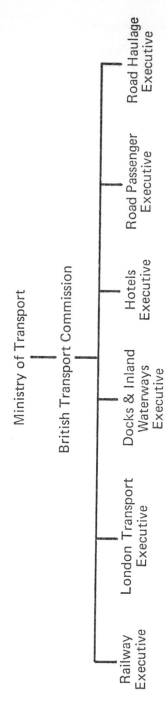

Ministry of Transport

British Transport Commission

Railway Executive

London Transport Executive

Docks & Inland Waterways Executive

Hotels Executive

Road Passenger Executive

Road Haulage Executive

Under the Act of 1953 all Executives, with the exception of the London Transport Executive, were abolished and were replaced by Boards of Management or Committees.

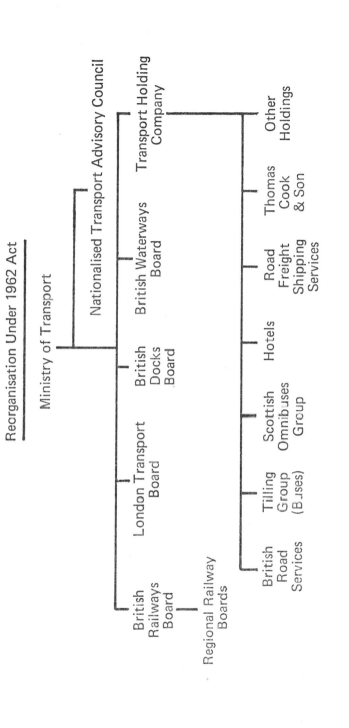

Reorganisation Under 1962 Act

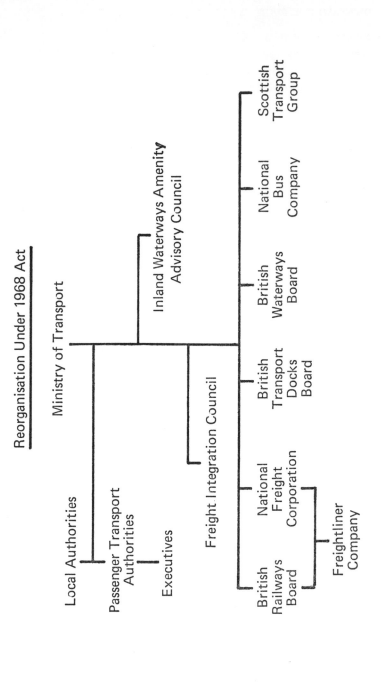

Reorganisation Under 1968 Act

Ministry of Transport

Local Authorities

Passenger Transport Authorities

Executives

Freight Integration Council

Inland Waterways Amenity Advisory Council

National Freight Corporation

British Railways Board

Freightliner Company

British Transport Docks Board

British Waterways Board

National Bus Company

Scottish Transport Group

functions and duties delegated by the BTC. In other words, they were operating agents with direct contact with the public. In turn the executives could organise their work on regional lines if necessary, subject to the consent of the commission. Thus the Railway Executive was divided into six regions, London Midland, Western, Southern, Eastern, North Eastern and Scottish.

Of the remaining provisions of the Act those relating to charging powers and financial matters were the most important and relevant. Apart from the duty of maintaining an adequate, efficient and properly integrated system of transport, the commission had to conduct its operations in such a manner 'as to secure that revenue ... is not less than sufficient for the meeting of charges properly chargeable to revenue, taking one year with another' (Sect 3(4)). In other words, in the long run the BTC was supposed to break even, though there was considerable vagueness as to the time period involved and the exact nature of the items to be charged to revenue.

In theory this meant that pricing policy would be the key factor in enabling the commission to fulfil its financial obligations, and also its duties with regard to the integration of transport services. Yet its freedom of charging was restricted in several ways. All revisions of charges had to be submitted to the Transport Tribunal (the old Railway Rates Tribunal)—in fact the commission was obliged to present draft charges schemes for all services within two years of the passing of the Act—which, after a public inquiry, the tribunal might accept, alter or reject as it saw fit. Furthermore, the minister could issue directives of a general nature relating to rates and charges, and though neither the minister nor the tribunal were expected to take action which would jeopardise the commission's efforts to break even, the rather vague phrase 'taking one year with another' was obviously open to abuse if either party interpreted it too loosely. In any case, the commission's freedom to manipulate charges was further restricted by the fact that the old nineteenth century statutory provisions relating to undue preference and discrimination were not repealed. However, the Act did not specify the manner in which charges should be determined, a somewhat glaring omission in view of the importance of the subject. Apart from the terms of compensation, the details of which are now only of academic interest, the remaining financial provisions related to the commission's borrowing powers. Fairly tight limits were imposed on the BTC's spending powers and ministerial approval had to be obtained for programmes of reorganisation and development involving substantial capital outlays.

Finally, because of the commission's fairly extensive ownership of inland transport facilities some form of protection was necessary for the consumer. Both traders and passengers were left free to choose that form of transport which most suited their needs, while special consumer consultative machinery (Transport Users Consultative Committees) was set up to protect the transport user from possible arbitrary acts of a public authority with semi-monopoly powers over inland transport facilities.

NATIONALISATION IN PRACTICE

It would be wrong to write off the 1947 Act as a complete failure in practice since the commission's powers and duties were soon to be modified by new legislation in 1953. Within a short space of time a considerable amount was accomplished though in the event the grandiose aims of the legislation were never realised. In its report for 1953 the commission presented a list of objectives which it had set itself, several of which were achieved by the early 1950s. The railways had been welded into a unified system, the former railway-owned docks had been regrouped, the waterways network had been rationalised, and a substantial road haulage fleet and organisation established. But in several respects, notably integration and charging policies, the commission's achievements had fallen short of what was desired. In part this failure can be explained by the difficulties involved and the deficiencies of the enabling legislation.

As far as the efficiency and adequacy of services is concerned the commission appears to have done its best at a time when resources were scarce and physical assets were in poor shape. The conceptual problems involved in any such assessment make judgement very difficult but there is little reason to believe that services were inadequate, since there was no sharp reduction in the amount offered, and given the conditions at the time the efficiency with which they were performed was satisfactory. The commission was also able to make a reasonable financial return in the early years since the railways were not then in serious deficit. It is clear however that some of the conditions laid upon the commission were incompatible. Efficient and economical operation in the commercial sense could never be attained as long as adequate services had to be provided since 'adequate' in the full public sense inevitably entailed the retention of unremunerative services and a degree of cross-subsidisation.

But it was on the question of integration and co-ordination of services that the BTC found the going hard. Initially the commission appears to have set its sights fairly high. In the annual report for 1950 it was observed that 'no opportunity has been lost to emphasise that integration is vital to the prosperity of the commission's undertakings . . .', and frequent references were made to plans for integration. But a reading of the annual reports leaves one in some doubt as to whether the commission had any clearly conceived ideas as to how this objective could be achieved. For the most part the commission appears to have concentrated its attention on physical means, that is structural changes of a piece-meal nature designed to achieve a more co-ordinated pattern of services. Several schemes for passenger road transport and trade harbours were prepared, in accordance with the provisions of the Act, together with partial schemes for the co-ordination of road and rail services. These only touched the fringe of the problem and the change in policy in the early 1950s cut short their implementation.

The slow progress achieved on this front was perhaps only to be expected. After all, in the early years the BTC was struggling with the problem of organising and shaping a transport monolith at a very difficult time, when capital and labour were scarce and much equipment, especially on the railways, required repair or renewal. Even so, it is doubtful whether an 'economical and properly integrated' system of transport in any full sense could have materialised from the provisions of the legislation. The machinery of organisation did not lend itself easily to the integration and co-ordination of facilities. Until the early 1950s the structure was highly functional and overcentralised. Though the BTC and its executive agents were responsible for managing and running the transport services under their command they were in a sense only delegated authorities since real and final power lay with the Minister of Transport who could override the decisions of the commission and its agencies. Any plan to co-ordinate services was likely to make slow progress in practice because of the functional and centralised nature of command. This meant that schemes for co-ordination stemming from the lower level had to pass right up the chain of command and on to the minister before a decision was finally reached, a process that was bound to cause delay and frustration. In any case, at the regional level integration of services was not likely to be encouraged since each executive tended to organise its regional structure differently. Eventually the railways had six regional divisions, the Waterways Executive five, and the Road Executive twelve.

The organisational problem was one that could have been solved given time and efficient management. More serious however were the incompatible obligations imposed upon the commission which made it difficult to achieve all the prescribed objectives at one and the same time. Apart from the prescriptions laid down by law the commission had a moral duty to fulfil certain social obligations, eg the provision of unremunerative social services, a duty which could hardly be reconciled with the writ to provide economic and integrated services. Moreover, failing satisfaction on pricing policy (see below) any attempt to provide economic and integrated transport facilities was dependent on some method being devised to ensure that each traffic was allocated to that mode able to transport it as cheaply and efficiently as possible. Here the commission's freedom to manoeuvre was restricted in several ways. Transport users were completely free to choose between alternative modes, while the BTC did not have a monopoly of all transport facilities. This was particularly the case in road passenger transport where the commission was expected to promote regional schemes for the co-ordination of passenger services whether by road or rail. Thus even had it been possible for the commission to direct or allocate traffic among its own services, its power to co-ordinate would still have been limited by the element of private enterprise, the activities of which increased in later years as a result of the partial denationalisation of road haulage in 1953 and the growth of own account transport.

Ideally of course the solution to integration rested upon a rational pricing system by which the prices charged for all services were related sensibly in some way to costs, in the expectation that each traffic would then take the least costly service. But in the matter of pricing the commission's hands were tied in several respects. It is true that there were no detailed specifications in the Act of 1947 as to how prices should be fixed and the initiative in formulating new charges schemes was left with the commission. The only specific provision was that it should not be prevented from making charges which would allow it to break even taking one year with another. However, in practice, when vetting charges schemes submitted by the BTC, the tribunal and the minister could, and did, interprete this provision rather loosely to justify rejections, delays or modifications of the proposed charges. Secondly, in the absence of specific recommendations on charging there was a danger that charges schemes would conform to the time-honoured principles of the past which meant an excessive averaging of charges and heavy cross-subsidisation. This is more or less what happened. Neither the tribunal nor the commission seemed readily disposed to undertake a radical revision of charging structures, and in fact by the early 1950s the new charges schemes still remained to be presented. Even by the end of the decade, when the new structures were more or less complete, it is doubtful whether pricing policies could be regarded as very much more rational and scientific than they had been before nationalisation.

There are several reasons why a rational pricing policy failed to emerge. In the first place the BTC only had a hazy notion about the costs of different services and therefore could not hope to price on the basis of cost throughout the system. Traditional practice ensured that value systems of classification still feature prominently in charging procedures, while the continued existence of restrictions against undue preference and discrimination did not help matters. Greater freedom was allowed in charging policies after 1953 but there still remained sufficient constraints in the system to ensure that the ideal policy was not attained. For example, political interference with new charging proposals sometimes upset matters. But this issue apart, the legislative framework tended to encourage cross-subsidisation rather than reduce it, a situation scarcely conducive to a scientific pricing policy. The fact that the BTC had fairly extensive control over inland transport left the way open for considerable cross-subsidisation, though in time as private competition increased, especially after the denationalisation of road haulage, the prospects of retaining sufficient remunerative traffic to allow this to take place steadily diminished. Furthermore, since the commission had the general duty of providing adequate services this appeared to presuppose that some of the less profitable services would have to be retained on social grounds. In fact, for most of its life the commission took its social obligations too seriously with the result that many loss-making services, especially on the railways, were kept open. Finally, the fact that the executives and the regions were not separately accountable left the way open for cross-subsidisation between services on a fairly wide scale.

The absence of a rational pricing structure severely limited the prospects of achieving a properly integrated system. As Gwilliam has noted: 'The failure to produce a new charges scheme which would meet this need was possibly the most serious and fundamental deficiency of the nationalised transport sector.'[11] These prospects were further diminished in 1953 when the Transport Act of that year denationalised road haulage and relieved the commission of its duty to integrate.

One further defect of the 1947 Act is that it paid little attention to the needs of modernisation and technical improvement in transport. The commission was obliged to provide an adequate and efficient system but it was never made clear how this should be defined, how it was to be achieved or what resources would be available. The railways in particular required a drastic overhaul and it could be argued that they deserved better treatment. Yet the Act contained little reference to this important matter and the commission's powers to raise money for investment were limited.

DENATIONALISATION OF ROAD HAULAGE

It is unlikely that the 1947 Act would have produced a viable, efficient and integrated system of transport since the commission's obligations and duties were such as to render the achievement of these objectives difficult if not impossible. However, given the fact that it was considerably modified before many of its provisions had been fully implemented it would be doing less than justice to describe it as a complete failure.

The Act of 1953 was clearly a politically inspired piece of legislation designed to abrogate certain provisions of the previous Act. Whereas the earlier legislation had been based on the assumption that unitary ownership was necessary for an efficient and integrated system the 1953 Act was based on the premises that competition would secure the best results. The white paper preceding the Bill maintained that the restoration of competition 'should lead to better and cheaper transport than could possibly result from the "integration" contemplated in the Transport Act [1947], which in any case would have tended to subordinate the needs of the trader to a plan, rather than to adapt transport to his needs'.[12] Accordingly, the commission's area of control over transport was reduced, its general duties modified, while certain restrictions relating to charging powers were lifted.

The major aim of the Act was to push through the denationalisation of road haulage. The commission was to dispose of its road haulage assets as quickly as possible through a specially constituted Road Haulage Disposals Board. In the event some difficulties were found in selling the entire fleet to the private sector and ultimately the commission was left with a small fleet of about 16,000 vehicles.[13] At the same time the commission was virtually debarred from acquiring further interests or control of any other transport undertakings in the private sector, while in the case of road passenger transport the minister could direct the commission to dispose of its existing holdings.[14] Subsequently the commission's remaining road services, as with private operators, became subject to the licensing provisions of the Road Traffic Acts of the 1930s, and the limitation on private hauliers imposed in 1947 was lifted.

The general duties of the commission and its structure were revised. Henceforth the commission was expressly limited to providing railway services together with other transport services and facilities in those fields in which it had a stake. Except for the case of London Transport, the former obligation to integrate or co-ordinate transport services was rescinded, including the obligation to prepare area schemes for road transport services. However, not all the general requirements contained in the 1947 Act were repealed since with respect to all its services and facilities the BTC had to pay due regard to 'efficiency, economy and safety of operation and to the needs of the public, agriculture, commerce and industry'. (Sec 25(i)).

As far as structural matters were concerned provision was made for the abolition of all the executives by Ministerial Order and this was subsequently accomplished for all except London Transport. Henceforth the individual branches of transport operated as constituent companies under the BTC the latter retaining control over general policy matters and financial operations. The idea behind these changes was to get away from the over-centralised and functional system of management which had previously existed but which had never worked very smoothly in practice. Secondly, by giving greater freedom and autonomy to the individual managements it was envisaged that they would be in a better position to operate in a commercial manner.This policy was carried furthest with respect to the railways where special provision was made for the abolition of the executive and the setting up of a decentralised management structure. Eventually Area Boards were established to administer the regional railway networks. These boards were not intended to be executive organs of day-to-day management, but were bodies roughly corresponding to the company boards which existed prior to 1948. It was the intention that the Area Boards should exercise general supervision of the railways in their areas and ensure that the policies laid down by the BTC were carried out. They were given a considerable degree of autonomy with respect to the formulation of policy at the area level and over the supervision of the work of the regional railway managers who were responsible for the day-to-day running of the railways.[15]

Some notable departures were made in the field of charging policies, these being partly designed to inculcate a greater degree of commercial freedom. The BTC was required to prepare and submit draft charges schemes to the tribunal for the railways, inland waterways, canals and port facilities, but not for road transport (except in the London area), which were to be dealt with by the road licensing authorities. Only maximum charges were to be embodied in the schemes and the BTC could fix charges as they saw fit as long as the maxima were not exceeded. Special provision was made for the temporary adjustment of charges to meet rising costs up to a maximum of 10 per cent. At the same time, to increase the competitive thrust of the railways, some of the former restrictions relating to equality of treatment and undue preference were removed. Nevertheless, some restraints remained. The tribunal retained the power to revise or reject the maximum charges schemes, and in certain cases, notably freight charges, to determine on appeal the reasonableness of particular charges.

It is difficult to accept much of the logic behind the Act of 1953 since in effect it was neither one thing nor the other. Basically the main ideas behind it were to provide greater competition and reverse the trend towards large scale unitary ownership established by the Act of 1947. But in the latter respect the government confined its attention to road haulage and the end result was to leave British Road Services with the rump of the vehicles which it could not sell. However debatable the advantages of scale may be in this sector the upheaval, after years of careful work in building the network, was enough 'to damp the spirits and blunt the initiative of those in charge.'[16] In any case, BRS was far from being a monopolist and if all that was desired was greater competition this could have been achieved by removing the 25 mile limit and relaxing the 1933 restrictions pertaining to road haulage licensing.

Increasing competition and the return of road haulage to private ownership meant further pressure on the railways' financial viability; cross-subsidisation between road and rail would no longer be feasible. Thus it became even more important, at least from the financial viewpoint of the railways, that charges should be related to costs, and, since coordination was to be effected increasingly through the market, that charges for all the commission's services should be based on sound costing principles. But, as with the earlier legislation, the Act of 1953 gave little guidance on this matter and judging by the subsequent progress on this front it is clear that not a great deal was achieved towards producing satisfactory pricing formulae.

Perhaps the major defect was that the Act did not really go far enough. It provided greater incentive for the exercise of commercial freedom but not enough to ensure the financial viability of the services operated. The management of the separate branches of transport was made more decentralised but the restricting influence of the BTC's overlordship was always lurking in the background. Indeed, it is somewhat difficult to see why the commission was retained in existence as a separate entity except for the ease with which the minister could communicate directives. Given the fact that each branch of transport was hived off into separate managements and that the commission no longer had the express obligation to integrate services there appears to be no valid reason why it should have been retained. The main raison d'etre for the commission had been its power to integrate services and once this obligation was removed its continued existence became an anomaly and in some ways a hindrance to progress in the separate branches of transport for which it was responsible.

THE BACKGROUND TO THE REORGANISATION OF 1962

The logical conclusion to the legislation of the early 1950s came in 1962 when the BTC was abolished and separate independent Boards were established for each of the main activities formerly managed by the commission. The background to this reorganisation is worth recounting in some detail.

The chief reason for the dissolution of the BTC was undoubtedly the failure to deal with the railway problem. By the late 1950s the railways were approaching financial bankruptcy. After 1955 they had failed to make a return even on their current account and by the early 1960s the current deficit was approaching £100 million per annum,[17] and the accumulated deficit of the BTC amounted to over £500 million most of which was accounted for by the railways. Greater commercial freedom and the modernisation plan launched in 1955, had done little to assist the railways in the face of mounting competition from road transport. Moreover there was every prospect of further deterioration unless drastic action was taken.

The BTC was not wholly to blame for the railways' financial circumstances, but it is clear from the searching criticism made by the Select Committee on Nationalised Industries in 1960 that on many counts the commission had failed miserably with respect to railway policy. In the first place, though the BTC had chosen the right priorities in the modernisation plan, it had not, for one reason or another, implemented them fully. Even worse the committee found that the plan had not been checked properly. Many of the estimates were based on guesswork and no proper attempt had been made to calculate the returns on each sector of the plan. In this respect the Ministry of Transport was as much to blame as the commission in not ascertaining the facts properly, with the result that large expenditures were undertaken on modernisation 'without any precise calculation of what the profitability of those parts will be on completion.'[18]

Secondly, the commission was reprimanded for the slow progress made in developing a satisfactory system of costing both on a national and regional basis. The commission still had only a hazy notion as to the real cost of most of its services, while little had been attempted in the way of regional accounting on the grounds that it was too difficult given the great interchange of traffic between regions. Be that as it may, the absence of a proper costing system undoubtedly had serious consequences. The area boards were unable to determine how efficient and profitable their main activities were, and hence they could not calculate the full effect of any modernisation proposals. Furthermore, ignorance on the matter of costs prevented the railways from charging economic fares and in turn this slowed down the rate at which un-remunerative services were withdrawn. The committee was further critical of the way in which policy had been based upon both economic and social considerations: 'this confusion in judging between what is economically right and what is socially desirable has played an important part in leading to the situation in which the Commission now finds itself'.[19] The implication was that the commission should have based its decisions on economic criteria alone and provided only such services as could be operated profitably. Where social considerations necessitated the continuance of uneconomic services it was up to the government to subsidise them.

Finally, the committee was not at all happy with the way the railways were controlled by a body responsible for more than one form of transport. The commission's transport responsibilities were too wide and the interest of the railways would have been better served by one single authority. 'It cannot have helped to achieve efficiency in the higher direction of British Railways that there should have been no one authority whose only duty in the whole field of transport was to ensure an efficient system of railways.'[20] It was hinted therefore that some structural reorganisation might be advisable though the committee did not specifically recommend the break up of the commission.

To some extent the criticisms made about the commission's activities were unfair since it was clear that the government was partly responsible for the failure of the BTC to fulfil its obligations towards the railways. The commission could point to the fact that revenue had been lost through fare increases being held up by the minister, that capital investment plans had been adversely affected by government interference, and that the government should have given a clearer mandate as to the future size and shape of the railway system and more explicit guidance on the matter of social obligations. But in the circumstances a scapegoat had to be found and the commission's apparent failings provided a convenient excuse for reorganisation.

The strictures of the select committee were no doubt sufficient to sign the death warrant of the BTC. Nevertheless, it is clear that the government was by this time seriously considering the question of transport reorganisation. In March 1960 the prime minister had intimated in the House of Commons that measures of reorganisation were iminent and he announced the setting up of a special inquiry, the Stedeford Committee, to advise on the structure of nationalised transport. The Advisory Group's report was not published but it is almost certain that it recommended a thorough overhaul of the existing structure and that its proposals were embodied in the white paper on transport which heralded the break-up of the BTC.[21] These events must be set against the background of a wholesale re-thinking regarding the basic objectives and financial obligations of nationalised industries as a whole. In April 1961 a white paper on their financial and economic objectives[22] marked the beginning of a new framework of control for nationalised industries which was designed to make them more commercially minded and give more explicit definition to their financial objectives.

THE TRANSPORT ACT 1962

The Act of 1962 completely reversed the provisions of that of 1947 since it reconstituted the transport services, which had been grouped under BTC, under separate authorities. The break-up of the commission meant the end of any prospect of integration and co-ordination of internal transport services as a whole, and in fact competition between services became the official policy. It was hoped, however, that by dividing up assets in this way, and giving the individual boards as much commercial freedom as possible, some improvement would take place in the financial position of the concerns, especially of the railways.

In place of the commission four autonomous transport authorities were established, the British Railways Board, the British Docks Board, the British Waterways Board and the London Transport Board. The remaining activities of the commission were grouped under a newly created Transport Holding Company. The latter covered a wide collection of activities the most important of which were road haulage and bus and coach services (see Chart p77).[23] Each board was to be financially autonomous which meant that cross-subsidisation between sectors was no longer possible. However, rather surprisingly in view of the new economic philosophy with regard to public undertakings, the financial duty of each board was very similar to that laid on the BTC, namely to balance the accounts taking one year with another (Section 18). The main exception to this rule was in respect of the Transport Holding Company which was given a clear commercial mandate to maximise profits.[24] From the beginning the company regarded itself as commercial enterprise rather than a nationalised concern,[25] and it subsequently demonstrated its ability to improve on the results achieved by the more centralised regime of the BTC.[26]

As might be expected the provisions relating to the railways were spelt out in some detail. The new board was to devote its energies almost exclusively to managing the railway system. The day-to-day management of the railways was placed in the hands of six regional boards which had greater autonomy and freedom from central control than the Area Boards which they replaced, though there was no requirement that each should maintain a separate regional trading account. The extent to which responsibility was delegated to the regions was a matter to be decided between the minister and the Railways Board, and decisions on certain key matters, eg finance, industrial relations and planning the shape and size of the railways system, were to be taken centrally. As far as financial matters were concerned the railways were treated generously. Nearly £500 million of accumulated debt was written off while approximately £700 million worth of commencing debt was suspended, thus relieving the railways of a considerable part of their interest burden. Since it was not expected that the railways would be able to pay their way in the first five years the minister was empowered to make grants of up to £450 million to cover operating losses, after which it was anticipated that the railways would break even.

Considerably greater freedom was given to the boards with respect to commercial matters. Common carrier and other statutory obligations were removed and the boards in theory were free to charge for their services as they saw fit. However, certain restrictions remained; in particular, fares in the London area were still subject to the jurisdiction of the Transport Tribunal, while it was still possible for the minister or government to intervene when changes in rates or fares were proposed.[27]

The reorganisation of nationalised transport in 1962 was largely inspired by the pressing needs of the railways. By placing them under one separate authority and relieving them of certain financial and commercial burdens it was hoped that this would lead to a more concentrated and dynamic effort on the part of the management. However, the legislation, while relieving the railways in the short-term, could do little to solve the long-term fundamental financial problems of the railways since it made no specific provision for tackling one of the main problems, namely the elimination of excess capacity and uneconomic services. Though the procedure with respect to closures was simplified no specific provision was made for subsidy payments in cases where consent to proposed closures was refused. Thus there was no clear indication that the new procedure would speed up the rate of closure and the future viability of the railways depended on the execution of plans then being prepared for reshaping the network.

The Act had little to say about the relationship between various forms of transport and this is hardly surprising given the fact competition was assumed to be the mainstay of the new policy. Provision was made for co-ordination of services in the London area through co-operation between the London Transport Board and the Railways Board, while a Transport Advisory Council was established to advise the minister on questions relating to co-ordination. But its terms of reference were confined to nationalised transport, which in effect rather limited its scope in relation to road and rail transport as a whole. In any case, if the competitive process was expected to produce the desired results it is difficult to see exactly what purpose the council was to serve.

If co-ordination and a rationalised allocation of resources was to be achieved through market forces it was essential that the latter should be allowed to operate. Yet it is clear that this could not be achieved without a rational system of pricing the services offered. In this respect the Act of 1962 went no further than that of 1947 since, though it retained the break even clause for each board and allowed much greater freedom in the realm of pricing, it made no specific pronouncement on the criteria for determining charges nor did it provide any relevant body to look into this question. Thus there was no guarantee that the board would behave any differently than the former management in this respect, in which case it was unlikely that all prices charged would reflect costs and as a consequence not all traffic would take that service least costly in terms of real resources.

LABOUR'S 'NEW DEAL' FOR TRANSPORT—THE 1968 TRANSPORT ACT
The dust scarcely had time to settle on the previous legislation before another upheaval was mooted. This final phase (at least as far as this book is concerned) was the biggest and most dramatic since 1947. It was inspired not by any immediate pressing problem, though the railways were still in trouble. Rather it was, as with the 1953 episode, the product of a change in government in 1964 which expressed dissatisfaction with the policy of their predecessors.

The Labour Government felt that the commercial approach had been tried and found wanting. A ruthless policy of rationalisation and commercial drive by the Railways Board (under the inspiration of its chairman Dr Richard Beeching) had not produced a markedly better financial turnout. More generally it was considered that by maintaining the principles laid down in the Act of 1962 the proper transport needs of the country were being neglected.

The new approach to transport policy was outlined in a White Paper published in July 1966.[28] It was clear from this statement that the government's main intention was to reverse the trend towards commercial freedom and the disintegration of transport services which had been going on since the early 1950s. While stressing the desirability of improving the efficiency of transport operations generally, the main emphasis was on the need to integrate road and rail services and to ensure that the transport system as a whole took full account of the social and economic requirements of the country. In place of the 'Victorian mentality' of trying to solve the transport problem by competition between autonomous enterprises, there would be a return to planning each part of transport 'as part of a coherent and integrated whole'.[29] As far as the railways were concerned this meant that commercial viability, though still an important consideration, would be of secondary importance. The railways could not be expected to play a proper role in the economy if they were required to comply with the provisions of the 1962 Act since, in the words of the White Paper, it took too little account 'of the interrelation of the railways with other forms of transport and of economic and environmental needs, whether national or regional.'[30]

In accordance with these new objectives the White Paper made several proposals, the full details of which were to be elaborated more fully in four official papers released in November 1967. First, the government intended to re-define the size and shape of the basic railway network so that it would accord more closely with the country's commercial and social needs. This meant that the network would be somewhat larger than that envisaged under the previous policy of widespread closure. Details of the revised network were published in a Ministry leaflet in March 1967.[31] Commercially viable services would be expected to pay their way but the government undertook to assume financial responsibility for losses incurred on services retained for social reasons. The Railways Board could then be given realistic financial objectives to enable it to move as soon as possible to a fully economic basis of operation. A working party, under a Joint Steering Group, was set up to examine key aspects of railway operations, including costing and pricing, investment appraisal, management structure and financial reconstruction. Despite its wide terms of reference its report dealt mainly with the latter two problems and for the most part its recommendations were accepted by the government without modification.[32]

The second main proposal related to freight traffic.[33] In place of the competition between road haulage vehicles of the Transport Holding Company and the equivalent rail freight services there was to be a combined organisation, the National Freight Corporation, to take over both. This new body, which was to be run on commercial lines, would take over the railways' Freightliner services, sundries division and cartage vehicles, together with the state-owned road haulage and shipping services operated by the THC. In effect this meant the railways would no longer be burdened with heavy losses on sundries traffic, but they would participate in the profitable Freightliner business by means of a 49 per cent holding in the Freightliner Company, a subsidiary of the new corporation. These proposals covered mainly those forms of freight which could be conveyed either by road and rail, and the general aim was to achieve a more efficient and integrated type of service and eliminate wasteful competition which would offer the customer an integrated door-to-door service by road and rail. To further this aim a new and, in some ways, more restrictive form of road haulage licensing would replace the existing A, B and C licensing system of the 1930s.[34] Its most important feature was the proposal to institute quantity control licences for heavy vehicles engaged in long-haul movement of bulk freights. The idea behind this form of control was that it could be used to promote the shift of traffic from road to rail wherever this could be done economically and without detriment to the consignor.

A fairly extensive reorganisation of public passenger transport was also envisaged[35] on the grounds that the existing units of control (primarily the local authorities in this instance) were often too small to carry out the proper planning and integration of transport services over wide areas. To overcome this problem Passenger Transport Authorities, traversing the boundaries of several authorities, were to be set up in major urban areas outside London; they, or rather their executives, would take over municipal bus undertakings and prepare plans for the integration of all transport services within their areas.[36] Since this would involve co-operation with the railways the government proposed to make grants to the executives in respect of the costs of any subsidies incurred in the maintenance of suburban railway services. Outside the major conurbations, bus transport was to be controlled by a National Bus Company (with a separate group for Scotland) which would acquire the bus interests of the Transport Holding Company. This undertaking and its Scottish counterpart would work in close conjunction with the Railways Board and the Passenger Transport Authorities, and would take over responsibility from the railways for securing the provision of bus services to replace withdrawn rail services.

The policy recommendations contained in the White Papers of

1966 and 1967 formed the basis of the mammoth Transport Bill presented to Parliament late in 1967 and which became law almost a year later. Its principal objective is to promote the integration of inland transport and in this respect it envisaged a move away from the Tories' concept of competition and a return to the concepts of the 1947 legislation. But there is a significant difference. Under the 1947 Act all forms of inland transport were lumped together under the single control of the British Transport Commission; this later proved to be a mistake since the range and diversity of transport activities were too great for any one undertaking to secure integration and efficient operation. The new Act therefore attempted to achieve integration on a sectoral basis by hiving off various types of transport under separate and autonomous authorities. Railways, docks and waterways were to remain as before under their respective boards, but a number of new agencies were created, namely the National Freight Corporation, two National Bus Companies and the Passenger Transport Authorities, while the Transport Holding Company, shorn of its activities, disappeared.[37] The new organisational set-up can be seen on the chart (page 78) and compared with that under the Acts of 1947 and 1962.

The organisational changes followed closely the lines detailed in the white papers preceding the Bill. In the first place a complete rationalisation of freight activities was to be carried out. The new central authority, the National Freight Corporation, acquired the road haulage and shipping services of the Transport Holding Company, all the assets used in British Rail's freightliner services except the trains, and the railways' sundries (parcels) traffic. The NFC was given commercial responsibility for freight traffic by road while the Railways Board had the same duty with respect to that carried by rail. Like the Transport Holding Company the new corporation is a holding concern which organises its various activities through several subsidiary companies.[38] The Act also established two new subsidiaries of the NFC. The first of these, the Freight Sundries Company,[39] is a wholly-owned subsidiary; it acquired the railways' sundries traffic for which it was to receive a subsidy to cover initial losses. The second agency is the important Freightliner Company, owned jointly by the NFC and BRB, which handles all traffic consignments on freightliner services. The Freightliner Company is to be run as a commercial concern and the British Railways Board charges commercial rates for the carriage of its containers.

Both the Railways Board and the Freight Corporation are charged with the general duty of promoting 'the provision of properly integrated services for the carriage of goods within Great Britain by road and rail'. The chairmen of both boards are members of a new Freight Integration Council whose task is to advise the minister on freight integration over the whole field of nationalised transport, including aviation. However, in this respect there is, as envisaged in the white papers, a clear indication that attempts will be made to shift traffic from road to rail whenever possible. In the execution of its duty the Freight Corporation is expressly required to secure that in the provision of (properly integrated) services, 'goods are carried by rail whenever such carriage is efficient or economic' due regard being paid to the needs of the consignor and the type of goods to be carried (Section 1a). In this respect the new road haulage licensing system, which replaces that of the 1930s, was to play a special role. All road haulage operators, including own account operation, must obtain an operator's licence for goods vehicles exceeding $1\frac{1}{2}$ tons unladen weight (all vehicles below this weight are exempt), and a transport manager's licence. These constitute the *quality* licence provisions designed to ensure safety, efficiency and proper accountability with respect to such operations. The more controversial measure was that providing for *quantity* licensing the objective of which was to ensure that rail services should be used where available unless the consignor could show that they were inferior to road haulage. 'Special authorisations' were required for goods vehicles of more than 16 tons gross weight engaged in hauls over 100 miles and for certain bulk materials suitable for rail movement. Applicants for such permits were to be made to the licensing authorities and the only bodies entitled to object were the NFC and BRB who must prove that rail has a definite advantage over movement by road. At the time it was suspected that the system would be used to divert traffic to the railways, but in fact these provisions have not so far been invoked.

As for passenger services one of the main objectives of the Act was to promote the co-ordination of local services within major urban areas. The minister had power to establish Passenger Transport Authorities anywhere in the country. So far five have been established,[40] while control over London Transport has been transferred to the Greater London Council and in effect constitutes a further PTA. The authorities are designated as virtually autonomous monopolists within the respective areas since all municipal bus undertakings are transferred to their executives, while the latter are virtually exempt from the powers of the Traffic Commissioners. The main duty of the PTA's is 'to secure or promote the provision of a properly integrated and efficient system of public passenger transport to meet the needs of that area with due regard to the town planning and traffic and parking policies of the councils of constituent areas and the economy and safety of operation' (Sect 9 (3)). In order to facilitate integration the PTAs are empowered to co-operate with the Railways Board, the National Bus Company and any other transport interests with respect to the provision of road and rail services.

All the bus interests of the Transport Holding Company including some of those belonging to the former London Transport Board are vested in the National Bus Company and the Scottish Transport Group. Both have a duty of reorganising passenger services and co-ordinating these services in conjunction with other transport operators. The Scottish Group also has powers over water transport in Scotland.

The financial clauses of the Act are important for they provided for an extensive system of subsidies and grants together with another capital reconstruction of British Rail. In part these were designed to ensure that the relevant transport authorities met the requirement to break even 'taking one year with another', a phrase seemingly enshrined permanently in the vocabulary of transport legislators, though they also served to fulfil a social purpose. The railways, as might be expected, were the chief beneficiaries. The interest-bearing capital debt of the Railways Board was reduced to £300 million. The railways were to be assisted by two forms of grants: up to £50 million, paid over a five year period (1969–73) on a tapering basis, was provided for track rationalisation, while grants, expected to be in the region of £55 million, were to be made towards the cost of unremunerative railway services retained for social reasons. The PTAs can also make payments to the Board for keeping rail services open and ultimately it was anticipated that they would assume financial responsibility for such services in their areas. The railways were also relieved of their unprofitable sundries traffic which was transferred to the NFC, the latter receiving a grant over a five year period for this item. Indirectly the railways would also be assisted by higher charges imposed on road haulage and the new road haulage licensing system. Several other grants or subsidies were to be made to bus operators towards fuel costs (to offset the duty), the cost of new buses and for major improvements to existing systems such as new track and passenger terminal facilities.

It is too soon as yet to say how the new arrangements will work in practice and in any case not all the clauses of the Act have been invoked. Quantity licensing for road haulage, for example, has not been brought into operation. Nevertheless, by 1970 most of the major changes had been introduced and the new transport authorities were in full operation.[41]

The Act of 1968 is certainly an impressive piece of legislation and most commentators would probably agree that it represented an improvement over that of 1962.[42] The latter had several notable defects including the failure to deal with the antiquated road licensing system, the absence of any comprehensive urban transport policy, the failure to deal with the contradictions in railway policy and the lack of any policy to determine the best use of road and rail resources in the public sector. By contrast, as one critic has noted 'In relation to the failures of the 1962 Act, we can see that Mrs Castle [the author of the Act] has dealt radically with road haulage licensing (but not with passenger transport licensing); has laid the foundations of a comprehensive urban transport policy; has resolved the contradictions in railway policy; and has produced a reshaping of the public freight sector which *could* bring about a new optimum use of resources. Vertical integration within the public sector is taken a step forward by this reorganisation, and has been encouraged (e.g. with the development of Inland Clearance Depots) outside the main transport policy measures; but it is still left as rather a Cinderella of policy, in spite of the more general acceptance of its importance'.[43]

LEGISLATIVE ACTION IN RETROSPECT

It would be out of place in a general survey to attempt a detailed criticism of the current legislation. However, it is worthwhile to cast some reflections on the legislative framework relating to inland transport as it has developed in the twentieth century.

Twentieth century transport has been dominated by massive organisational changes. Since the second world war major legislative reorganisations have occurred with monotonous regularity and the nature of these changes has been partly determined by political considerations, or swings in the political pendulum, and partly by a belief, on the part of politicians and civil servants, in the virtues of institutionalism, that is the idea that economic problems are best solved by altering the institutional framework rather than by formulating policy which will solve these problems. There are times of course when there is good reason to alter or adapt the structure when institutions have 'seized up' or outlived their usefulness, as in the case of the British Transport Commission. On the other hand, there is a case for arguing that organisations are only as good as the management makes them—witness for example the relative success of the Railways Board under Beeching, the varying fortunes of the airways corporations under different managements, and the failure of the BTC which suffered from indifferent management.

Be that as it may, there is no doubt that frequent structural changes have not been conducive to progress in transport. The constant upheaval has produced an unsettling effect on managements and, as Munby has noted in the case of the railways,[44] has prevented over-stretched managements from doing what they should have been capable of doing. The shock imparted by the denationalisation of road haulage had an almost nightmarish quality about it and the road haulage sector of the BTC, after years of hard work building up its network, was left in a demoralised state.[45] The Transport Holding Company was particularly critical about the way in which transport was exposed to a constant political cross-fire. In its last report the company complained that the impending threat of dissolution or dismemberment was scarcely conducive to the proper and profitable development of a business undertaking. Moreover it proceeded to launch a swingeing attack on the frequent upheavals caused by political dominated transport legislation of the post-war period:

> Approximately thirteen years out of the twenty-one were spent waiting for major Transport Acts of Parliament, whether good or not-so-good, and in reorganising after them. . . . Moreover, each Act has represented another swing of the political pendulum. There has also been, over the twenty-one years, a whole series of lesser Acts, Statutory Instruments and White Papers, not to mention the reports of Committees of Inquiry. Each of these has given rise in turn to the usual political exchanges, and . . . the British Transport Commission (or its successors) was thereby exposed to a form of severe crossfire which certainly did not improve its image or its effectiveness.

> . . . surely the moral of the last twenty-one years as a whole is that political intervention shall be kept within bounds that are not only reasonable, but also clearly and precisely defined, and above all that a concensus view must be arrived at, as a political settlement, as a result of which the transport industry will be freed from the consequences of reversable Acts of Parliament every few years, and will at last be granted a due amount of stability.[46]

Nor was this the end of the matter. Apart from the major upheavals, there has been increasing political intervention and control of one form or another so that nationalised transport undertakings have not even been allowed the degree of commercial freedom laid down by law. Frequent Ministerial intervention has been exercised with respect to pricing policy and investment programmes which in some cases adversely affected their performance. No doubt such intervention was sometimes misguided, but in other instances it could be argued that there was insufficient control. The most notable example is the apparent failure of either the Treasury, the Ministry of Transport or anyone else to check the viability of the railway modernisation plan of the 1950s. A more glaring disaster it would be difficult to find.

Apart from the unsettling effects of massive upheavals in transport structures, it has been suggested that the emphasis on organisational changes was largely irrelevant to the transport problems of the twentieth century.[47] The enormous growth in the use of private motor transport and the concomitant decline in the importance of public transport have given rise to the problem of adapting and modernising the latter sector while at the same time reallocating resources within the sector as a whole. Since the resources available for the transport sector are limited it therefore becomes essential that they should be allocated efficiently and that consumers of transport should choose that type of service which costs least to provide in real terms. To achieve the desired results it is necessary to ensure that appropriate criteria are devised for pricing transport services and for allocating investment and that suitable financial targets are prescribed for transport undertakings.

Little of the twentieth century transport legislation has made much contribution towards tackling these issues. In most cases, from the Railways Act of 1921 through to the Transport Act of 1962, the dominant theme, or even obsession, has been reorganisation and the crucial economic issues have been ignored or neglected. Thus, for example, very little attempt was made to relate the provision of public transport to that in the private sector in terms of the allocation of scarce resources. The associated problem of urban transportation has been virtually neglected. Policy guidelines to nationalised undertakings on financial and economic matters have also been minimal. Practically the only financial direction contained in the Acts has been the obligation of such undertakings to balance their books 'taking one year with another', a requirement with little meaning or significance, especially in terms of modern needs, unless more specific guidance is given on the criteria to be followed with respect to investment and pricing. On these matters the law has remained silent. The result has been that not only has financial performance varied a great deal, but also that a wide variety of pricing and investment criteria have been used the success of which is far from obvious. In the absence of sound criteria it was almost inevitable that resources would be misallocated, either through over-investment in certain sectors, or the failure to invest in those areas where normal market forces could not reflect a need in social terms. Thus in the case of the London Midland electrification scheme in the 1950s no proper criteria were used for assessing the economics of the project nor were any alternatives even considered, that is whether a diesel operated line would have been a better bet, or even doing nothing at all. Or to take a more recent example, the question of whether to subsidise rail or bus services on social grounds; in 1971 some £30 million was spent on subsidising rail services as against only £1 million on buses though the latter, in direct monetary terms, are much cheaper to run. Some individual single railway journeys cost the taxpayer £2 each, or over £1000 a year per passenger. At this rate it would be cheaper to buy the passenger a new car every year.[48]

During the 1960s there was some change for the better and in part this was reflected in the most recent legislation of 1968. Attempts were made, both within and outside the government, to identify the chief features of the transport problem and the sort of policies which should be applied to resolve that problem. This involved not only the exposure of the problem in terms of hard facts—eg the extent of the urban traffic problem, the likely demand for transport in the future and the consequences of the withdrawal of public service facilities[49]—but also the way in which more refined economic analysis could contribute towards dealing with these matters. The most notable example in this respect was the progress made in the application of social cost-benefit analysis which could help to determine the correct amount of investment or disinvestment to make in cases where market forces were either absent or too weak to resolve the issue.

Official thinking and practice on these matters was also making steady progress. A beginning was made in 1961 when the financial targets of public undertakings were defined in more precise terms[50] and this was later followed by a further white paper which defined, for the first time, the criteria to be used for pricing and investment.[51] Briefly this advocated that prices should be related to marginal costs, that all important projects should make use of discounted cash flow techniques, and that financial targets should reflect sound investment and pricing policies. It was also recognised that certain projects might require appraisal by social cost benefit analysis which would be undertaken by government departments.

Not all these developments are reflected in the Transport Act of 1968 by any means. The time-honoured principle of breaking-even taking one year with another still stands, while little reference is made to investment and pricing criteria. On the other hand, it may be argued that there was no real need to specify in detail on such matters since the latter could be left to consideration outside the law, and, in any case, the fact that more sophisticated economic analysis is now widely accepted in government circles suggests that it will be more readily applied in the future. There are grounds for some reservations on this score however. It is doubtful for instance whether the Passenger Transport Authorities come within the scope of the government's new thinking. Secondly, it would seem that there has already been some relaxation in the strict vetting of major transport investments which has operated since the late 1960s. The £35 million first stage of the Fleet underground line in London has gone through despite some doubts about its merits both on commercial and social benefit grounds,[52] while so far we have heard little about the economic viability of the electrification of the West Coast trunk railway line from Weaver Junction to Glasgow now reaching completion. If this sort of thing becomes a common occurrence the whole economic exercise of the last few years will have been in vain.

In other respects however the 1968 Act does represent an advancement on what has gone before. For the first time a serious attempt is made to grapple with the urban transportation problem; the provision of specific subsidies for loss-making but socially desirable services is a welcome departure from previous practice, while the prospects of improved integration of freight transport hold out promise. Much remains to be done, particularly with respect to co-ordinating the policies of so many separate authorities, both publicly owned and local authority, and relating these to activities within the private sector. Whether the new developments are successful still remains to be seen.

CHAPTER FOUR

The changing pattern of transport demand in post-war Britain

SINCE THE WAR the transport sector has not only grown faster than the economy as a whole but there has also been a significant shift in the pattern of demand and hence a change in the relative importance of different branches of transport. This has been true on both the domestic and international fronts. As far as inland transport is concerned this comprised a shift from rail to road transport, and secondly, a move away from public towards private transport, especially on the passenger side. There was, in addition, a marginal swing towards air transport. These changes in demand patterns have almost been matched on the international side; here there has been a dramatic shift from sea to air travel, though on the freight side air transport has hardly challenged shipping's monopoly in freight movement. The origins of most of these changes can be traced back to the inter-war period but undoubtedly their most spectacular impact has occurred since 1945. Indeed, it would be necessary to go back to the rail/canal era to find changes of similar dimensions. However, before discussing the nature of these shifts in more detail it is essential to consider the importance of transport in the economy as a whole.

TRANSPORT IN THE NATIONAL ECONOMY

The main indicators suggest that transport as a whole has been an expanding sector of the total economy in the post-war period, though the data on this matter are not altogether free from ambiguity. Index numbers of output for transport and communication show that this sector expanded at a slightly slower rate than industrial production and gross domestic product up to 1963, after which there was some acceleration.[1] However, the index also includes communications, while the series for transport is by no means comprehensive in that it does not fully reflect the contribution of private car ownership.

It is not easy to estimate very precisely the size of the transport sector as a whole. Probably the best approach is to compile a composite figure of the expenditure generated by each branch of transport from the national income series, though even this runs into difficulties. The breakdown of the figures suggests that there may be an element of double counting in certain cases, while some of the series, notably those for road haulage expenditure, are not very reliable. Moreover, there is no series for expenditure on ocean freight transport, and the treatment of private car transport is not altogether satisfactory.

Despite these difficulties an attempt has been made to construct a uniform series of transport expenditures for the period 1954–1969. This includes current expenditure on passenger and freight transport by road, rail, sea and air, together with capital expenditure on all types of transport including roads, docks and harbours. The series for private cars and road haulage vehicles includes consumer and business expenditure, taxes and estimated depreciation of vehicles, but excludes the actual purchase of new vehicles. Expenditure on sea freight transport is excluded as a reliable series could not be found for this item. The final result of these calculations is given in table 3. Given the incomplete coverage and the tentative nature of the estimates in some cases it cannot claim a very high degree of accuracy. But the fact that uniformity has been maintained in the compilation over time does mean that it can be used to illustrate the trend movements. From table 3 it can be seen that total transport expenditure has formed a steadily rising proportion of gross domestic product; the share in 1954 was just under 16 per cent but by 1969 it had risen to over 20 per cent. As might be expected, capital expenditure, which excludes the purchase of private vehicles, has fluctuated quite sharply in certain years and as a proportion of total capital formation the upward trend was checked quite sharply after 1960, though more recently the trend has again been reversed.

Table 3 *Estimated total expenditure on all forms of transport 1954–1969 (£millions at market prices)*

	Current expenditure	Capital expenditure (1)	Total transport expenditure	Total transport expenditure as a proportion of gross domestic product	Capital expenditure on transport as a proportion of gross domestic fixed capital formation (1)
1954	2448·3	388	2836·3	15·86	15·20
1955	2653·3	427	3080·3	15·86	15·27
1960	3803·9	845	4648·9	18·24	20·51
1965	5848·5	977	6825·5	19·28	15·47
1968	7412·0	1374	8786·0	20·59	17·43
1969	7919·1	1440	9359·1	20·38	17·73

(1) Excludes purchase of private vehicles
Sources: *Annual Abstract of Statistics; National Income and Expenditure; Passenger Transport in Great Britain; Highway Statistics* (all HMSO)

Clearly then transport has been anything but a stagnant sector of the economy in the post-war era. Even if some of the estimates are open to question the magnitude of the rise in the share of the transport sector leaves little room to doubt that it has expanded both absolutely and relatively. This expansion has also been accompanied by a marked shift in preferences for different modes of transport.

INLAND PASSENGER TRANSPORT

The most dramatic growth has been in passenger transport, especially that within Great Britain. Consumers' expenditure on all passenger transport (including sea and air, both inland and overseas) as a proportion of total consumers' expenditure almost doubled between 1946 and 1970, from 5·95 to 11·79 per cent (table 3). Inland transport accounted for much of this growth. Volume indicators show that the average person was making more journeys in 1970 than twenty years earlier. By the latter date the number of passenger miles travelled per capita was more than double (4682) that in 1950 (2106). Throughout the period as a whole per capita movement within Great Britain increased at a rate of just over

4 per cent compound per annum compared with 2·8 per cent for gross domestic product.

All this expansion is virtually attributable to the spread of private car ownership. In fact, all other forms of inland passenger transport have declined both absolutely and relatively; the only exception has been air transport but this is still only a very marginal supplier of inland transport services. The swing away from public transport (road and rail) was already under way by the beginning of the period and by the later 1950s passenger miles travelled by private car had exceeded those by public means. Some ten years later, in 1970, private transport accounted for over three quarters of the passenger movement within the country. On a per capita basis passenger miles travelled by public transport fell by nearly 50 per cent between 1950 and 1970 whereas those performed by the private car rose more than six times.

The changing distribution of passenger traffic between different modes of transport can be seen clearly from Table 4. In 1950 public transport accounted for over 70 per cent of the inland passenger movement and private road transport for around one

Table 4 Total Passenger Mileage travelled in Great Britain 1950–1970 (estimated passenger mileage, 000 million passenger miles)

	Air (incl. Channel Islands & Northern Ireland)	Rail (1)	Road (public service vehicles)	Public Sector (road & rail)	Road (private transport)	Total
1950	0·08	23·9	50·2	74·1	28·8	102·98
1955	0·2	23·8	49·8	73·6	54·3	128·1
1960	0·5	24·8	43·9	68·7	89·4	158·6
1965	1·0	21·8	39·2	61·0	144·7	206·7
1970	1·2	22·2	34·1	56·3	196·2	253·7
Percentage shares of total						
1950	0·08	23·21	48·75	71·96	27·97	
1955	0·15	18·58	38·88	57·96	42·39	
1960	0·31	15·64	27·68	43·32	56·37	
1965	0·60	10·54	18·96	29·40	70·00	
1970	0·50	8·80	13·40	22·20	77·30	

(1) Includes London Transport Railways
Source: *Passenger Transport in Great Britain* (HMSO)

quarter or more. Since that date the share of the former has declined steadily in every year so that by 1970 the relative shares had been completely reversed. Within the public sector bus and coach travel has suffered the worst. Traffic carried peaked out around the earlier 1950s, when it accounted for about 45 per cent or more of all passenger movement, and within the next two decades it fell by almost one third so that by 1970 its share was a mere 13·4 per cent. Passenger movement by rail held up rather better; here the traffic peak was as late as 1957 and the decline since that date has been quite modest at just over 11 per cent. Even so, by 1970 the railways accounted for only 8·8 per cent of total passenger movement as against nearly one quarter in 1950. The remaining sector, air transport, has in fact experienced even more rapid growth than private road transport, but it started from a negligible base and even today it accounts for a mere one half per cent of all passenger movement. Moreover, there is some indication that air travel within the UK may have peaked out recently as a result of improved long distance rail transport and further penetration of the private car.

The data on consumers' expenditure confirm the trends depicted by the physical volume indicators. Table 5 provides the

Table 5   Changes in consumers' expenditure on transport 1946–1970
(percentage shares in total transport expenditure)

	Expenditure on private motoring as % of total consumers' expenditure on transport	Expenditure on public transport (bus/rail, sea/ air) as % of total consumers' expenditure on transport	Expenditure on rail and bus as % of total consumers' expenditure on transport	All consumers' expenditure on transport as % of total consumers' expenditure.
1946	28·77	71·23	NA	5·95
1950	32·34	67·66	NA	5·69
1955	54·42	45·58	38·02	7·81
1960	64·12	35·88	28·67	9·41
1965	68·50	31·50	22·96	10·28
1970	72·18	27·82	18·21	11·79

Source: Derived from *National Income and Expenditure* (HMSO)

key data in the form of percentage shares of expenditure on different modes in total transport expenditure. Private motoring expenditure includes running costs and the purchase of vehicles, while for completeness a calculation has been made for all public passenger transport expenditure, including that on sea and air travel between Britain and other counries. The growth of expenditure on private transport has undoubtedly swamped all other transport expenditure even when expenditure on overseas travel, virtually all of which is publicly operated, is included. Whereas just after the war the public share of transport expenditure was over 70 per cent and that of private transport less than one third, the relative shares had been almost exactly reversed by 1970. Within the public sector only air transport has increased its relative share.

Thus, in a period when passenger transport has expanded rapidly the private road vehicle has swept all before it. It has not only created new traffic but it has also creamed off much of the traffic from the public sector with the result that the latter has contracted substantially. As yet there seems to be no sign that this diversion has been completed even though private transport accounts for nearly three quarters of all inland passenger movement.[2] Private motoring now accounts for a similar share of total expenditure on transport. Moreover, according to the Family Expenditure Survey, household expenditure on transport in 1970 was the second largest category of household expenditure, accounting for 13·7 per cent with food at 25·7 per cent and housing, the next largest, at 12·6 per cent.[3]

INTERNATIONAL PASSENGER TRAFFIC

There has been an equally dramatic change in the volume and distribution of passenger traffic to and from the UK. The main difference compared with inland transport is the absence of any diversion from public to private transport since the two modes, air and sea transport, are almost exclusively publicly operated. Since 1950 total passenger movement from the UK has increased by more than five times and both sea and air travel expanded through to 1970.[4] However, air traffic has experienced by far the most rapid growth; between 1948 and 1970 it rose twenty-fold whereas passenger travel by ship barely trebled. Before the war air transport had only been a marginal supplier of passenger transport services, accounting for less than 4 per cent of total outward movements. The war itself gave a boost to aviation development and, partly as a consequence of an incapacitated mercantile marine, travel by air rose sharply in the early post-war years; by 1948 it accounted for nearly 21 per cent of UK passenger departures. Thereafter the relative share of air transport increased continuously and by 1970 it was approaching two thirds of the external passenger traffic to and from the UK.

The penetration of air transport has varied considerably according to the length of route involved. On long distance routes air traffic had easily surpassed that by sea in 1960 (the North Atlantic was the first route to be captured from shipping) and within the next decade sea travel on such routes dwindled to insignificant proportions. To all intents and purposes air transport accounted for the bulk of long-distance international traffic by 1970. On most other routes air penetration has been slower and travel by sea has continued to increase steadily. This can partly be explained by the fact that the cruising element has retained some attraction on the shorter sea voyages, though cost differentials are also important (see below). Thus is was not until 1963 that air traffic to the European Continent and Mediterranean area exceeded that by sea, and the latter continued to increase slowly

Table 6   UK passenger movement by sea and air 1938–1970 (000s)

OUTWARD

	Air	Sea	Total	Air as % of Total
1938	101·2	2156·9	2618·1	3·87
1948	537·3	2056·8	2594·1	20·71
1950	723·3	2461·7	3185·0	22·71
1955	1422·2	3189.4	4611·6	30·84
1960	2956·0	3368·0	6324·0	46·74
1965	5589·0	4326·0	9915·0	56·37
1970	10844·0	5761·0	16605·0	63·31

Source: *Annual Abstract of Statistics* (HMSO)

despite further penetration by air. In 1970 outward air traffic to this area numbered 7,637,000 passengers compared with 4,758,000 by sea. Traffic to the Irish Republic has been the least receptive to air transport and by 1970 the division of traffic between air and sea was about equal.[5]

INLAND FREIGHT TRANSPORT

The trends in inland freight transport have been similar to those on the passenger side though somewhat less pronounced. The volume of goods traffic by all modes, including inland waterways, coastal shipping and pipeline (measured in ton-miles), increased by 2·9 per cent per annum between 1952 and 1970, a rate of growth very similar to that in gross domestic product, but substantially less than that in total passenger transport. The main growth sector has been road transport and again there has been a marked diversion from rail to road transport, though not quite so dramatic as in the case of passenger traffic. Nevertheless, by 1955 the share of freight carried by road exceeded that of rail and at the end of the decade road haulage accounted for one half the total goods movement within the country. Since then road freight has continued to increase in importance and in the late 1960s it accounted for about 60 per cent of the total. Rail freight has declined absolutely and the share of the railways has fallen from around 45 per cent in 1952 to 20 per cent in the late 1960s (see table 7). In terms of actual tonnage carried the railways' share is even less, not much more than 10 per cent in 1970 compared with 84 per cent for road haulage.

Other forms of transport only made a small contribution to total freight movement, though in the later 1960s coastal shipping appears to have hauled the same amount as the railways. However, the statistics on coastal shipping have been revised so frequently that there remains some doubts as to their reliability. Coastwise shipping is mainly concerned with long hauls of one or two bulk commodities such as coal and oil,[6] and in terms of tons carried it accounts for only one quarter of the tonnage by rail. It still remains, however, one of the cheapest forms of transport for bulk hauls. The smallest sector, pipelines, has experienced the most rapid growth, but it still remains a marginal specialist supplier

Table 7   Freight Transport in Great Britain 1952–1970 (000 million ton-miles)

	Rail (1)	Road	Coastal Shipping	Inland Waterways	Pipelines	Total
1952	22·4	18·3	9·0	0·2	0·1	50·0
1955	21·4	23·0	9·0	0·2	0·1	53·7
1960	18·7	30·1	11·9	0·2	0·2	61·1
1965	15·4	42·1	15·3	0·1	0·8	73·7
1970	16·4	50·8	14·2	0·1	1·8	83·3

Percentage shares

	Rail (1)	Road	Coastal Shipping	Inland Waterways	Pipelines	Total
1952	44·8	36·6	18·0	0·4	0·2	100·0
1955	39·8	42·8	16·8	0·4	0·2	100·0
1960	30·6	49·3	19·5	0·3	0·3	100·0
1965	20·9	57·1	20·8	0·1	1·1	100·0
1970	19·7	61·0	17·0	0·1	2·2	100·0

(1)   From 1969 onwards includes estimates for former freightliner and sundries traffic by rail now handled by Freightliners Ltd and NCL.

Source: *Annual Abstract of Statistics*

even though by the late 1960s the throughput tonnage was almost as large as the traffic carried coastwise. Pipeline transportation is a very recent development which poses a challenge to both road and rail. Though Britain laid a network of pipelines during the war to service military airfields it was not until the early 1960s that commercial application of this new mode of transport began on any scale. The Pipelines Act of 1962 gave the government considerable powers of direction and control over construction of pipelines. Since that date a network of lines has been established for the transportation of liquid products, notably gas and oil, and by the end of the 1960s some 8 per cent of all oil movements in the UK were made by pipeline, that is almost as much as conveyed by British Rail. Great Britain now has three main crude oil pipelines, and several for refined products with the number continually increasing. Natural gas was first piped ashore at Easington in 1967 and since then there has been rapid development in this field. The next phase will be the piping of North Sea Oil which should come on stream during the mid 1970s.

The pipeline has certain advantages over traditional forms of transport. It provides a continuous flow movement, there is no problem with regard to return loads, the pipeline does not suffer from congestion or the hazards of trans-shipment, and it is very economical of space and light on manpower. On the other hand, it is very inflexible, construction costs are heavy and the final costs of piping depend upon a number of factors. The costs of conveyance vary according to the degree of fluidity of the product—e.g. crude oil is more expensive to pipe than light petroleum products —while there are important scale economies to be had from increasing the diameter of the piping installation. As one might expect, costs vary inversely with the degree of capacity utilisation. If pipelines are used to maximum capacity unit costs can be kept low and hence they compare favourably with those of other forms of transport, but units costs rise very rapidly when throughput falls below the optimum.

Pipeline transportation is not likely to develop on the same scale as in the United States since surface distances in the UK are comparatively short. Nevertheless, the pipeline has presented a competitive threat to both road and rail, especially for the conveyance of oil, since, except for small quantities, the unit costs are generally lower. Road transport is not so seriously threatened however since most tankers are employed in the later stages of distribution, while coastal shipping still remains cheaper except in cases where the tanker route is considerably longer. It certainly seems likely that pipelines will penetrate further into the market for the movement of liquids, but whether they will become a viable alternative for the transport of other commodities depends on how easily they can be converted into a liquid or semi-liquid state and then reconstituted, as in the case of certain chemicals, and the technical feasibility of moving solids in an encapsulated form. In actual fact the movement of solids by pipeline, a derivative of municipal domestic sewage systems, has quite a long history, since as early as 1913 pieces of coal up to five inches in size were being conveyed for 600 yards from a Thames wharf to Hammersmith power station at the rate of 50 tons an hour. By the 1950s several industrial hydrotransport pipelines were in use carrying a variety of solid-liquid mixtures, usually in the form of coarse slurries. Such products as coal, chalk, certain types of asphalt, iron ore, concrete and cement can be carried in this manner, and a 57 mile pipeline for Portland cement operates near Rugby. However, as yet there are no great economic benefits to be dervied from moving solids by pipeline except over relatively short distances.

In contrast to the situation in passenger transport there has not been any marked shift towards private haulage, that is mainly on own account (the C licence traffic). In fact it is rather the reverse, though for earlier years it is difficult to state the exact position owing to the lack of reliable statistics of traffic carried by various types of vehicle. It seems almost certain that up until the early 1950s there was a trend towards own account operations, no doubt partly resulting from the reaction to nationalised road haulage undertakings and the disorganisation following therefrom. Certainly there was a massive jump in the number of C licence vehicles—between 1946 and 1954 they more than doubled whereas only a very modest increase occurred in the number of vehicles operating for hire or reward. Thereafter the rate of expansion of own account vehicles slowed down, while those for hire and reward increased more rapidly than previously, partly as a consequence of the denationalisation of road haulage in 1953. A sample inquiry carried out in 1958 suggested that hire and contract work had developed more rapidly than own account operations since the early 1950s. Increases in the size and carrying capacity of vehicles, industrial changes and the easing of some restrictions on operation were the main factors responsible.[7] Since 1958 there has been a marked trend away from private haulage according to the estimates presented in *Highway Statistics*. The mileage performed by vehicles on hire or reward expanded more rapidly than own account operations and by 1970 accounted for 61·4 per cent of the total compared with 52 per cent in 1958, and around 46 per cent in 1952. On the basis of tons carried own account operations were still slightly more important, though again the tonnage figures show a clear trend away from this sector.[8]

The remaining branch of goods transport—that of international freight—need not detain us long. Though the volume of overseas freight business has expanded steadily in the post-war period there has been no substantial diversion from one mode of transport to another. The bulk of overseas freight still goes by sea though there have been some remarkable improvements in handling methods in recent years. Air freight has expanded rapidly in the last decade or so but it is confined for the most part to valuable or perishable cargoes of low bulk. As yet air transport only performs a marginal role in freight movement though the potential for further penetration into this sector is considerable.

DETERMINANTS OF TRANSPORT DEMAND

The changes in the volume and pattern of transport demand since the war are of such magnitude that it is worthwhile to attempt some assessment of the causal factors at work. In certain cases the forces determining the growth in demand for a particular service or the diversion of traffic from one mode to another are fairly obvious. For example, there is no great mystery as to why air passenger traffic has grown so rapidly and why shipping has lost out to the airways on certain routes. Two factors predominated here—speed and price.[9] Rapid technical development in aviation has brought forth an enormous improvement in the reliability and speed of aircraft. Before the war cruising speeds of 180 to 200 mph were just about attainable with the new DC3's. By the early 1950s this had been lifted to around 300 mph and within the matter of little more than a decade cruising speeds had almost doubled. Thus the Boeing 747, with a cruising speed of 585 mph, could reduce the Atlantic crossing to a 'commuter trip', while Australia can be reached within just over a day's travel whereas the sea voyage takes about one month. The time saving involved has obviously been crucial to business travellers, and no doubt accounts for much of the traffic lost by shipping lines on long distance routes. That factor apart, the airlines have undoubtedly generated much of their own traffic through cost-reducing technical innovation, particularly the employment of larger aircraft.[10] As a result the price of air travel has fallen substantially. In 1951 the lowest available normal return fare on the New York—London run was $711; by 1969 it was $420, which represented a real reduction of more than 50 per cent. The following year saw the introduction of even lower special fares of \$250.[11] Given these changes it is not surprising that air passenger traffic on this route has grown from negligible proportions in 1948 to over 6 million passengers in 1970 by which time air transport had captured about 95 per cent of the total market. On many other routes average air fares in real terms have been reduced by about 50 per cent over the past fifteen years and market penetration by air transport has increased accordingly. In fact, on most long distance routes air travel is now cheaper than sea transport.

This is still not the case on shorter routes specially those to the near continent. Surface transport remains cheaper but air transport has a premium in terms of speed. However, this has not been sufficient to outweigh the higher costs and hence, though market penetration is increasing, sea transport retains a substantial share of the market though much of it is accounted for by short cross-channel journeys, especially car ferry services. In this context the development of hovercraft services in the last decade or so has given a new lease of life to cross-channel ferry traffic. The commercial application of this new form of travel has been very rapid indeed. The first practical demonstration took place in 1959, the first commercial services were started in the early 1960s and within the matter of a few years traffic levels approaching half a million passengers were being recorded. Most of the services so far have been confined to the south coast ports though feasibility studies are being carried out for other routes. The two main companies in the market are Hoverlloyd and British Rail's Hovercraft subsidiary; the latter began operations in the middle of the 1960s and by 1971 it was carrying over one million passengers and nearly 100,000 cars across the English Channel and to the Isle of Wight. The market share of hovercraft services on these routes has risen very rapidly indeed; by the early 1970s hovercraft carried 20 per cent of the car and passenger traffic across the Dover Straits at speeds five minutes less than by air.

The reasons for the remarkable progress of hovercraft travel can quite easily be identified. In terms of speed and cost, and possibly also safety, it scores over other forms of transport. Large hovercraft require only about one third of the power required by conventional displacement vessels to achieve speeds of over 40 knots, while operating costs are further reduced by lower manning requirements. Thus it is able to offer a speedy service at modest prices both of which compare favourably with those offered by the traditional ferry and air transport. It caters also for car ferry traffic which is a rapidly growing market. Furthermore, it is a very flexible form of transport which can be operated without the need for elaborate terminal facilities so that the potential for extending services to many minor ports is considerable.

Given the potential of hovercraft services doubts must be raised as to the wisdom of further investment in alternative transport media for cross-channel services. This applies to both conventional sea ferry services and air transport, but above all to the whole question of the much and long debated Channel Tunnel the trial boring stage of which has recently been given official sanction. Estimates of the cost of the project vary considerably but it is unlikely to be less than £800 million allowing for interest and inflation; moreover, it is anticipated that the Tunnel would make a considerable loss during the first ten years of operation. Some traffic which would use the Channel Tunnel could be carried as quickly and as cheaply by 15 to 20 large hovercraft costing about £3 million each, at early 1970s prices, while even conventional ship services with accompanying terminal facilities could provide the necessary means of transport at a fraction of the cost of the Tunnel. Nevertheless the advantages with potential expansion of through bulk rail transits with next day delivery cannot be ignored. In view of the considerable cost differentials there would appear to be a case for reassessing the economics of this controversial project.

There has been nothing spectacular in the growth of inland freight transport. The rate of increase has been more or less what one might expect in accordance with the expansion of gross domestic output, and there is no special reason why it should expand at a rate much different from the latter. Of more interest is the distribution of traffic between different modes, and in particular why the railways have lost traffic and why road transport has been the main growth sector. The railways have of course lost some of their heavy traffic as a result of the decline in the staple industries such as coal, but at the same time they have failed to participate in the expanding sector of the freight business, notably merchandise. Indeed the railways have lost some of their former traffic in this category to road transport. It is unlikely however that this diversion of traffic can be explained simply in terms of cost differentials between road and rail even though costs have been moving against the latter. Within certain limits it is probable that relative price differentials have played only a small part in the choice of transport mode. Many firms and traders are unaware of the true nature of transport costs and this is especially the case with firms which operate their own vehicles since no proper costing is usually carried out. A selected inquiry made in the mid 1960s found that only one third to one half of the firms surveyed were aware of the transport costs by alternative modes for some or all of the consignments about which they were asked. Over one quarter of the consignments despatched by professional operators (road, rail etc) were sent by modes which were more expensive than the cheapest alternative, while nearly one third of those consignments not sent by the cheapest method went by a mode that was 25 per cent more expensive than the cheapest alternative. Many traders stressed that their transport requirements were determined by the speed of service, ready availability and convenience, all factors which would tend to tilt the balance in favour of road rather than rail transport.[10] However, the ownership of road vehicles by firms was not a significant influence on the distribution of traffic between modes. In this respect the type of consignment and length of haul were more important in the selection of mode. Own account transport was preferred by firms which produced goods destined for final consumption and for fragile, perishable and high value commodities. Much of this traffic consisted of relative short hauls. On the other hand, as the length of haul increased and the products carried moved further away from the final stage of consumption (eg raw materials and intermediate products), so the share of traffic going by professional operators increased. The length of haul was not a particularly significant factor in the choice between road haulier and rail though the latter was slightly favoured for very long hauls. There were other factors, weight of consignment, which were also important in determining modal choice in specific cases. But for the most part the modal split between road and rail depended upon the nature of the goods and the length of haul, while the convenience element also weighed heavily in favour of private rather than public transport. The price factor on the other hand had little effect on modal choice. Demand for freight transport is very price inelastic, a fact borne out by the large number of consignments sent by modes which are more expensive than available alternatives.[13]

The most interesting developments have of course been in inland passenger transport, notably the big rise in the number of passenger miles travelled and the massive shift towards private transport. For this sector it is easier to make a more detailed analysis of the determining forces because of the ready availability of data. However there are certain complications. For one thing the number of relevant variables is fairly large, including disposable income, income distribution, the price of transport, the size of population, the age and sex distribution of population, density and spatial distribution of population, family size and the level of car ownership. Most of these factors have been included in urban and regional models of traffic flows, but in a macro-approach using time series data some of these variables are inappropriate for one reason or another. Some of the variables cannot be rendered meaningful in a national context, while in certain cases continuous time series data are not available. In any case, to try and represent all the variables in any estimating equation would lead to undue complexity. Secondly, the existence of private transport complicates the situation, especially with regard to explaining the division of traffic between modes. The private car owner does not normally make a rational assessment of alternative transport costs and when competition takes this form 'the economics of the whole matter becomes much less calculable, because costs appear to lose, and convenience to gain, in importance.'[14]

The fact is that cost considerations have not been the only

determinant of the spread of car ownership or the use made of private transport. If this had been the case then it would be legitimate to assume that the great post-war boom in private travel would never have taken place, since the cost per mile of using one's own car has been much higher than that of public transport. Calculations made for the late 1950s (in pre-decimal pence) show that the total costs per mile of running a car (assuming an average occupancy of 1·5 persons) were 5·0d for a car in the 1001–1265 cc range, and 6·4d for one in the 1266–1500 cc range. If running costs alone are taken the relevant figures work out at 2·1d and 2·7d per mile, which is still higher than the comparable charges by public transport.[15] In 1958–59 the average receipt per passenger mile on British Railways was 1·49d, on BTC and provincial and Scottish buses 1·4d, on London Transport buses 2·1d, and on London Transport trains 1·8d. Though these price relatives have changed somewhat in favour of the private car since that date it still remains true that private motoring is more expensive than public transport except when average car occupancy rates are high.

Clearly then, if the total cost of private motoring had been the prime consideration involved the shift away from public transport would never have occurred. But in fact motorists generally base their calculations, if at all, on the price of fuel alone which means that their costs compare favourably with those of public transport. Moreover, non-cost considerations probably play a more important part in the decision to purchase a car and the use to which it is put. Despite increasing congestion the car has the edge in terms of convenience and service, while the deterioration in public transport facilities has no doubt favoured the growth of car ownership, though the cause and effect relationship in this respect is debatable.[16] Furthermore, the fact that the car is a conspicuous product has undoubtedly produced a strong demonstration motive for purchasing a car. It is a well-known fact that car ownership has risen much faster than average incomes in the post-war period. Calculations made in the early 1960s show that for every one per cent increase in incomes the car stock (in monetary value) rose by 2·4 per cent, while other factors produced an additional increase in the stock of about 3 per cent per annum.[17] Once a purchase is made there is every incentive to use a car as much as possible since unit costs fall with increased mileage. These considerations appear to support Ray's contention that 'it is not the cost of railway travel which leads people to buy cars; and once the car is bought, the owners will tend to use it whenever it is more convenient, without elaborate cost calculations. The fact the total cost per mile of car travel is usually—for one or two persons—much higher than the railway fare is no deterrent; for car travellers, if they work out the cost of their proposed car journey at all, will tend just to calculate the cost of fuel and ignore any additional depreciation and main-tenance'.[18]

The above arguments appear to rule out the possibility that price relatives have been significant in determining the changing pattern of transport demand. However, since the early 1950s the trend of costs has moved very strongly in favour of the private car and against public transport,[19] and it is difficult to believe that this has not had some effect on the choice of modes. Between 1956 and 1969 for instance, the average price of rail travel rose by 85 per cent and that of bus travel by 97 per cent, whereas estimated car running costs rose by only 37 per cent and the purchase cost of cars (new and second-hand) remained more or less static.[20] Overall this has meant that expenditure per passenger mile has risen less rapidly in the case of private transport with the result that rail and bus transport have become steadily more expensive in relation to motoring costs. In table 8 consumer outlay per passenger mile by private car (which includes both the running and purchase

Table 8   Consumers' expenditure per passenger mile on different modes

	Bus and coach	Rail	Car	Bus as % of car	Rail as % of car
	p	p	p		
1953	0·51	0·45	0·84	60·59	53·57
1960	0·71	0·59	1·14	62·28	51·75
1969	1·16	0·91	1·26	92·01	72·22
1970	1·29	1·01	1·36	94·85	74·26

Source: based on data in *National Income and Expenditure* and *Passenger Transport in Great Britain*

costs of vehicles) is compared with that on rail and bus transport for selected years. For much of the 1950s expenditure per passenger mile on rail and bus transport averaged between 50 to 60 per cent that on private motoring. During the following decade there was a sharp increase in the former so that by 1970 average expenditure per passenger mile by bus was almost the same as that by private car, while rail transport had reached nearly 75 per cent of that level. The relative increase in the cost of public transport can be explained largely in terms of increased labour costs which are relatively unimportant in the case of the private car. Moreover, car operating costs do not reflect the demand for scarce urban road space, noise and pollution costs etc, so that the pricing system has tended to work in the motorists' favour.[21]

However, regression analysis does not reveal the price variable as being a very potent explanatory force. Calculations for the period 1956–1969 show that only in the case of rail transport was the price variable significant, and the results indicated that price elasticity was the major cause of the declining share of rail travel in total passenger mileage.[22] In the case of bus and car travel the price factor turned out to be insignificant. Income, and to a lesser extent population, growth were however, significant factors in the expansion of passenger travel (that is by private car).

We may conclude therefore that changes in price relatives have not been important either in determining the volume of passenger travel or the shift in demand between modes. Income growth has been an important determinant which has reflected itself in the spread of car ownership.[23] However, there are many less tangible factors such as convenience, comfort, status etc, which have promoted the popularity of having one's own transport. Such forces have undoubtedly played a significant part in the expansion of personal travel in the post-war period. Finally, time savings have in certain cases induced a shift of traffic from one mode to another. General gravity models show that traffic flows between two places will increase as the travel times between them decrease, and usually this results in a shift in the volume of traffic to that mode which offers an improvement in service. Obviously this process cannot be demonstrated on a national basis but there is reason to suppose that the increasing use made of the private car, especially in areas where public transport is slow and infrequent, is partly explainable in terms of the time savings which accrue from doing so. Similarly, the speed up of train services between London and the North-west of England as a result of electrification of services in the mid 1960s resulted in a considerable swing from air to rail travel although the shift from car to rail transport was negligible.[24]

The trends and causal forces outlined above provide, along with the legislative changes discussed in chapter 3, the background to the development of Britain's transport system since the war. The following chapters examine some of the consequences of these changes as they affected public operators in the separate branches of transport.

CHAPTER FIVE

The Railways

UNDOUBTEDLY THE RAILWAYS HAVE PROVIDED the most intractable problem in British transport during the post-war period. At a time when the aggregate demand for transport has been growing rapidly the railways have lost traffic and their share of the total internal transport market has fallen dramatically so that at present they account for 10 per cent or less of the total passenger and freight traffic.[1] Even more depressing have been the large and mounting financial deficits which in 1962 and 1967 surpassed the £150 million mark (inclusive of interest charges). The pressing financial difficulties have led to several reorganisations and reconstructions of the railway system but all to no avail, though the position would no doubt have become even worse had no attempt at all been made to revive their fortunes.

The post-war history of the railways falls conveniently into three phases. The first period covers the years up to 1962 when they were under the care of the British Transport Commission. This was probably the most disastrous period, a time when many opportunities were lost. The second phase spans the two Transport Acts of 1962 and 1968 when a serious attempt was made to grapple with the problems under Beeching style management. The Act of 1968 gave legal recognition to the third phase since it acknowledged the social obligations of the railways and paid for them accordingly. It is convenient to examine their development within these three periods.

THE BTC ERA

It was somewhat ironic that the railways were to have their finest hour in the years shortly before nationalistion. During the war the railways were utilised almost to breaking point as a result of heavy traffic demands and longer hauls. Total passenger movement almost doubled, from 18,993 million passenger miles in 1938 to 35,248 million in 1945, while freight traffic rose by 50 per cent between 1938 and the peak year of 1944 (16,266 to 24,444 million ton miles). Financially the railways also did very well; there was a large net revenue surplus in every year, though a good part of this was creamed off by the government under the control arrangements made with the railways at the beginning of the war.[2]

The British Transport Commission inherited a railway system which was in poor physical shape in 1948. Investment and repair work had been neglected during the war while traffic had fallen sharply from the peak levels recorded in 1944–45. Moreover, the task of structural and administrative reorganisation following nationalisation proved a more difficult and protracted problem than at first envisaged. Thus in the first few years the BTC was preoccupied with reorganising the system and maintaining it in reasonable working order rather than projecting plans for the future. Fortunately traffic volumes in these years remained well up on prewar while the full threat of road competition was restrained by wartime restrictions, notably petrol-rationing. Thus until the early 1950s the railways continued to break even on working account, though when central interest charges are taken into account there was a small deficit in every year except 1952.

Soon afterwards it became clear that the railways could not even manage to cover their current working expenses. In 1956 a deficit on current account of £16·5 million was recorded and this rose steadily to a peak of £104 million in 1962, the last year of the commission's existence. The overall deficit, allowing for the railways' contribution to central charges, mainly interest payments on capital based on a 70 per cent allocation, rose from £57·7 millions to £156·1 million over the same period. Thus financially the railways were in a very much worse position than before the war and their financial return was distinctly poor compared with the other activities controlled by the BTC, most of which, except for the waterways, were profitable.

The question of the railways' interest charges merits some comment at this point since it has sometimes been argued that these were unduly high in relation to the earning power of their assets. It is true that the commencing debt of the railways was high, reflecting on optimistic valuation at the time of compensation to former stockholders. But even if these assets had been written down in value, or had the railways been relieved of their interest payments altogether, losses would still have occurred except in the early 1950s. After 1955–6 the railways' share of central charges remained fairly stable and it was the operating account that really became the problem. By the end of 1962 there was a cumulative deficit on this account alone of over £200 million, after allowing for the surpluses made up to 1955. Moreover, the railway accounts were favoured in at least two ways. Not all rolling stock was depreciated on a replacement cost basis so that the allowance for this item was lower than it should have been. Secondly, after 1957 interest on advances from the Ministry of Transport to cover revenue deficits, together with interest on new borrowings for capital purposes, were transferred to a special account and thereby excluded from the returns. If these two items had been taken into account they would have outweighted any relief afforded on interest payments to former shareholders.[3]

Thus however one might care to juggle with the figures the fact remains that the railways have not paid their way since the war. Even if we ignore the interest charge burden the railways still did not manage to break even on their working account after 1955, and by the early 1960s the shortfall had reached astronomic proportions. The main question to be answered therefore is why the BTC failed so miserably in running the railways. Several possible reasons have been put forward to explain the poor financial performance but first it is necessary to see how far this can be attributable to loss of traffic.

THE VOLUME OF TRAFFIC

As we said in an earlier chapter the railways failed to share in the boom in demand for both passenger and freight transport after the war, virtually all of which was captured by road transport.

The absolute volume of railway traffic also began to decline steadily after the mid 1950s though not by as much as one might have expected. However, this was compensated in part by an increase in the average length of haul so that the volume of traffic, measured in passenger and ton miles, was considerably higher throughout the 1950s than in 1938. In later years there was some falling off in traffic, especially on the freight side, yet even by the early 1960s the level of traffic compared favourably with that of 1938 (see table 9). This suggests that it would be incorrect to attribute all the railways' financial difficulties simply to a sharp decline in traffic carried.

The stagnation in railway traffic, both passenger and freight, can be attributed to two main factors: road competition and the decline or slow growth of those sectors for which the railways remained the major carriers. Much of the loss on the freight side can be attributed to this latter factor.[4] The collapse of the coal trade and the stagnation in other mineral traffic hit the railways hard. The tonnage of coal carried declined from a peak of just over 175 million tons in 1953 to 145 million in 1963 and there has been a further sharp drop since. In mineral traffic the railways tended to specialise in those sections which were growing least rapidly, eg iron and steel products.

Table 9   British Railways traffic 1938, 1948–1962

Net ton miles (millions)

Passenger journeys (millions)	Tons of freight (millions)	Passenger miles (millions)	Mer-chandise	Coal and Minerals	Coke	Total
1938	1,237	266	18,993	4,980	3,182	8,104	16,266
1948	1,024	273	21,022	6,949	4,926	9,582	21,457
1955	994	274	20,308	6,087	5,075	10,191	21,353
1960	1,037	249	21,547	5,706	4,840	8,104	18,650
1962	998	228	19,772	5,200	3,600	7,304	16,104

Source: *Annual Reports and Accounts of the British Transport Commission*

More serious was the loss of potential traffic to road transport. On the freight side the most rapidly expanding branch was general merchandise and here the railways failed to penetrate this market.

This was partly inevitable since a good deal of it was derived from industries whose work was especially suited to road transport. Moreover, it is likely that for part of this period much of the competition in road transport was accounted for by traders using their own vehicles. One estimate suggests that C licensed vehicles and contract A vehicles (that is on long term contract to one particular user) gained 90 per cent of the traffic lost by the railways between 1952–1961.[5] In the case of passenger traffic, it was the private car that was responsible for the enormous upsurge in passenger movement and not the public road passenger transport industry, which lost more traffic than the railways. The greater degree of convenience, and the cost trend in favour of the car were the chief causes of the railways' relative losses in this field, though it should be remembered that much of the passenger road traffic was not competitive with rail anyway. As it was the railways did well to maintain their passenger mileage throughout the 1950s.

In effect therefore, the expansion of private road transport was largely responsible for checking the growth of railway traffic. Not all traffic need have been lost to this sector; a more determined effort to exploit expanding passenger and merchandise freight markets should have paid results. On the other hand, it must be recognised that since the use of the private vehicle represented a convenient rather than an economic choice of transport, whatever the policies adopted by the railways it was unlikely that they could have restricted the growth of road transport or benefited from it to any great extent. Hence in these circumstances the railways were obliged to make the best of what they had got.

It has been argued that the above factors were incidental rather than basic causes of the railways' financial difficulties.[6] The basis of this contention is that though declining industries may experience a contraction in activities they should be in a position to adapt their business to avoid making large deficits. Secondly, in view of the fact that the railways were able to maintain their prewar traffic levels for much of the period there seems little reason why they should have made such large deficits unless it could be shown that competition from road transport forced the railways to adopt uneconomic charges for the services they offered.

Thirdly, bus and coach companies suffered far more serious contractions in traffic but many of them have managed to produce a better financial outturn than the railways.

The upshot of this line of reasoning is that the railways could have improved their financial performance had they pursued the right policies. Given that there was little prospect of attracting large increases in traffic the railways were inevitably forced on the defensive. In railway operation the proportion of costs which are fixed or inescapable in the short-term is high, so that in conditions in which traffic is stagnating or tending to decline in certain sectors unit costs rise rapidly. To ensure profitable operation in these conditions it is essential that careful defensive policies are adopted. Three main lines of attack were open to the railways. First, it was crucial that the correct pricing and costing policies should be chosen, in particular that prices were adjusted to costs wherever possible. Secondly, there was an urgent need to reduce costs wherever possible either by the elimination of excess capacity or through more efficient use of resources. And thirdly, it was necessary to make every effort to modernise and improve the system so as to attract as much traffic as possible or prevent further loss. In all three respects the railways under the BTC failed to approach the ideal.

THE PROBLEM OF PRICING

For much of the twentieth century the railways have faced two main problems with regard to pricing policy. First, railway charges as a whole have persistently lagged behind the rise in costs of operation, and secondly, specific services have rarely been priced on the basis of true operating costs. Thus pricing policy generally had failed to reflect costs properly and the system as a whole has contained a large element of cross-subsidisation. As we shall see, the long term financial viability of the railways has been severely affected by inadequate pricing procedure.

The lag in prices behind costs dates largely from the first world war when charges were frozen. This was repeated during the 1939-45 war and afterwards. The effect was dramatic. By 1961 railway expenses were more than 300 per cent higher than in 1938, whereas rates and charges had risen by less than half this amount. A substantial part of this increase in costs occurred during and shortly after the war, whereas in the 1950s the rise was more moderate. Even so costs continued to outstrip the rate at which charges were adjusted, and the discrepancy was most marked on the passenger side where the railways' losses were greatest. Wage costs were the main problem since they accounted for some 60 per cent of working expenses and absorbed about 80 per cent of gross revenue. Between 1948 and 1961 wage costs more than doubled and it is not surprising that total railway expenses followed very closely the pattern of wage costs.

Given this discrepancy it was only a matter of time before the railways ran into deficit. In the early post-war years the position was cushioned to some extent by fairly high traffic levels. But when in the 1950s traffic volumes began to level off and decline, and costs continued to escalate, losses were bound to occur unless large scale economies in railway operation were achieved. In fact the railways were never able to counteract the rising trend in costs in this way and in only two years, 1958 and 1959, did they manage to achieve a reduction in working expenditure.

The British Transport Commission made known that it was fully aware of the dangers involved in failing to adjust charges to match the new pattern of costs.[7] Why did it do so little to rectify the situation? For one thing it was felt that if charges rose too rapidly the railways would simply lose traffic to road transport or even to the airways. Up to a point this was true though both the commission and the Transport Tribunal assumed mistakenly that all traffic was equally affected by competition and that it was the duty of the railways to retain all the traffic they had got. Thus when the railways secured greater commercial freedom in 1953 they embarked on an excessive lowering of many freight rates regardless of the marginal nature of some of the traffic they were trying to retain. What both the commission and tribunal failed to understand properly was that rate adjustments should have been much more discriminatory, so that bad or unprofitable traffic would be priced out of the market and the good paying traffic retained by appropriate price reductions where competition was severe.

B.T.—I

Delays in presenting and implementing new charges schemes were also responsible for the slow adjustment of charges. These were not drafted until the 1950s and were then subject to considerable delay by the tribunal and minister. The first main Passenger Charges Scheme of 1951 was subject to eleven months delay at an estimated cost of £100,000 a day to the commission, while in 1958 the commission's application for increasing fares was held up for over a year while the tribunal deliberated. It was nearly two years before the Draft Charges Scheme of 1955 was passed. And even after these long delays there was no guarantee that all the commission's requests would be granted. There can be little doubt that these prolonged deliberations affected railway earnings adversely. 'In the past . . . both by the time taken to reach decisions and by the nature of the decisions themselves, the Tribunal has severely cut down the Commission's earnings'.[8] Even worse the commission had to face obstruction from the minister as well. In 1952 and again in 1956 the minister intervened to prevent increases in passenger and freight charges even though these had been passed by the tribunal. The cost of these interventions was estimated at between £15 and £23·5 million.[9]

Only limited progress was made towards developing a more scientific pricing policy. In its early reports the commission emphasised the need to abandon the old system of charging, and to charge the customer the real cost of the services he selected; to facilitate progress along this front a traffic costings organisation was set up in 1951. The Transport Act of 1953 should have facilitated progress in this respect since it allowed the commission greater freedom in charging matters, though the Transport Tribunal still kept tight control over maximum charges. Nevertheless, the move towards a more rational structure was hesitant and piecemeal. The main advances were a sharp rise in the price of cheap concessionary tickets in 1953 on which the railways made heavy losses, while the new freight charges scheme of 1957 provided for a scale of maximum charges based on the 'loadability' of freight, which was a more reliable guide to the costs of conveyance than the old value classification. Yet even the new maximum charges of 1957 entailed carrying about 10 per cent of goods traffic at a loss and it was not apparent from the new schedules that all indirect costs would be covered by the charges for each class of traffic.

Thus despite some improvements in methods of charging the railways were, by the early 1960s, still a long way from pricing all their services and traffics on the basis of real costs. And for a good part of the time the old system of charging, value and distance for freight, and distance for passengers, prevailed. Consequently, since charges failed to reflect costs there was a high degree of cross-subsidisation throughout the system and this in turn gave competing transport modes an opportunity to cream off the best traffic and leave the railways with that which was least profitable.

There are several reasons why the commission made such little headway in this respect. Both the ministry and the BTC maintained that services could not be priced properly because of the difficulty of finding out where the losses were made. The permanent secretary to the Ministry of Transport told the Select Committee of 1960 that 'one of the most difficult things in the Ministry is to discover where the money is actually being lost'.[10] The BTC also confessed that, despite nearly ten years experience, its accounting system and costing techniques were not sufficiently developed to show precisely where the losses occurred.[11] This was a weak excuse and in any case it was not entirely accurate. Though every service and traffic had not been costed properly there was a good idea where the major losses were being made. As early as 1950 the commission had shown the great variations which existed in the costs of operating different passenger services (eg between main line express and branch line services), yet continued to charge a standard fare to all passengers.[12] Similarly on the freight side it was known on which routes and services the railways' advantages lay. It was known that a fair proportion of the merchandise traffic was making a loss, whereas coal and mineral traffic were relatively profitable. Yet here again little attempt was made to adjust charges accordingly.

It would of course have been difficult for the commission to have priced all its services properly simply because in some cases, eg commuter and branch line services, the increase in charges required would have raised a public outcry. It is quite certain that neither the tribunal nor the minister would have allowed such charges to go through, though the case was never put to the test since it ran against the grain of the commission's own thinking. It is very doubtful whether the commission would have taken such drastic action even had it been free to do so. The BTC was clearly under the impression that it knew too little about costs to do this properly. Secondly, old traditions die hard and it is clear that the commission found difficulty in relinquishing the former railway practice of retaining as much traffic as possible whatever the cost of carrying it. It is also clear that the commission was torn between conflicting objectives. It wished to make the railways pay by pricing properly yet at the same time it was still attached to the old idea of providing a public service, that is a service which normally accepted the obligation to carry all traffic offered regardless of cost and without undue discrimination between users of that service. In effect the commission appeared to be under the impression that cross-subsidisation, a public obligation to carry and a pricing policy based on costs could be run as compatible objectives. But in a competitive market the obligation to carry cannot be compatible with financial viability, since the average cost charging required by the obligation would leave the carrier in danger of losing all traffic which costs less than the average to carry, while it would retain the unprofitable traffic which costs more than the average. The failure to recognise that the former railway monopoly had long since disappeared may explain in part why more positive action was not taken to adjust the pricing system.

The absence of positive action on pricing policy was clearly due to a complex set of interrelated forces. Failure on this score certainly contributed substantially to the railways deteriorating financial position. It also determined the rate at which the railways could secure economies from the elimination of excess capacity.

ELIMINATION OF EXCESS CAPACITY

If the commission did not do its sums correctly then delay in eradicating the uneconomic parts of the system was inevitable. An inadequate knowledge of the costs of services would leave the commission in ignorance as to which parts should be cut out, and/or would preclude it from using pricing policy to divert traffic away from the uneconomic sections so that they could be closed down.

It was no secret that a good part of the system was unprofitable. Many small branch and rural lines had been uneconomic from the moment they were built and at the time the railways were nationalised it was estimated that about one third of the route mileage could profitably have been scrapped.[13] Initially however the commission made little reference to the necessity of closing down parts of the system, and it was not until the launching of the modernisation plan in 1955 that the urgency of drastic action was stressed in order to secure a more compact railway system as a complement to the modernisation programme. Yet progress in pruning the structure proved to be painfully slow. By 1961 only just over 400 services had been withdrawn from about 4000 miles of route, while fewer than 1000 stations and depots had been closed. Since many stations and routes had to be kept open because only one type of traffic was withdrawn the actual route mileage completely closed to all traffic amounted to only just over 1050 miles, that is about 5·3 per cent of the 1948 total. The savings arising from these closures were minimal, amounting to about £4·2 million per annum.

In fact by the early 1960s only the fringe of the problem had been tackled since many of the early closures had consisted of very small branch lines. The failure to press forward the closure policy more rapidly cannot be entirely attributed to the commission's inability to identify the unprofitable sections, nor to its conscious regard to social obligations. The procedure for vetting closure proposals was complex and often entailed inordinate delays, while public outcry against such proposals often resulted in the BTC abandoning schemes of closure altogether. One application for closing a line in Wales, for example, took over two and a half years to get through the vetting machinery.[14] Each application had to be scrutinised carefully by the railway management; it was then passed to the relevant Transport Users' Consultative Committee which, after a detailed inquiry, passed its recommendations to the central committee; the latter reviewed them and then passed the application to the minister for the final decision. The effort and time spent in this process may well have deterred the railways from making as many applications as they might have done.

Given the limited nature of the closure policy the railways could not hope to achieve large economies from this source. Indeed the BTC never really contemplated that such a policy would revive the ailing financial situation of the railways. By the middle of the 1950s the commission had turned its attention to more constructive action, namely modernisation of the railway system, which was far more likely to meet public approval than the negative action of reducing services. Closure of services was written into the plan, as we have seen, but it never featured prominently in the execution of the modernisation project. It was only after the break-up of the BTC that a concerted effort was made to contract the system.

INVESTMENT AND MODERNISATION

The Modernisation Plan, launched in 1955, was an attempt to make up for the past neglect. During the early post-war years no firm plans had been formulated about the future shape and structure of the railway system. The railways were regarded as a low investment priority and severe shortages of both labour and materials meant that the railways could do little more than try to catch up with arrears of maintenance. As a result total disinvestment on railways between 1937 and 1953 amounted to £440 million at 1948 prices, or £650 million at 1960 valuations. By the latter date the railways had still not worked off their arrears of investment despite the modernisation programme of the 1950s.[15] Not surprisingly the railways were badly in need of modernisation by the time the plan was published.

The main idea behind the modernisation programme was to reduce the cost of railway operations and improve the efficiency of services so as to attract more traffic. Only by a thorough overhaul of equipment would it be possible to exploit the railways' natural advantages as bulk transporters. Thus an ambitious programme of re-equipment was envisaged including improvements to track and signalling to allow higher speeds, the replacement of steam by diesel and electric traction, the modernisation of stations and passenger rolling stock, and the drastic remodelling of freight services partly through rationalisation. The cost of all this was estimated at around £1240 million—this was later revised to £1660 million—and the whole operation was to be complete within 15 years, though all the main components of the plan were to be started within the first 5 years. It was anticipated that the economic benefits accruing would enable the railways at least to break even, and even more optimistic noises on this score were made when the plan was reappraised in 1959.

In fact the plan was little more than a pipe-dream; it was a last-minute rescue operation, hastily conceived and ill-thought out, and accepted by the ministry and government largely because they had nothing better to offer. No detailed or proper scrutiny of the economic implications of the programme was carried out either by the commission or any outside body. The Treasury told the Select Committee of 1960 that it was 'merely a hotch-potch of the things that the Commission was saying it was desirable to try to achieve by 1970, ill-qualified and not really explainable'.[16] The commission had only a hazy notion of the total costs involved and the financial results likely to accrue from modernisation. How they arrived at the conclusion that the railways could break-even by 1961–62 is beyond comprehension. Very few of the components of the programme had been costed properly, and in this respect the Ministry and Treasury were as much to blame since they underwrote the plan without bothering to check the details. The most glaring example was the case of the London Midland electrification scheme which accounted for about 10 per cent of the total investment. Here no proper calculation had been made of the expected rate of return—the commission, Treasury and ministry all had different ideas about investment criteria—and no one knew what the cost of alternatives, eg diesel traction, would be. As it turned out *ex post* calculations showed that the profitability of the scheme was likely to be marginal at best.

Despite these drawbacks the programme was implemented fairly rapidly until it was brought to a halt in 1961 pending further reorganisation. Railway investment in the years 1955–62 was running at three times the level of 1948–54 and much of the planned capital investment was spent in these years. Of course the programme was never completed and the expected returns never materialised, but the visible benefits of modernisation were there for all to see. Perhaps the most obvious was the rapid switch to diesel traction. Steam locomotives were rapidly phased out (the last delivery was made in 1960) and by 1963 diesel and electric power accounted for some 62 per cent of the total traction miles run compared with about 13 per cent in 1955. Progress in this respect was more rapid on the passenger side and was accompanied by improvements in rolling stock and the modernisation of some stations. Achievements on the freight side were less spectacular though some progress was made in rationalising and modernising Britain's out-of-date freight services. Freight rolling stock was reduced substantially, larger wagons introduced, freight trains were speeded up and traffic was concentrated at fewer and more modern goods terminals and marshalling yards. Priority was also given to developing the high speed movement of bulk freight in specially designed wagons and containers for use by road and rail. The most notable case was the Condor express container service started in 1959 between London and Glasgow. However, much still remained to be done as regards improving the efficiency of freight services as was to be shown in the 1960s.

Finally, a start was made towards overhauling the antiquated signalling system and improving the track, though progress in this field certainly did not match that of traction. Improvements in both respects were essential if higher speeds were to be attained with the new forms of traction and to allow equipment to be used more intensively. On many main-line routes, especially where electrification was involved, extensive reconstruction or complete renewal of track and signalling equipment was required to permit faster and safer travel. Even so progress in the early years of the modernisation programme was very slow indeed. By the end of the 1950s only 200 miles of track had been equipped with long-welded rails, though subsequently the rate of advance was rather more rapid. The introduction of colour-light signals and power-operated signal boxes made greater headway, though only a small proportion of the track had been re-equipped by the early 1960s. At the end of 1963 multiple aspect colour-light signalling covered 3600 single track miles, less than half of which had been installed since the inception of the modernisation plan. These new systems necessitated the construction of modern signal boxes controlling large sections of the track, and as a result the number of signal boxes had been reduced to 8552 by the end of 1963, or nearly 1200 less than in 1955. The wider adoption of automatic warning system of train control reinforced one of the railways' major advantages over other forms of travel, namely safety. At the end of 1962, 1232 route miles of main line had been equipped with the Standard Automatic Warning System of train control, while 5445 locomotives and 1482 multiple unit cabs had been fitted with the corresponding drivers' warning apparatus.

Though improvements were certainly visible there was still much more to be done, especially on the freight side, by the early 1960s when the modernisation programme was suspended. Since the developments were so piecemeal and the plan was far from complete by the early 1960s it is impossible to assess properly the economic benefits. Certainly diesel traction brought some economies; in 1964 it was estimated that the savings from this source were over £10 million, while all the major passenger modernisation schemes resulted in a sizeable increase in revenue. But whether they were all profitable is to be doubted. Moreover, the total economies derived from this source were limited since the BTC did not press forward with a policy of reducing the network. In any case, whatever the gains these were more than outweighed by the rise in costs since the deficit of the railways continued to escalate in these years.

EFFICIENCY OF BRITISH RAILWAYS

It is doubtful whether the railways gained very much from improved efficiency either. Despite the modernisation programme and a 25 per cent reduction in the labour force between 1948–1962, output per worker rose by only 15 per cent during this period and

most of the gain was secured before 1955. Labour productivity
however, is only a partial measurement of efficiency and Deakin
and Seward suggest that productivity of all factor inputs combined
may have declined slightly between 1952–1962.[17] This conclusion
appears to be borne out by the very limited improvement in the
utilisation of rolling stock.[18] In comparison with European railways British performance showed up very badly in this respect.[19]
The record in productivity was dismal to say the least and suggests
that the BTC devoted far too little attention to this important
matter.

THE BTC'S RECORD

The Transport Commission's record with regard to the railways
can hardly be written down as a success story since the financial
position of the railways became steadily worse as time went on.
Admittedly the commission had a difficult task on its hands in
trying to manage a declining undertaking subject to heavy pressure
from road competition, while its policies were sometimes inhibited
by undue government influence and legal impediments. Nevertheless, it was not an impossible task and the commission itself must
share some of the blame for failure. It suffered from a lack of good
managerial talent and this resulted in weak and tentative policies.
In particular, it waited nearly eight years before producing a
programme of modernisation and when it did the plan was found
to be faulty. It had no firm policy with regard to closures and
rationalisation of the structure, while the mistakes in pricing
policy stemmed partly from an inadequate costings procedure.
Finally, it failed to press forward with productivity improvements.
Not surprisingly therefore the commission had little to offer to
counteract rising costs and the deficit rose accordingly. Whether
the government or Ministry of Transport should also be held
partly responsible for failing to give the commission adequate
policy guidelines is another matter. After all the BTC was responsible for managing the railways and it was up to that body to
draw up appropriate policies and then await ministerial reaction.
There was nothing to prevent it devising the right policies and if
these had been rejected then it would have been absolved from

blame. But lack of proper initiative in the first place cannot pass without rebuke.

BEECHING TO THE RESCUE?

By 1960 it was becoming apparent that the financial problems of the railways were not likely to be solved by the commission's policies of modernisation and piecemeal improvements. The large railway deficit was causing some concern within govenment circles. The upshot was a further inquiry, the appointment of Richard Beeching in May 1961 to manage the railways, and a drastic reorganisation of the nationalised transport system by the Transport Act of 1962.[20] This, as we have noted earlier, abolished the BTC and set up separate boards for each transport activity. The railways were given almost complete commercial freedom and a drastic financial reconstruction was carried out to reduce their interest burden.[21] The minister was also empowered to make grants of up to £450 million to cover operating losses over a five year period after which it was expected the railways would break even. The idea behind these measures was to assist the railways to secure financial solvency.

Beeching was given a clear commercial mandate by the government, namely to make the railways pay. His first task therefore was to carry out a thorough survey of the system to find out which services paid their way and to determine exactly where the losses were being made. The results of this survey appeared in the now famous report *The Reshaping of British Railways* published in March 1963. This was in fact the first detailed cost study of the railway system and it confirmed what had always been suspected that the greater part of the railway system was uneconomic. Much of the system was under-utilised. One third of the route mileage carried only about one per cent of the freight and passenger traffic (measured in ton and passenger miles), while one half of the route mileage only accounted for around 4–5 per cent of the total traffic. In other words, the traffic density was so low on half the system that it was barely sufficient to cover the cost of providing the route (that is track and signalling), with nothing to spare at all for movement and other costs. Conversely, the remaining half of the system

earned enough to cover its route costs more than six times. Under-
utilisation of stations and rolling stock was also prevalent. One
third of the stations produced less than one per cent of total
passenger receipts, and one half produced only two per cent, while,
at the other extreme, 34 stations, less than one per cent of the total,
earned 26 per cent of total passenger receipts. Roughly one third
of the freight wagons were surplus to requirements and many
passenger coaches were available simply to cater for peak service
needs.

Most types of traffic were losing money, though some more than
others. On the passenger side the most unprofitable services were
stopping trains, which made an overall loss of £66 million in 1961.
In many cases traffic densities were so low that there was little
prospect of making the services pay. Suburban services all but
covered their direct costs, but made an overall loss of £25 million;
many were uneconomic because of the peak nature of the traffic
and the low fares charged. Potentially the most profitable type of
passenger traffic was that on the inter-city routes; direct costs were
well covered though an overall deficit of £22 million was incurred.
Most freight traffic was uneconomic and its handling badly in need
of reform. Much of it moved in single wagon consignments, a
legacy of the nineteenth century. The worst section was general
merchandise which accounted for two thirds of the total losses
made on freight traffic. Here the scope for improved handling
methods was enormous. In contrast, mineral and coal traffic performed better; both covered their direct costs and coal actually
produced a profit of £2·6 million. These traffics were handled
more efficiently than merchandise though there was still plenty
of scope for improvement.

The proposals for reform contained in the report were drastic
but given the facts it was difficult to conceive otherwise. Many
uneconomic lines, stations and services would have to be closed to
all traffic. Details of the freight closures were not provided, but it
was envisaged that over 400 passenger services would have to be
withdrawn or modified and over 2000 stations and 5000 route miles
of track closed to passenger traffic. The second main proposal
was for selected development and rationalisation of the inter-city

trunk routes, details of which were published later in February 1965. About 3000 miles were selected for intensive development which could be capable of handling the estimated traffic flows up to 1984. Altogether it was envisaged that about 8000 route miles out of a total of 17,000 would eventually be retained. Most suburban services in large cities would have to be retained though fares should be aligned more closely with costs. The remaining proposals were concerned largely with the modernisation and reform of rolling stock and freight traffic. The amount of rolling stock was to be reduced and modernised while the phasing out of steam traction would be continued. Freight handling methods would come in for drastic overhaul, and a new type of service—the liner train—was to be introduced to provide combined road and rail movement of containerised merchandise.

On the financial side the report was fairly optimistic. Savings were expected to be of the order of £115 to £147 million if the plan was adopted in full. 'If the plan is implemented with vigour, however, much (though not necessarily all) of the Railway's deficit would be eliminated by 1970'.[22] As we shall see, this optimism was not borne out in practice.

The *Reshaping Report* was clearly a radical and exciting document which attracted criticism from many people. The popular outcry was against the passenger closures which were likely to deprive certain areas of railway services altogether. More fundamental criticism by economists pointed to the dubious nature of some of the statistical work. One economist felt the plan was disappointing not so much in what it recommended 'as in the inadequacy of the facts, the thinness of the arguments in several places, and in the extent to which it accepts official railway viewpoints without critical scrutiny'.[23] Certainly many of the estimates were extremely tentative, especially those relating to freight traffic, and many of the projections appeared to be based more on wishful thinking than hard facts. It was difficult to determine exactly what savings would accrue from the reform of freight handling methods, and the plans for this sector were based on rather vague, and as it turned out optimistic, assessments of the volume of goods traffic in the future. A significant increase in freight traffic was anticipated, especially in merchandise and oil where a trebling of volume was expected over the period 1964–1984. It was also stated that there was much potential rail traffic then being carried by road hauliers, possibly some 93 million tons suitable for rail conveyance, though after further analysis this was reduced somewhat. Given the shaky basis of some of the calculations it is not difficult to see why the overall financial projections should not be taken too seriously. In any case, these did not make proper allowance for probable cost increases while the reforms were being implemented. Wage costs were bound to rise, and interest payments were also likely to move upwards despite the capital reconstruction proposals contained in the Act of 1962. One estimate suggested that interest charges alone might rise from £52 to £90 million between 1962 and 1968[24] so that to break even within a five year period would require the board to turn an operating deficit of around £80 million (1962) into a surplus of £90 million, no mean achievement within such a short space of time.

The implementation of the Beeching proposals proceeded rapidly after the publication of the report, though some slowing down in the pace of progress had occurred by the end of 1966 since by then the new Labour government was having second thoughts about the wisdom of this course of action. In July 1966 a white paper on Transport Policy rejected commercial viability as the first objective of railway policy and urged that the railway system should be designed to accord more closely with the country's economic needs. In effect this spelt the end of the Beeching programme (Beeching had left the board in May 1965) in its original form, especially with regard to passenger closures, though many aspects of the plan continued to be implemented. Thus by 1968, when the Transport Act was passed, the railways were much slimmer, more efficient but still financially destitute.

The details of the implementation cannot be described in full but it is worthwhile to examine briefly some of the main aspects of the policy if only to appreciate the dramatic changes which took place. Within the space of five or six years the British Railways Board achieved very much more than the BTC had done in 14 years. As regards the purely negative aspect of cutting out the excess capacity this was done with remarkable speed, and included rolling stock as well as the more familiar station and passenger closures. Some idea of the scope of the cuts can be seen from table 10. Between 1962 and 1968 the number of locomotives and freight vehicles was roughly halved, the stations open declined by more than 50 per cent, the route open for traffic fell by some 5000 miles, the number of marshalling yards was cut by more than two thirds and manpower requirements were considerably reduced.

The decline in the number of locomotive units was especially impressive, a reflection both of the greater efficiency of diesel traction compared with steam (which was phased out completely during the 1960s) and improvements in efficiency of operations. Moreover, this contraction was not, as in the 1950s, compensated for by a corresponding increase in the number of diesel or electric multiple powered units. These were introduced on many short and medium distance routes but because of the closure of many services and improvements in the utilisation of rolling stock the number of multiple units actually fell slightly between 1962 and 1970 (Table 10). Overall therefore there was a sharp drop in the total number of powered units (locomotives plus multiple units) of nearly 35 per cent.

Table 10   Assets of British Railways

	Dec 1962	Dec 1968	Dec 1970
Locomotives	12,628	4,658	4,449
Passenger coaches: of which	33,821	19,544	18,678
loco hauled	22,715	8,386	7,699
diesel and electric multiple powered units	11,106	11,158	10,979
Freight vehicles	862,640	437,412	370,917
Stations	6,801	3,235	2,868
Marshalling yards	602	184	146
Route mileage for traffic	17,481	12,447	11,749
Employees (rail only)	475,222	296,274	251,797

Source: British Railway Board, *Annual Reports and Accounts*

Even so progress was not quite as rapid as originally intended and there still remained scope for further cuts in 1968; the Railways Board was particularly dissatisfied with the rate at which closures were implemented and complained bitterly about the lengthy procedure required to effect them. In some extreme cases the procedure caused delays of nearly three years, and by early 1966, when about three quarters of the passenger closures had been decided, the Board was incurring losses of £7 million a year on those cases still outstanding. Much excess capacity still existed both in terms of track and rolling stock. The chairman of the board (Sir Henry Johnson) remarked in 1968 on the size and nature of the wagon stock in the following terms: 'The existing wagon fleet, comprising more than 400,000 vehicles, restricted in speed and designed and built to Victorian standards, is the biggest and least efficient in Europe. It must be replaced by a modern fleet of, say, 100,000–150,000 wagons, capable of running at least at 60 mph, fitted with power brakes, and needing little maintenance'.[25]

This enormous reduction in assets was more than sufficient to counteract the further decline in traffic during this period so that most productivity indices rose sharply. Deakin and Seward record a growth in total factor productivity of 4·03 per cent per annum for the years 1962–65 as against a negative value of 0·64 per cent for 1952–62.[26] Nearly all specific indices of productivity showed marked increases through to 1968. Thus labour productivity rose by 49 per cent, net ton miles per freight wagon nearly doubled, the average wagon load rose by 33 per cent, while traffic units per track mile increased by 29 per cent (1962–68).[27] However, in some cases even sharp improvements failed to make up for ground lost since the war. In 1968, for example, the average wagon turnround time was still longer than in 1948, while the average passenger trainload was slightly down on that recorded earlier.

The constructive side of the board's work was equally important. The transfer from steam to diesel and electric traction continued and by the end of 1966, 96 per cent of the total coaching train miles and 77 per cent of the freight train miles were operated by diesel and electric traction, as against 81 and 22 per cent respectively in 1962. Within two more years steam was a thing of the past. At the same time the board was able to improve the standard of service for passengers on many of its inter-city routes. For example, in the 1965 timetable there were 636 start-to-stop runs of 60 mph or more each weekday compared with only 200 in 1962. In 1966, 151 runs between scheduled stops of 70 mph each weekday were recorded as against 133 in the previous year, while further improvements in time-schedules were made in subsequent years. Faster journeys were made possible in some cases by eliminating intermediate stops and during the later 1960s British Rail were actively 'exploiting the capability of 100 mph sections of line'. The big attraction of this period of course was the completion of the London Midland Electrification project (the last major piece of work of the original modernisation programme) which cut journey times between London and the North-West by about one third and enabled British Rail to offer passengers the experience of travelling comfortably at 100 mph.

Improvements on the freight side appear even more remarkable, possibly because through past neglect the scope for reform was somewhat greater than elsewhere. Here the main aim was to transform the unit of traffic from the wagon load to the train load by developing high-speed freight in through-train loads, while also diversifying the composition of freight traffic so as to reduce the railways' dependence on staples such as coal. The development of train-load working accounted for about one half of the railways' steel and general freight traffic by 1968 as a result of the introduction of three basic types of train, the company train, the merry-go-round train for coal and the freightliner. Company trains were designed to cater for the needs of particular customers and they formed the centrepiece of the railways' attempt to secure through working and win new traffic by long term contracts. By 1968 about 1500 company trains were being run each week compared with 600 in 1963; they were used extensively for the conveyance of raw materials, chemicals, cars and vehicle components, and oil. In some cases, notably oil, impressive gains have been registered. As a result of contracts signed with major oil companies rail carryings of oil rose from 5 million tons in 1961 to over 14 million in 1968, and accounted for a fifth or more of the general freight traffic ton mileage. Important long-term agreements were signed for conveying a number of other products. Similarly the handling of coal traffic, both for domestic and industrial use, was rationalised. Distribution of coal was concentrated at a number of large centralised depots, while in 1963 an agreement was signed with the Central Electricity Generating Board covering the conveyance of coal to new power stations specially equipped to accept permanently coupled trains of wagons, and to existing power stations subsequently converted for handling such trains. With this type of merry-go-round operation between pithead and power station, forming a sort of non-stop conveyor belt circuit, the modern high-capacity coal wagon can do 20 times the work of the old system. However, because of various difficulties this method got off to a slow start and in 1968 only about 7 per cent of coal traffic was carried in this way, though it is anticipated that by 1975 it will be around half.

The most impressive and well-known innovation has been the freightliner. This was designed to improve the handling of merchandise freight and formed the logical extension of earlier container services, Condor and Speedfreight introduced in 1959 and 1963. The main idea was to provide a speedy service based on the joint use of road and rail for door-to-door transport of containerised merchandise, composed of consignments too small to make good individual trainloads. Potential traffic for the new service was estimated to be about 30 million tons rising to 40 million over ten years. The new service got off to an inauspicious start for various reasons including union opposition, and the original plans were later scaled down. The first service started between London and Glasgow in 1965 and by the end of 1968 the network comprised 45 routes. Nevertheless the freightliner service has not been an unqualified success. Though it attracted a number of new customers the annual throughput in 1968 was only $2\frac{1}{2}$ million tons and the whole operation showed a loss of £2 million in 1969. Part of this may no doubt be explained by teething difficulties but there have been certain miscalculations of the economics of the scheme, notably regarding estimates of the costs of collection and delivery and load factors, and the mileage at which the freightliner service scores over road haulage.

To accommodate the new techniques of handling traffic constant improvements had to be made to the track, structures and signalling. This was particularly true in the case of the main trunk routes where higher speeds required more durable track and the extension of modern signalling techniques. Hence during the 1960s steady progress was made with the modern techniques introduced in the 1950s. By the end of 1966 for example 2870 route miles of track had been fitted with continuous welded rails and concrete sleepers, and by the early 1970s this total had been raised to 6400 miles (end 1972). Modern methods of track maintenance were introduced in 1964 which subsequently revolutionised the upkeep of the greater part of the permanent way. By the early 1970s nearly 4000 route miles and the majority of locomotives and multiple unit cabs had been equipped with the automatic warning system of train control, while most of the freight train mileage was worked by trains fitted with power brakes which permitted faster and safer running with heavier loads. Initially progress was somewhat slower with the installation of modern signalling equipment, though in 1966 a national signalling programme was launched. This contemplated the introduction of colour-light signalling on all the main trunk routes and areas of heavy traffic, with control exercised by a comparatively small number of strategically placed, power-operated signal boxes. By the early 1970s this system had been extended to 8600 out of a total of 23,000 single track miles and it is contemplated that eventually about 60 signal boxes will regulate traffic on at least one half of British Rail's route mileage. The chief aim of signalling systems is of course safety rather than economy, though the adoption of modern signalling techniques has meant not only the elimination of many small, uneconomic manual signal boxes— over 1100 alone were scrapped in the three years 1969–71—but also the disposal of much surplus track since improved traffic regulation as a result of the enlargement of control areas made possible better utilisation of the existing track. Estimates suggest that where track rationalisation is allied to new signalling systems, then the throughput of busy traffic can be raised by up to 15 per cent. The recently completed signal complex at Bristol, for example, which controls 114 route-miles, replaced 61 older signal boxes and led to the elimination of some 17 per cent of the track mileage in the area covered by the scheme. One of the lessons of modernisation has been that track rationalisation and track circuit signalling with central control need to be carried out simultaneously to achieve the greatest economies. And apart from the obvious operational economies, such developments have helped to raise the speed of main-line working while at the same time improving the safety of travel.

In sum these changes marked a significant step in the right direction but towards the end of the decade there was still much to be done. Despite the rapid run-down in equipment and rational-isation of handling methods excess capacity still remained and much of it antiquated at that. Methods of freight handling still left much to be desired. Coal and coke traffic continued to bulk large in railway freight operations and most of it was handled in the traditional way. Moreover, of British Rail's total freight tonnage in 1970 about one half continued to be hauled in wagonload con-signments.

No FINANCIAL PANACEA

The seemingly impressive reforms of the Beeching era had remarkably little impact on the financial outturn. The key statistics are detailed in table 11. Though the board managed to reduce or contain the operating deficit between 1963 and 1966 (the figures for 1962 and 1963 are not strictly comparable) it still remained large and it rose again in 1967. Interest charges tended to rise throughout the period so that by 1967 the overall deficit was higher than in 1963. Moreover, these figures understate the true position since they do not allow for the payment of any interest on the accumulated deficits of the railways since 1962.

At least the Railways Board was able to contain the operating deficit which was something the BTC had not been able to achieve. But in view of the hectic pace of reform in the 1960s the record appears a dismal one. And the question is why was this so, given that the cost savings were far from negligible? Was the situation beyond the control of the board?

Table 11   Railway Operating Results 1962–1970 (£millions)

	Receipts	Expenditure	Operating result	Interest charges	Net receipts
1962	465·1	569·1	—104·0	52·1	—156·1
1963	525·2	599·0	—75·8	58·1	—133·9
1964	530·9	593·4	—62·5	58·4	—120·9
1965	530.6	602·1	—71·5	60·9	—132·4
1966	527·5	598·0	—70·5	64·2	—134·7
1967	506·5	593·0	—86·5	66·5	—153·0
1968	529·1	609·2	—80·1	67·3	—147·4
1969	611·2	555·0	56·2	41·5	14·7
1970	658·3	606·6	51·7	42·2	9·5

Source: British Railways Board, Annual Reports and Accounts

Notes: 1. From 1963 onwards the returns include ancillary activities of the railways. 2. The figures from 1969 onwards are not comparable with those for earlier years and they can only be interpreted with reference to the financial provisions of the 1968 Transport Act.

The savings stemming from the transformation were close to expectations. Between 1962 and 1967 annual savings amounted to £138 million, but unfortunately these were swallowed up by rising costs of operation, £112 million being absorbed by wage and other price increases. Labour earnings increased faster than any measure of labour productivity. Moreover, despite the attraction of some new traffic, especially on the freight side, the railways were continuing to lose traffic as a result of the further penetration of road competition and a decline in some of the railways' main customers. The reduction was most marked in coal and coke and passenger traffic as the figures in table 12 show. Thus output in terms of total traffic units (passenger-miles and net ton-miles combined) fell faster than costs through to 1968 and hence expenses per unit of traffic rose from 1·58p in 1963 to 1·67 in 1968. Although there was a small rise in receipts per traffic unit this was no more than sufficient to allow the railways to mark time financially.

Some of the rationalisation proposals were held up or their implementation rejected largely on social criteria grounds but by 1968 most of the planned targets contained in the Reshaping Report had been achieved so that losses incurred on proposals still in the

Table 12   Railway Traffic 1962–1970 (millions)

	Passenger miles	Net ton-miles Total	Coal and coke	Other freight traffic
1962	19,728	16,104	7,304	8,800
1963	19,230	15,398	7,805	7,593
1964	19,874	16,052	7,470	8,582
1965	18,713	15,429	7,005	8,424
1966	18,453	14,825	6,868	7,957
1967	18,089	13,609	5,997	7,612
1968	17,835	14,693	6,277	8,416
1969	18,400	15,120	6,307	8,813
1970	18,895	16,392	6,247	10,145

Source: *Annual Abstract of Statistics*

Notes: 1. Figures for passenger traffic from 1969 onwards omit some 154 million passenger miles as a result of the transfer of the Barking-Upminster line to London Transport in 1968.

2. After 1968 an estimate is made in 'other freight traffic' for the rail share of Freightliners Ltd as a result of structural changes contained in the 1968 Transport Act.

pipeline or rejected were relatively small. In any case, most of the projected savings had materialised; in this respect therefore the report had not been widely optimistic. Where it did err was in not allowing sufficiently for wage and price increases which cancelled out most of the gains, and in its optimistic assumption that the railways would secure substantially more freight traffic through greater efficiency and the introduction of new services. The extension of the latter was not as fast as anticipated while the expected returns from the new freight services were far from being accurate.

There were of course still many economies to be made. There was no shortage of excess and uneconomic capacity to be eliminated and the scope for further measures of rationalisation was enormous, especially on the freight side. Moreover, the railways were still burdened with heavy social obligations in respect of suburban and short-distance passenger traffic which accounted for the bulk of the railway losses on the passenger side. The board complained bitterly about this in their annual report for 1965: 'the railways can never become wholly viable without further action to relieve them of social burdens which, if they must be met, should be financed from sources other than railway revenue'.[28] Without any relief on this account the railways had little prospect of eliminating their deficit for even with a further massive rationalisation effort the savings were unlikely to exceed those already secured between 1962 and 1967. And in the latter year the railways were making an overall loss on all their traffic and only express (inter-city) passenger traffic and coal managed to produce a worthwhile surplus over direct costs.

Some criticisms can be made about the board's financial and commercial policies though deficiences on this score certainly did not contribute very much to the deficits. The perennial problem of pricing remained. Though the board knew far more about its cost structure than the BTC, it did not for the most part take the opportunity to make its pricing procedure more flexible, given the freedom under the 1962 Act. Generally speaking, the board did not charge according to costs and competitive strategy. The Prices and Incomes Board was highly critical of the railways' pricing procedure: it argued that they had concentrated too heavily on general increases with a failure to discriminate between traffic and that little attention had been given to estimating the effects of tariff increases on revenue. 'The marketing information available is, however, so sparse that it is not certain that all the proposals for fares and charges increases will, in fact, increase net revenue. ... General increases in fares and charges have diminished total traffic, and increased unit costs, the increase leading to increased fares, with each turn of the screw aggravating the problem. ... We are disposed to be sceptical of the value of standard increases, and to attach greater importance to the need to particularise, in other words to increase net revenue by pricing more flexibly in line with particular marketing possibilities, even granted that the information available for doing this is limited'.[29]

No doubt progress was impeded in this direction by the continuing lack of knowledge about the costs of particular services though the matter became a much more complicated one as a result of the increasing pressure to conform to marginal cost pricing. The 1967 white paper advocated that long-run marginal cost should be charged wherever possible though it recognised the difficulties involved in adopting this procedure in industries where the area of unallocable costs is large and not easily definable. The railways provide a good case in point since a high proportion of their costs are joint and difficult to allocate. As the Prices and Incomes Board pointed out, to determine long-run marginal costs in this case, costs must be studied in terms of systems analysis and this was not yet possible since the major strategic decisions about the total size and balance of the traffic had yet to be made as part of a corporate planning exercise instituted by British Rail at the end of 1967.[30]

However, several doubts have been expressed about the wisdom of using the marginal cost procedure and it is doubtful whether any sophisticated policy could do much to reduce the deficit. The fact is that the railways have fought a losing battle with the general rise in costs since the war and have been unable to recover these by raising their charges sufficiently; nor have they been able to attract much new traffic by selective reductions since for much of their traffic they are, so to speak, on a kinked demand curve, that is demand falling off when prices are raised but failing to respond when lowered.[31] This does not of course preclude some use of the price mechanism in either direction to exploit cost or market elasticities in certain cases. It has always been anomalous that the railways kept for so long their standard mileage charge for full-fare paying passengers given the great cost variations between services. It is only recently that the railways have begun a more selective and discriminatory pricing policy on their inter-city routes, a policy which has been rewarded with some success.[32]

Another area in which the railways appear to have fallen short is in respect of investment appraisal. During the 1960s the Treasury, in conjunction with the sponsoring departments, took the initiative in tightening up the control of investment planning in nationalised industries and promoted the use of new investment appraisal techniques. The main criteria were outlined in the white papers of 1961 and 1967. Discounted cash flow techniques, using an 8 per cent discount rate, were recommended for all important projects, while in some cases a social cost/benefit appraisal might be more appropriate. Accordingly, the Ministry of Transport took active steps to improve the techniques used by the transport industries. It requested that the railways submit a five year 'rolling' programme of investment and that the case for undertaking any specific investment should be accompanied by an assessment of the profitability of existing facilities and of any feasible alternative investment. This tighter control by the ministry was timely since it led to a cut back in investment and hence avoided some of the rather wasteful and uncosted investment undertaken by the BTC. However the Select Committee on Nationalised Industries of 1968 was rather disturbed by the ministry's report on the alleged reluctance of the Railways Board to utilise the new methods. The ministry claimed that many projects put forward for approval did not show an adequate rate of return and that the board failed to make adequate use of the discounted cash flow procedure. Of the 57 projects submitted to the ministry for approval as part of the 1966 investment programme only 10 were accompanied by the dcf assessment when originally submitted (and 3 more were added at the ministry's request), but in many cases no rate of return at all was cited. The neglect was most conspicuous in the replacement field. The Railways Board was clearly having difficulties with the new techniques— it complained of not having the number of staff with expertise as the ministry had—and it was not altogether happy with the ministry's close scrutiny which appeared to question the board's commercial judgement. On the other hand, there was some justification for the ministry's concern since the Railways Board was obviously content to press forward investment projects 'on general grounds that the service must go on where, on strict economic and commercial grounds, this should not be done'. However, the ministry's claim that lack of proper appraisal of replacement investment was largely responsible for the board's financial difficulties, was clearly wide of the mark.[33]

The upshot of this clash was the setting up of a joint review to resolve the matter of investment appraisal, though quite how this will get round the railways' investment difficulties remains to be seen. The railways have a big plan for capital spending in the 1970s, notably a £350 million programme for the Southern Region commuter network, and the costs of the London–Glasgow electrification scheme. Yet internal resources are limited and some of the projects clearly will not satisfy the new criteria, in which case Treasury assistance would not be forthcoming. But perhaps the ministry and Treasury will relax the rules to allow the show to go on. Indeed, the sanctioning of the Weaver Junction–Glasgow electrification project without (as far as we know) having passed a rigorous investment appraisal, would seem to indicate that they are prepared to let by-gones be by-gones.

REORGANISATION ONCE AGAIN

The new Labour Government of 1964 was clearly unhappy about the transport situation as a whole and the departure of Dr Beeching from the Railways Board in May 1965 provided the opportunity for the government to reorganise transport policy. It was committed to a new national plan for inland transport including a new deal for the railways. The full details of the new policy were released in a series of white papers which formed the background to the Transport Act of 1968.[34] As far as the railways were concerned, the government rejected commercial viability as the prime objective of railway policy and stated that the railway system should be designed to accord more closely with the country's economic needs. As a consequence the future network of the railway system was redefined. In all some 11,000 route miles were to be retained as against about 8000 under the original Beeching formula and 13,500 then in existence. The additional 3000 miles, that is the difference between Beeching's proposed figure and the new plan, consisted mainly of commuter and rural services and routes deemed to be of value in regional planning despite their cost. Apart from the basic network of 11,000 miles, a further 2500 route miles were not selected for specific development. Not all these services would be closed, but each would be reviewed on its merits. It is difficult to see how the figure of 11,000 miles for the basic system was chosen since little explanatory detail was given in the document outlining the revised network.

Despite the downgrading of commercial objectives the government was very much concerned about the financial position of the railways, the more so now that it had enlarged the future network. Large deficits had a demoralising effect on both management and workers and it was deemed essential to eliminate these if maximum effort and efficiency were to be attained. Hence the board was to be given a new financial framework within which it was expected to move as soon as possible to a position of financial equilibrium. This comprised a capital reconstruction, the subsidisation of socially desirable services, specific grants for track rationalisation, and the removal of the unprofitable sundries traffic.

The Transport Act of 1968 gave effect to these proposals. First it made provision for a major capital reconstruction whereby the Board's commencing capital debt was scaled down to £365 million (from £1562 million). This relieved the railways of about £30 million in annual interest payments and £20 million in depreciation charges, though partly because of a rise in other interest charges they were still paying over £41 million in 1969 compared with £67 million the year previously. However, it was anticipated that this was a realistic figure which could be met out of the railways' revenue. Secondly, the long advocated method of subsidising uneconomic but socially necessary services was accepted for the first time. Specific grants were to be made for each service retained on these grounds, and in 1969 about 300 services were assisted at a total cost of £61 million, with a similar grant being made in 1970 and 1971. Grant-aid covered nearly every type of service including a few Inter-city routes, though the provision of financial assistance did not preclude closure at some future date.[35] The third type of assistance comprised track rationalisation grants. Up to £50 million was to be paid on a tapering basis over a five year period to help defray the cost of maintaining surplus track and equipment pending its elimination. Finally, the railways were relieved of responsibility for road bridge maintenance, while compensation was promised for subsidies paid to bus operators providing services after the withdrawal of rail.

There was also some financial relief on the freight side as a result of the new integration proposals. Two major sectors, sundries and freightliner traffic, were hived off to a new body, the

National Freight Corporation but the board retained a 49 per cent stake in the Freightliner Company. National Carriers Ltd., a wholly owned subsidiary of NFC, was to take charge of the sundries traffic, with a subsidy of up to £60 million over a five year period to meet initial losses. The railways however secured an immediate gain of some £20 million through this latter deal. Indirectly the railways also stood to benefit from more onerous road haulage charges and a system of quantity licensing which appeared to be designed to favour the railways, though these provisions have not so far been invoked.

FUTURE PROSPECTS

A combination of unfavourable circumstances placed the railways in an invidious financial position in the post-war period. The rapid expansion in road transport inevitably forced the railways onto the defensive since they lacked the convenience and flexibility which motor transport could offer. But to match capacity to demand in a situation of contracting traffic poses far greater problems than in the reverse case, and the process was hindered by various obligations, both legal and social, and by government policy. Hence, the railways became a high cost industry which reduced their competitive power even further. However, factors outside the railways' control were not the only problems. For the first decade or more after nationalisation railway management was not up to the task of adapting the system to meet the changing conditions or to devising policies that would exploit railway potential to the full. In particular, the BTC completely misjudged the long term trends in the pattern of transport demand and hence its policies on investment, pricing and closure were geared largely to maintaining the *status quo* rather than to revamping the system for future needs. Its policies were ill-defined though in this respect it can be argued that it lacked guidelines from the government.

During the 1960s the railways proved ready to respond to drastic solutions. A large scale rationalisation programme was carried through and a more commercial response was shown by the management. By this time however, it was too late. Market penetration by road transport had already reached a high and unassailable level and the railways were still losing traffic from some of their former customers. Moreover, the cost-price situation had by that time passed the point of no repair and as fast as economies were made these were eaten up by rising costs. The deficit therefore came to be accepted as inevitable and in 1968 a wholesale salvage operation was put in hand.

However, it is difficult to accept that this shot in the arm will be the last. The total financial relief in 1969 (including release from the sundries traffic losses) amounted to some £160 million which allowed the board to turn in a profit of nearly £15 million, but two years later this had been reversed into a deficit of equal magnitude, and according to the chairman's report the prospects looked bleak. A decline in coal and steel movements and rapidly rising costs, especially wages, were partly to blame,[36] but apart from these factors the underlying trends are not promising.

It was generally accepted that given the financial provisions of the Act and the estimates for future traffic the railways would be able to break even in the 1970s. Several reservations must be expressed on this score and in fact even the board itself is having second thoughts.[37] In the first place many of the grants taper off over time and it is difficult to conceive that the railways will be able to earn sufficient revenue to finance their anticipated investment and re-equipment programme without further financial aid. Indeed, additional assistance, notably for the cost of investing in urban railway networks, has been promised since the 1968 Act.[38] The alternative of course would be a further dose of rationalisation: there is still much excess capacity to be eliminated, and labour costs, which form 60 per cent of total expenses, could certainly be reduced. But it seems unlikely that the government will contemplate another drastic pruning of the network. The main prospect for cost savings therefore lies in improved efficiency though gains on this count are not likely to be sufficient to match rising costs.

As regards traffic trends the prospects are far from promising. Projections made before the 1968 Act suggested that the railways would be able to balance their accounts provided that all freight traffic and services which could not be made profitable were discontinued. These forecasts were based on a number of assumptions: that total output and wages would expand at 3 per cent per annum over the period 1967–75, that there would be no change in the prices of materials and services purchased by the board, and that freight traffic other than fuel and steel would double, while total rail freight would expand by 1750 million ton miles (12 per cent) by 1975, leaving the railways with a 22 per cent share in the national market. These projections were unduly optimistic to say the least and on the basis of past trends it seems very unlikely that the railways will be able to retain their share in the total freight market. The original Beeching estimates of freightliner traffic, for example, were later considerably downgraded as a result of an underestimation of the railways' competitive break-even distance. Moreover, given the railways' kinked demand curve any increase in charges, which are almost inevitable given the cost pressures, are likely to result in a further loss of traffic. And the biggest problem will almost certainly be the pressure on costs. Most of the economies made in the 1960s were whittled away by wage increases, yet apart from a very modest 3 per cent rise in wages the board expected costs to remain fairly stable, a view which has already proved to be unfounded.

Passenger transport presents less of a problem and the prospects are somewhat brighter for the future. Indeed, recently passenger traffic has been increasing for the first time for many years and in 1969 passenger receipts exceeded those derived from freight. Here of course the BRB has benefited immensely from the massive subsidies and though these alone are not likely to do much to boost traffic the board obviously has a vested interest in retaining the subvention when cases come up for review. The social subsidies are not likely to continue indefinitely and much will depend on how far local authorities and the Passenger Transport Authorities are prepared to help out. It is on the Inter-city routes however where the greatest potential lies. Given flexibility in pricing structures and improvements in service the railways could win back traffic from road transport. The success achieved on the electrified routes from Euston over the past five years augur well for the future. Passenger traffic has roughly doubled, about 40 per cent being newly generated and the rest representing a diversion from the airlines and road transport (40 and 20 per cent respectively). Speed appears to be the crucial element since railway experience indicates that a one per cent increase in traffic can be gained from an additional extra mile an hour of speed in passenger service. The prospects of a further boost to train speeds with the introduction of the High Speed Train (HST), capable of speeds of 125 mph on existing track, and the 150 mph Advanced Passenger Train (APT) which it is hoped will bring new and sophisticated technology to BR should enhance British Rail's attraction, though against this there is the probability of increased competition from vertical take-off aircraft and motorway express bus services at very much cheaper fares.[39]

Thus the railways have in effect been given a clean bill of health by the Act of 1968. Their difficulties however are by no means over and many doubts still remain. As this volume closes for press (Spring 1974) the government is assessing the whole railway policy yet again and indications suggest that it has finally been accepted that the railways never can be profitable. Much still depends on how well they are able to exploit their assets by vigorous commercial policies, and improve their public image. They have much to offer but it will be the consumer who decides whether the service is worthy of purchase.

CHAPTER SIX

Road Transport

UNDOUBTEDLY THE MOST SPECTACULAR DEVELOPMENT in British transport since the war has been the rapid expansion of motor transport. This had already made considerable headway in the inter-war years with over 3 million vehicles of one sort or another in use at the end of that period, but this scarcely bears comparison with the sheer magnitude of volume growth soon after the war. The war checked expansion and in 1946 the number of vehicles in current use was very similar to that in 1938. Yet a decade later, in 1955, the number had doubled to over 6·6 million, and this figure doubled again by 1965. More recently there has been some slowing down in the rate of growth; nevertheless, the total number of motor vehicles licensed in 1970 was over 15 million. Most of the expansion can be accounted for by private cars and goods vehicles. As can be seen from the table 13, the number of private cars and vans rose nearly six times between the late 1940s and 1970 and at the latter date accounted for nearly 12 million (and nearly 13 million if we include motor cycles and scooters) of the 15 million or so vehicles then in existence. The other main growth area has been that of goods vehicles whose number more than doubled over the same period though they amount to only a fraction of the number of private cars. By contrast public passenger transport vehicles have declined steadily since 1950 and in 1970 they numbered a mere 105,000, including taxis.[1]

The rapid penetration of own account passenger transport has been a phenomenon of the post-war period. Before the war road

Table 13   Motor vehicles currently licensed in UK, 1938–1970 (000s)

	Private cars and private vans	Motor cycles, scooters, mopeds.	Public service vehicles(1)	Goods vehicles(2)	Other vehicles(3)	Total
1938	1,984	448	89	504	114	3,139
1948	2,002	544	131	785	344	3,806
1950	2,307	739	140	916	409	4,511
1955	3,609	1,242	105	1,134	533	6,623
1960	5,650	1,829	95	1,433	659	9,666
1965	9,131	1,640	98	1,642	748	13,259
1970	11,802	1,062	105	1,659	695	15,323

Source: Highway Statistics (HMSO)

Notes : (1.) Includes taxis and trolleybuses but excludes tramcars.
(2.) Includes agricultural vans and lorries
(3.) 'Other vehicles' covers agricultural and general haulage tractors, trench diggers and mobile cranes, three wheelers, pedestrian controlled vehicles, Crown and exempt vehicles.

transport as a whole (both public and private) accounted for well over one half the total passenger miles travelled in this country and it was public transport rather than the private car which made the major contribution.[2] This was still true in the immediate post-war years since the shortage of cars for the home market and limitations on their use as a result of petrol rationing severely restricted the growth of private transport. In fact public transport had its last moment of glory in the war and early post-war years and actually increased its share of the market. In 1950 public road and rail transport accounted for about 75 per cent of the market, while the volume of transport by private car (in passenger miles) was little changed from that in 1938. Rail passenger traffic however remained static and it was bus and coach travel which set the pace. Between 1938 and 1950 passenger mileage by bus and coach rose from 19·4 to 50·2 thousand million passenger miles and accounted for nearly one half the total market as against less than one third before the war, while road transport as a whole accounted for about 75 per cent of all mileage travelled.[3]

The position was to change rapidly as the car revolution got under way from the early 1950s. During that decade the number of vehicles in use more than doubled and in 1960 nearly 30 per cent of all households had the use of one or more cars. An indication of their increased use can be gained from the fact that in 1960, 47 per cent used a car for their annual holiday as against only 21 per cent 10 years earlier. During the 1960s the dream of car ownership became a reality for a large section of the community; the car stock more than doubled again and in 1970 over one half the households of Great Britain possessed a car. The extent of the penetration of the mass market can be judged from a survey of car ownership by social class carried out by the AA in 1965. This showed that of those who owned cars from before 1945 nearly 70 per cent were in the top social brackets, A, B, and C1, whereas nearly 60 per cent of those owning cars since 1956 only were in the lowest social groups, C2 and DE.[4] Even so, on the basis of American experience there is still some way to go before saturation level is reached; as early as 1960 there was one car for every three people in the United States whereas in Britain in 1966 the ratio was about one in five and it is now closer to one in four. Moreover, there are significant regional variations in the density of car ownership. In 1966 this ranged from 213 cars per thousand persons in the South West region to 114 in West Central Scotland, while some counties, eg Surrey, Oxfordshire and Worcestershire, had twice as many cars per head as Lanarkshire, Durham or West Lothian. As one might expect, there is a strong tendency for regional car ownership to vary with income, though population density also exerted a strong influence in some cases, as in rural Wales where car density was as high as in the South East despite a much lower average income per capita.[5]

Some of the general influences determining the growth of car ownership and mileage travelled by car were examined in chapter 4. We saw that the expansion in the car stock was closely related to the change in personal incomes (after tax) but that the increase was considerably faster than incomes. This implied that independent, non-income factors exerted a powerful influence. The fact that car purchase costs have remained static in monetary terms and have fallen sharply in real terms and relative to the cost of public transport no doubt had some influence though it is unlikely they were of major importance. Costs do feature to a certain extent in the decision to purchase a car though not very explicitly, and there is no doubt that in the absence of income growth and favourable cost trends the level of car ownership would have been checked. On the other hand, non-economic considerations, such as convenience and social status, have shifted the consumer preference function in favour of car ownership at the expense of other articles of consumption and these would have exerted a powerful effect in the absence of cost and income changes. Thus cars may be bought in the first instance for leisure purposes or for journeys for which public transport does not cater. Secondly, there is no doubt that the car has become a powerful symbol of social prestige and the pressures to conform to the car way of life have been overwhelming. One author has vividly described the process in these terms: 'it is quite remarkable to trace from the earliest days what a prominent place in social values the car was to have, with the American example projected seductively via the cinema, and with high powered advertising keeping up a constant pressure in this country, the urge for possession became overriding. It became the new liberator in democratic terms; it was the new emancipation for the lower middle class and the new skilled worker. Place in society is reflected too obviously with other possessions: one's home and residential area too clearly reflect one's earning power and status. But the car is different: the driver of a typical family saloon can be (and frequently is) drawn from very wide sectors of society; his station is unknown and unknowable; the car is at once a concealer of his status and a herald of his stake in mid-mass. As a democratising medium it is a passport to a social recognition formerly denied him; as a destroyer of traditional class barriers it is supreme.'[6]

So much for the purchase of cars. Once bought there is every incentive to use the car as intensively as possible since, given the high proportion of fixed costs to total running costs, unit costs drop very sharply as mileage run increases. It is doubtful whether the owner conceives the economics of the situation in these terms; it is more likely, if any consideration at all is given to the matter, that he regards the fixed costs, interest on foregone capital, tax and insurance, driving licence and garaging, as irretrievable sunk costs. In effect this provides an even greater disposition to utilise his car since it is primarily short-run marginal costs which are taken into consideration; these include mainly petrol, oil and possibly tyres and maintenance—the cost of his own labour and of the congestion caused are ignored. These short run costs compare very favourably with those of any alternative form of transport especially when more than one occupant per car is involved. But possibly more important are the quality and service functions. Even with increasing road congestion the car still has the advantage in terms of time, convenience and comfort and these factors count increasingly as public transport deteriorates with the ever growing volume of traffic. Apart from these factors there has been a considerable shift in both residential and work locations since the war of a type which reduces the accessibility of public transport and necessitates the use of one's own car. Moreover, as affluence increases the desire for greater mobility also increases, and since much of this is associated with leisure activities it is again of a type which cannot easily be satisfied by public transport.

Whatever the causes of the growth of car ownership and use there is no doubt about its magnitude. Since the early 1950s travel by private car has increased more than five times and in 1970 it accounted for 77 per cent of all passenger miles travelled in Great Britain. Moreover, since mileage per car is constantly increasing this inexorable growth seems likely to continue even beyond car saturation point. Apart from the obvious and visible impact it has had in terms of congestion and urban planning,[7] the private car has hit the public service operator severely and the history of this sector has been one of almost unbroken decline.

Public passenger transport

Before examining the effects and causes of the long-term stagnation in traffic a few background details on the changing structure of the industry are required. During the 1930s the industry had crystallised into four main groups: municipal operators, associated or territorial companies, independent operators and the road interests of the railways. The latter bought their way into road passenger transport by acquiring an interest in some of the large territorial companies, notably Thomas Tilling, British Electric Traction and the Scottish Motor Traction Group, which controlled around two fifths of the buses in Britain by 1939. Entry into the industry and conditions of operation were rigidly controlled by the licensing system passed in 1930.

Provisions for road passenger transport in the nationalisation measure of 1947 were defined very loosely compared with those for other forms of transport. The Act did not nationalise outright bus and coach services and initially the British Transport Commission simply inherited the railways' bus interests. However the BTC was given powers to acquire undertakings and these it used to negotiate for the outstanding shares in Thomas Tilling and the Scottish Group; attempts to take over the BET group failed however and this company remained independent, though with a large minority state holding, until 1968. In addition, the BTC also acquired a number of smaller, independent companies including Red and White Services, Youngs Bus Services, and Griffin and Ralph Transport. All these interests were administered by the Road Transport Executive until 1949 when a separate Passenger Transport Executive was created to deal with this sector. London Transport, which was taken over in its entirety, was administered by a separate executive.

Thus by the early 1950s over half the bus and coach industry was controlled by the state or municipal authorities; they accounted for about 43,600 vehicles as against nearly 38,000 controlled by independent operators.[8] In practice nationalisation had little impact on the company organisations which had existed previously since for the most part the BTC or its Executive retained the existing structure for operational purposes. Powers of the commission to prepare area co-ordination schemes for passenger transport never advanced very far and in any case they were cut short by a change in government policy in 1953. The Transport Act of that year prohibited the BTC from acquiring further undertakings and empowered it to dispose of the existing interests, but these powers were never invoked. In the same year the Thesiger Committee reported favourably on the licensing system and rejected the suggestion that easier entry conditions into the industry should be allowed, though it made little investigation into the economic and organisational problems of the industry. In effect therefore, the status quo was retained and the only notable change was the transfer of the BTC's bus holdings to the Transport Holding Company under the 1962 Act. This authority was given much greater freedom than other nationalised undertakings to operate as a commercial enterprise and in this respect it proved remarkably successful despite its rather short life.[9]

Labour's new plan for transport in the 1960s placed considerable emphasis on the need to provide 'an attractive and efficient system of public transport' particularly within cities.[10] This was the motive for the creation of Passenger Transport Authorities (by the Transport Act of 1968) to control public transport in the major conurbations and whose duties were to provide a properly integrated and efficient system of transport within their areas. To achieve this they were to work in conjunction with the railways and the National Bus Company which was created to take over the bus interests of the Transport Holding Company. Scottish buses were dealt with separately; these were handed over to a new Scottish Transport Group which also included shipping and ferry services. Under separate legislation London Transport was handed over to the Greater London Council though its country area buses were transferred to the National Bus Company. In addition, the bus industry was to receive considerable financial assistance including capital grants, subsidies for unremunerative services and an increase in the fuel duty rebate.

In 1970 therefore, when the restructuring process was more or less complete, the pattern of ownership fell into three broad groups. First, there was the state-owned sector comprising the NBC and Scottish Transport Group with a nucleus of the three major pre-war bus groupings in which the railways had invested together with a number of smaller undertakings which had been acquired since 1947. Both groups operate as holding companies— the NBC has over 50 subsidiary companies—with a decentralised organisational structure which allows considerable autonomy to the individual companies. In 1970 the state sector accounted for over one third of the total buses and about one third of all passengers carried. The second grouping comprises the municipal sector but which effectively consists of three different types of operator. There are the municipal undertakings proper which after the 1968 Act were reduced to about 68 as a result of the formation of the Passenger Transport Authorities. By 1973 five had been set up (for Tyneside, Merseyside, the West Midlands, South East Lancashire & North-East Cheshire and Glasgow) out of an amalgam of several local authority undertakings. They have much wider powers than the other municipal operators over public transport within their areas and they are exempt from the control of the Traffic Commissioners. Finally, London Transport is now under the control of the GLC though in many respects it bears much resemblance to the PTA's. This sector as a whole accounts for less than one third of all vehicles but well over 50 per cent of all passenger journeys, and the range in size of undertakings varies from the one extreme of London Transport with over 6000 vehicles to local authorities operating only a handful of vehicles. The remaining sector comprises independent private operators. In terms of the number of vehicles this sector ranks with the other two, accounting for over one third, but it carries a much smaller fraction of the total passengers. The number of operators is very

Table 14 Public passenger transport: ownership of vehicles and passengers carried by type of operator. 1970

	Vehicles owned	Passenger journeys (millions)
National Bus Company	21,839	2,573
Scottish Transport Group	4,696	464
Passenger Transport Authorities	6,124	1,378
London Transport	6,153	1,502
Local authorities	10,227	2,462
Other operators	24,899	775
Total	73,938	9,154

Source: Passenger Transport in Great Britain, 1970 (HMSO, 1972)
Note: A few trams and trolleybuses owned by municipal undertakings are included in the figures. Total journeys by these modes amounted to only 44 million.

large, over 5000, but the majority of firms are very small and many own but a single vehicle. Much of their work consists of contract and private hire work though they do make some contribution to stage services especially in sparsely populated rural areas.

THE DECLINE IN TRAFFIC

During the war and immediate post-war years passenger traffic increased very considerably partly because of the restrictions on private motoring. Once these were removed demand peaked out sharply and from 1953 onwards there has been a steady and uninterrupted decline. Between 1953 and 1970 passenger mileage travelled by public service vehicles declined by about one third while the number of passenger journeys fell by nearly 44 per cent (inclusive of tram and trolley bus journeys). However, not all types of services suffered contraction. As table 15 shows, stage services, which were by far the most important, experienced a dramatic decline but other types of operators fared much better. Contract services experienced a steady rise in traffic through to 1970, express services expanded until 1966 after which a decline set in, while excursion traffic tended to fluctuate on a gently declining trend. The specialised nature of contract work has provided a resilience that no other sector shared.

Table 15   *Bus passenger journeys by type of service 1953–1970* (millions)

	Stage services	Express services	Excursion services	Contract services	Total
1953	15,728	56	41	258	16,083
1960	13,274	69	37	300	13,680
1965	11,193	76	34	349	11,652
1970	8,645	69	27	413	9,154

Source: *Passenger Transport in Great Britain* (HMSO)

Note: The figures also include journeys by trams and trolleybuses, which amounted to 2739 million journeys in 1953 and 44 million in 1970.

Probably the worst hit services have been those in cities and rural areas. Urban traffic began to decline as early as 1950, whereas for stage services other than those of local authorities and London Transport, passengers carried did not reach a peak until 1955. Most city undertakings saw their peak loadings in the late 1940s or early 1950s, though in one or two instances, eg St Helens and South Shields, the turning point in traffic volume came later. But by the late 1950s nearly every authority was experiencing a fall-off in traffic and in some cases the magnitude of the decline was substantial. In Manchester, for instance, traffic carried dropped by about one half between the peak in 1949 and 1969 and by the latter date it was well below the pre-war level. Glasgow's transport system registered an even sharper decline from 804·6 million passengers in 1950 (the peak year) to 343·4 million in 1969, compared with 651·8 million in 1939. Similarly in London the volume of traffic carried by road fell by about 50 per cent over the same period though in terms of passenger mileage the decline was much steeper. Not all city undertakings have fared quite so badly—in Leicester the decline was only one third—but all suffered substantial declines in traffic, and allowing for the switch from trams and trolleybuses the overall decline in passenger journeys has been the order of one half or more from the peak through to 1970.[11]

With falling traffic and increasing costs, including city traffic congestion costs, many operators have been faced with increasing financial stringency. The widespread practice in the industry of cross-subsidisation between routes has become increasingly difficult since the number of really profitable routes diminished steadily over time. As early as 1956 the chairman of London Transport reported that about one half of London's bus routes were unprofitable, while in 1958 the Midland Red Company estimated that 32 per cent of its mileage and 64 per cent of its services were unremunerative. Local authority accounts indicate that an increasing number of transport undertakings ran into deficit. From a survey of 69 municipal transport concerns it was found that 17 reported losses in 1954–55 and 31 in 1967–68.[12] However, profitability is perhaps not a very meaningful concept in respect of municipal undertakings since many authorities as a matter of policy subsidise their transport services or at best they aim to break even.

The bus industry as a whole has not experienced anywhere near the degree of financial stringency of the railways. This is partly because fares have risen sharply in the postwar period and thus have matched the rise in costs. Outside the municipal sector rates of return have been reasonable. The state's holdings performed consistently well both under the BTC and the Transport Holding Company with an average rate of return on net assets of between 7–8 per cent,[13] while a survey of 143 non-municipal operators by Beesley and Politi for the period 1960–1966 showed that returns were far from negligible.[14] The higher content of inter-urban and express services, where returns are high, partly accounts for this respectable performance though these could prove less viable with the continued decline in traffic levels. Indeed, the recent disastrous financial performance of the National Bus Company does not augur well for the future.[15]

THE RURAL PROBLEM

The decline of the rural bus industry is in some respects more serious since it has caused serious social hardship. Many of these services were cross-subsidised from the beginning but this became increasingly difficult as traffic declined across-the-board. However, from the early 1950s traffic on rural routes declined rapidly with the spread of personal transport so that many services became even more unprofitable. In the later 1950s no fewer than 80 per cent of the stage routes of the Highland Omnibus Company were operating unprofitably. Services therefore began to be abandoned in the 1950s and the Jacks Committee in 1961 reported that there was little prospect of adequate services being retained without external assistance. 'Experience over the country seems to be that where services are finally abandoned there is no eagerness by other operators to provide them. This is hardly surprising because it usually follows only after the service has for long made a loss'.[16] Since then the rural transport problem has become a great deal worse with the abandonment of rail services and many more bus services. By 1970 many areas were virtually without any public transport services, and yet according to the Maud report on local government, as many as 41·7 per cent of the rural population of

10 million possessed nothing more than bicycles and many relied on the goodwill of neighbours.[17] The Transport Act of 1968 paid some recognition to the problem by providing a subsidy to be paid to rural bus operators by local authorities one half of which might be defrayed by the government. Initial reaction to the measure was far from enthusiastic since local authorities were reluctant to accept the burden. However, further and more substantial assistance was announced by the Minister of Transport Industries in 1971 which may yet secure the sector from further decline.[18]

PROBLEMS OF THE BUS INDUSTRY

That the spread of car ownership has been responsible for the decline in demand for public road transport there can be little doubt. As we have already noted, the private car scores over public transport both in terms of convenience and cost, in the latter case largely because the motorists' cost calculations turn out favourably in comparison with those of bus operators. The main problem for the public operator on the demand side is that the purchase of a car may be motivated quite independently of the type of service he can offer, and that once the transfer to personal transport is made there is a trade-off between private and public transport which works to the detriment of the latter.

It is unlikely that the quality of public transport (except in cases where it is almost non-existent) has had much influence on whether a car is purchased or not. Several possible factors were put forward in an earlier section to explain the rise in car ownership but basically it amounts to the fact that 'most individuals will buy a car just as soon as they can afford it, irrespective of the merits or dismerits of public transport, traffic congestion, or even whether they will always be in a position to use it'.[19] However, the quality of public transport does affect the use made of cars, especially by commuters, since the private-public transport trade-off is relatively responsive to changes in fares, relative travel times, comfort and convenience. Once the switch is made the relative unattractiveness of public transport becomes more noticeable and as the number of car travellers grows the process has a feed-back effect. More car travellers mean fewer bus passengers and increasing street congestion which in turn leads to higher fares and a deterioration in the quality of services offered by bus operators. And as the quality of service declines so the substitution effect accelerates. Moreover, what is even more depressing is that once passengers are lost there is little likelihood of them ever returning to public transport whatever the inducements offered.[20] A sample survey of Leeds car-owners who used their cars for work suggested that they were relatively insensitive to improvements in public transport services, in terms of faster travel times, reduced fares or better frequencies. Even the prospect of a free bus system attracted few potential transfers.[21] The fact is that public transport has acquired a poor image over the years and is rapidly being regarded as the mode of travel for the poor, the sick and infirm, children and elderly people. In these circumstances it is difficult to conceive that bus companies will be able to attract back traffic unless severe restrictions are placed on the use of personal transport. Indeed, there is every likelihood that further losses will occur as greater premium is placed on time and convenience in daily life. At present many car owners do not use their car for work purposes largely because of limitations on parking space.

The most awkward aspect of the industry's demand schedule is its skewed nature. Much of the traffic is carried during a few hours of the day, the early mornings and in the late afternoon and early evening, and it has been suggested that for mass-transit facilities, about 80 per cent of the traffic volume occurs during 20 hours of the week.[22] The peak problem is common to all urban transport undertakings which deal with large amounts of commuter traffic though most transport concerns experience peak demands of one sort or another (eg seasonal). Moreover, there is some indication that the problem has increased since the sharpest fall-off in traffic has occurred during week-ends, evenings and other off-peak times. Thus in 1960–61, 58 per cent of all passengers were carried on London's undergound railways in the maximum peak evening hour compared with 47 per cent in 1936–37.[23] Such changes can be explained partly by new patterns of leisure activity, notably television which has cut recreational travel during the evenings and week-ends, and partly to the fact that personal transport is better adapted to servicing leisure and other off-peak travel requirements.

The peak traffic problem imposes a serious financial burden on transport operators since it requires undertakings to maintain large fleets of vehicles many of which are severely underutilised and therefore cannot recover their full costs. The Tilling Bus Group, for instance, required 8000 vehicles to service their daily peak requirements in 1967 but only 5000 or fewer were needed for the off-peak periods.[24] Many municipal corporations require at least double the number of vehicles and staff to cope with peak demand,[25] and in some cases the position is a good deal worse. Much of the equipment may be used for no more than two or three hours a day though the problem is eased somewhat in the case of staff by shift working. Moreover, the fact that off-peak traffic has suffered the sharpest decline means that the scope for the cross-subsidisation of peak services has become less and less possible.

Given the nature of the demand situation it is difficult to see what the industry could have done independently to improve the position. Some solutions to the problem are available but these would require the collaboration and consent of external authorities. Partial attempts have already been made to deal with the situation. Considerable financial assistance has recently been announced for bus operators both in rural and urban areas. However, subsidisation contributes little towards solving the urban travel problem as such since it will not entice passengers to use public transport given the nature of the demand curve for urban transport. Only measures designed to achieve some restriction on the use of cars in towns and allow buses priority of way are likely to lead to a revival of the demand for public transport. These include severe restrictions on through traffic, high parking charges, road pricing and reserved bus lanes, or whole areas in the central zones of cities reserved for buses only. Several experiments have been made in various cities though most of them are of a very limited and tentative nature. However, the few radical experiments that have so far been made—for example, the busway reservations systems in Reading and Runcorn—suggest that the problem may be far from insoluable.[26]

THE INDUSTRY'S OWN SOLUTIONS

The bus industry has been faced with a similar problem to that of the railways, falling demand and rapidly rising costs, but with even less scope for reviving demand than the railways. In this situation one would expect that the industry, like the railways in the 1960s, would have adopted drastic measures to reduce costs and improve efficiency to offset the situation. In fact however progress in this respect has been very limited.

The position is best summarised by the unenviable productivity record of road passenger transport. Both labour productivity and output per unit of input fell continuously from 1952 to the mid 1960s and the rate of decline accelerated in the early 1960s, a performance which was very much worse than even that of the railways.[27] Though passenger traffic fell by around one third between 1953 and 1968, the labour force declined from 324,000 to only 263,000 while the number of vehicles in operation and vehicle mileage run contracted very little indeed. In these circumstances it is hardly surprising that the industry experienced severe cost pressures but the question is why were factor inputs reduced so little in the face of a sharp contraction in demand.

One problem has been the difficulty of rationalising the route and service structure. Though uneconomic routes and services have been abandoned, especially in sparsely populated areas, there is a limit to such a policy because of the absence of alternative transport services for people without cars.[28] Second, the widespread practice of cross-subsidisation has tended to conceal the need to cut out parts of the system, since by and large bus companies have not been forced to take drastic action by dint of heavy deficits. In large urban areas the problem has been complicated in several ways. The decline in traffic tends to be spread fairly evenly over the route structure, while the increasing predominance of peak traffic means that large amounts of rolling stock are required, as much of which as possible might just as well be used for off-peak services so long as running costs are covered. In any case, municipal authorities are under some community obligation to provide a reasonable network of services, especially if this helps to relieve congestion. If anything the geographical extent of urban services has tended to increase in order to serve new residential areas as a result of the outward shift of population from the cities. Thus in Manchester the route mileage operated by buses increased steadily from 313 miles in 1948 to 404 in 1969, but the actual bus mileage run remained static and the number of passengers carried fell from 360 million to 252 million.[29] The extension of services into less trafficked areas coupled with the secular downward trend in demand has had a dramatic impact on productivity. In Aberdeen the number of buses and bus route mileage doubled between 1948 and 1969 but the average number of passengers per bus mile declined by about 30 per cent.[30] Increasing traffic congestion has also had an adverse effect on productivity by reducing average speeds and the annual mileage per bus.

The scope for technical and structural economies has also been rather limited. It is doubtful, for instance, whether there are any significant economies to be derived from increasing the degree of concentration, though opinion differs on this matter. The white paper of 1967 hinted that the optimum size of unit might be in the region of 1000 buses which provided one of the reasons for the creation of the Passenger Transport Authorities.[31] Though concentration has increased significantly since the early 1930s—by 1968 about one per cent or more of the operators ran over half the total buses—the size of unit varied enormously. The average size of state fleets was 950, that of municipal undertakings 190, while over 4000 operators had 9 or fewer buses apiece. Many of the smaller operators served specialised markets and the scope for scale economies is probably very limited. Moreover, in the case of municipal operation, a recent study suggested that if anything diseconomies tended to accrue as the size of unit increased, though the authors admitted that very large units such as the PTAs might benefit from scale economies. However the evidence is by no means conclusive and Lee and Steedman were inclined to favour constant returns to scale.[32]

Unlike some other branches of transport, notably aviation, there have been no significant cost-reducing technical break-throughs in bus operation. Minor improvements have been made as with the introduction of more efficient vehicles, better maintenance which permits larger mileage between engine overhauls, and system planning of route operation etc., but these have had a negligible effect on productivity. A number of imaginative ideas are now current but their application still lies in the future. However, the most promising area for cost reduction would seem to be on the labour side since operative costs (wages of drivers and conductors) account for nearly 50 per cent of total expenses while total labour costs are around 70 per cent. The main difficulty in this respect lies in the indivisable nature of the operating unit which makes large scale labour economies difficult to achieve, though the Prices and Incomes Board in its many reports on the industry has suggested several ways of improving efficiency. The main hope would appear to lie in the extension of one-man operation which has been used extensively abroad for many years but which has hardly made any impact in this country until recently. At the end of 1966 fewer than 10 per cent of the industry's vehicles were operated without conductors.[33] One-man buses have been used on rural routes for some years but only since the legalising of one-man operated double-decker buses in 1966 have they been used to any great extent on urban routes. Since then many companies have resorted to one-man operation in an effort to overcome staff shortages and counter rising wage bills, and by the early 1970s up to one third or more of all vehicles had been converted. The savings vary depending on circumstances, though they can be quite substantial even when increased pay is awarded to staff. A study of 37 corporations which had converted about 20 per cent of their buses by 1969 suggests that there were considerable savings to be derived from converting to one-man operation (an average of nearly 14 per cent), though these were insufficient to outweigh the substantial increase in the real costs of bus operation over the period 1964–69. The scope for further savings from conversion still remains considerable, though these may diminish as conversion is made on less suitable routes. Such benefits are only likely to accrue so long as fare scales and methods of collection are simplified otherwise the increased running times involved, especially in peak periods, may well lead to additional costs greater than the costs of the conductor. Moreover, it has been suggested that the potential saving from conversion may also be diminished by large increases in stopping times, which in turn impose community costs in terms of delays to bus passengers and increased congestion. The necessity of finding a solution to this problem is evident.[34]

THE LICENSING SYSTEM

Since 1930 the bus and coach industry has operated within the framework of a fairly elaborate licensing system. It has been amended in detail but until recently no major breaches were made in the system of control. The Road Traffic Act of 1930 gave wide powers to regional Traffic Commissioners to regulate the industry by means of a series of licences. These fell into two categories: discriminatory and non-discriminatory licences. The first included drivers and conductors licences, public service vehicle licences and certificates of fitness. They were issued on the basis of objective criteria without discrimination between operators since anyone who satisfied the requirements obtained a licence automatically. For the most part these requirements were in the interests of safety and consumer protection and so little quarrel can be made about them.

The second type of licence, the road service licence, was quite a different matter. This provided the real teeth of the system, for each operator had to obtain a separate licence for every service, except for contract carriage, on which passengers were carried for hire or reward. The considerations which the commissioners were to take into account in dispensing such licences were defined as: the desirability of the service in the public interest, the suitability of the route, the adequacy of existing services and the needs of the area as a whole in relation to traffic, including the provision of adequate, suitable and efficient services and the provision of unremunerative services, and the co-ordination of all forms of transport, including rail. To assist the commissioners in their task restrictions could be attached to the licenses over fares, time-

B.T.—M

tables and stopping points. Fares, for example, were to be reasonable and fixed at a level to avoid wasteful competition.

Clearly the legislation gave the commissioners very extensive control over the industry. But their job was difficult partly because the provisions in the Act were vaguely defined while some of them were inconsistent. The terms public need, wasteful competition and adequate services were not defined explicitly, while no guidance was given on how co-ordination was to be achieved. The provision of efficient services was also difficult to reconcile with that of unremunerative services. Moreover, the commissioners were not equipped to deal with such economic matters in any meaningful way. In effect therefore, the application of the law developed largely according to the whims of the commissioners who placed emphasis on legal and administrative questions rather than economic ones. Against the background of excessive competition in the 1920s there was innate bias towards order and stability. This was reflected in two ways. First, competition was reduced since, by giving priority and protection to established operators, the commissioners made it difficult for newcomers to gain entry into the industry. Secondly, given the tendency to grant route monopolies and the absence of any guidance on pricing policy the commissioners were able to follow a pricing policy based on the principle of cross-subsidisation. This ensured the provision of unremunerative services, one reason why the Thesiger Committee was so happy with the system.[35]

Recently the licensing system has been roundly condemned[36] and certainly on strict economic grounds it is difficult to uphold. By restricting entry into the industry and thereby protecting the established operators it stifled competition and innovation in the industry and hence was not in the best interests of the public. Secondly, cross-subsidisation means that prices charged are not based on costs and this in turn leads to a misallocation of resources since the output produced does not adequately reflect the true state of demand. Moreover, from the industry's point of view it entails the retention of many uneconomic routes. However, though on economic grounds a strong case can be made for the removal of the licensing system it is doubtful whether this would be, as Hibbs might have us believe, in the best interests of public welfare. In the absence of external subsidies for uneconomic routes greater competition and a shift towards a cost-based pricing policy would almost certainly have led to the abandonment of many unremunerative routes and services. And in conditions of falling demand it seems unlikely that this loss would have been counterbalanced by new developments or services of any significance. The only reservation here might be in the case of rural areas where the rigidity of the licensing system tended to inhibit the introduction of services specially adapted to meet requirements. Under a competitive system only that part of consumer demand prepared to pay the price and accept the quality offered would be satisfied.

On social grounds therefore, a case can be made for the retention of the licensing system. Recent developments however would seem to indicate otherwise. The 1968 Transport Act removed the Passenger Transport Authorities from the control of the Traffic Commissioners. Various forms of grants and subsidies for bus operators were announced between 1968 and 1971, while the National Bus Company made known that it could no longer continue to cross-subsidise many of its more unremunerative services. These changes have done much to undermine the licensing system and it is significant that the Minister of Transport Industries announced in July 1971 that substantial modifications would be made. This would be consistent given the move away from cross-subsidisation and the recognition that specific services of a social nature should be subsidised.

ROAD HAULAGE

Road haulage differs in several respects from the passenger transport side. For one thing growth has been rapid since the war both in the public and private sectors with the public sector gaining ground,[37] and the industry's productivity record has been good. Secondly, the structure of the industry is somewhat different, being composed of many small units, while the industry has been subject to greater political controversy than public passenger transport. Thirdly, despite the licensing system there has been considerably more competition in the industry than in the case of passenger transport, a feature which is reflected in the pricing system and the relative absence of cross-subsidisation.

CHANGES IN OWNERSHIP AND STRUCTURE

Before the war road haulage was dominated by the small operator, though a number of large firms did exist and it was these through which the railways gained their entry into the industry. Control of road haulage during the war involved the Ministry of War Transport in creating a more organised structure. In 1943 the Road Haulage Organisation was set up which gained control over many of the large units engaged in long distance haulage. Altogether about 34,000 vehicles came under its supervision but they were handed back soon after the war. It was this sector however which was soon to be nationalised by the Transport Act of 1947, in an attempt to secure the integration of public transport. All long distance road haulage, defined as traffic carried more than 40 miles in one or more vehicles, one or more of the vehicles being at some time more than 25 miles away from their operating centres, were to be taken over by the British Transport Commission. All own account or C licence vehicles were exempt as were all vehicles operating within 25 miles of their base. These latter vehicles continued to come under the control of the licensing authorities but not those of the BTC.

Integration of freight transport soon fell by the wayside. No real guidance was given to the commission in this respect and in any case there were too many obstacles which lay in the path of achieving it. Traders were free to choose the type of transport which best suited their needs—there were no restrictions on C licence vehicles so that many traders acquired their own fleets— while the limit of 25 miles on public hauliers was not imposed until 1950. But apart from these factors the BTC and its relevant executive (the Road Transport Executive being split into two in 1949) were too busy building up the road haulage organisation to bother about the question of integration. This was a more difficult task than at first imagined since there were so many small units to contend with. A few years elapsed before all the long distance firms were acquired but by 1951–2 about 3800 concerns with 42,000 vehicles had been taken over and organised into an integrated unit, British Road Services.[38] A network of long distance services organised under one management would seem to have obvious advantages, and on the whole BRS performed its functions reasonably efficiently. However, judging by the rapid growth of own account vehicles in this period traders were not over-anxious to utilise the services of a nationalised concern.

No sooner had the organisation been completed than a change of government in 1951 reversed the policy. The Conservative Government was committed to returning road haulage to private enterprise and injecting a greater degree of competition into transport as a whole. Hence the Transport Act (1953) made provision for the disposal of most of BRS's vehicles, the 25 mile limit on other hauliers was lifted, and certain relaxations were made in the licensing system to make entry into the industry easier. Sale of the vehicles proved more difficult than expected, many of them had to be sold in very small lots, and eventually BRS was left with 16,000 vehicles when denationalisation was finally abandoned in 1956.[39] When the BTC was broken up in 1962 the state's road haulage commitments were handed over to the Transport Holding Company. The latter was given much greater commercial freedom than any other nationalised undertaking and it considerably improved the rate of return on the road haulage assets.[40]

Further significant organisational changes were made as a result of the Labour Government's Transport Act of 1968. With the abolition of the Transport Holding Company the State's road haulage activities were transferred to the new National Freight Corporation which also became responsible for most other nationalised freight traffic, including the railways' sundries division and the freightliner service.[41] In effect the NFC was given charge of all nationalised traffics which started or finished by road, irrespective of whether or not the main part of the journey was by rail. The main idea behind this move was to achieve a better integration of road and rail traffic, though wherever economically possible the new body was expected to ensure that goods were sent by rail. The Act also introduced a radical overhaul of the licensing system, following its condemnation by the Geddes Committee in 1965, but discussion of this aspect is deferred to a later section.

Throughout the period the nationalised sector remained by far the largest unit in the industry. Nevertheless, the state sector has never had anything approaching a monopoly of road haulage. Even at its peak (1951–52) British Road Services owned less than 12 per cent of all road haulage capacity, while in 1970 the NFC owned only about 42,000 powered vehicles out of a total of 1·6 million, and, inclusive of the rail element, accounted for a mere 12 per cent of estimated expenditure on freight transport.[42] It is true that the NFC's fleet is around six times larger than that of any other company but this comparison is somewhat misleading since many of its haulage activities are run by semi-autonomous subsidiary companies the fleets of which are obviously much smaller than the whole. Nevertheless, each subsidiary is larger than most independent road haulage firms, the main exception being the Transport Development Group, one of the few publicly quoted companies, whose fleet has grown from 400 vehicles in 1957 to 4663 in 1970. The state sector apart, the industry is dominated by the small unit. As table 16 below shows, about 84 per cent of all operators in the public sector had five or fewer vehicles apiece (and 50 per cent had only one vehicle!), while a further 15 per cent had 50 or fewer. These two groups owned 78 per cent of all vehicles plying for hire or reward. Only 50 concerns could be classed as large (100 vehicles or more) and most of the vehicles in this group belonged to the nationalised sector. In numerical terms own account or C licence vehicles were by far the largest, accounting for 80 per cent of all road vehicles, though their importance in terms of output was far less.[43] The size of fleet varied considerably from those engaged in local delivery work to the large fleets owned by major companies.

The existence of many very small units is not altogether surprising, but the virtual absence of very large firms (here we exclude the state sector where economies have not determined size) makes one suspect that scale economies are not a feature of the industry. The survival of small units has been facilitated by the licensing system which made entry more difficult,[44] and this has also restricted expansion of existing units though there has been little attempt to expand by take-over. The nature of the market served also favours the small man. Most hauls are short (under 25 miles) and services requiring specialised local knowledge and personal contact are common. Moreover, small operators can escape some of the overhead costs of large firms, though this point applies equally well to other industries.

Table 16 Estimated number of public haulage operators in Britain by size of fleet at 31 December 1963

Size of fleet	No of operators	% of operators	No of vehicles	% of all vehicles
1– 5 vehicles	39,130(1)	84·5	69,100	34
6– 50 vehicles	6,940	15·0	90,900	44
51–100 vehicles	160	0·4	10,100	5
101–200 vehicles	33	} 0·1	6,600	3
over 200 vehicles	17		28,900(2)	14
Total	46,280	100·0	205,600	100·0

(1) of which 23,130 had one vehicle only
(2) Inclusive of 24,000 vehicles owned by the railways and British Road Services.
Source: Ministry of Transport, *Public Haulage Operators: Analysis by Size of Fleet, 1963* (1964, Statistics Division of Ministry of Transport, 1964), Table 2.

The question of economies of scale in road haulage has frequently been debated but the evidence is not particularly conclusive. At first glance it might seem that the scope for scale economies is very limited given the indivisible nature of the unit of production, that is one truck plus a driver. On the other hand, the larger firm should be in a position to derive managerial and organisational economies, as well as lower costs from employing larger vehicles, though these may be affected by the difficulties of planning the utilisation of capacity fully in a market which is so heterogeneous and therefore does not lend itself easily to centralised control. It is significant that the nationalised sector of road haulage has always operated on the basis of autonomous decentralised units. But the balance of advantage one way or another has not been proved conclusively. 'The industry is too heterogeneous, with too many different sub-markets and too many variations from any theoretical average, to permit any clear advantage one way or another.'[45] Expert opinion appears to favour constant returns to scale which leaves the small haulier at no disadvantage *vis à vis* his larger counterpart.[46] Whether the recent trend towards larger units has any significance in this respect remains to be seen.

DEMAND FOR ROAD HAULAGE

As we noted in an earlier chapter the aggregate demand for freight transport has grown at a rate very similar to that of total domestic output in the post-war period. But the output of the road haulage industry has expanded very much more rapidly than the average. Between 1952 and 1970 ton-miles hauled by road rose by about 5·8 per cent per annum, that is twice the rate of growth recorded for all freight movement in Great Britain. The success of road haulage can be attributed to two things: first a diversion of traffic from the railways, and secondly, and by far the most important, the industries most suited to road haulage have grown faster than the average. As a consequence road haulage became the dominant supplier of freight transport. In 1952 it had a smaller share of the market than the railways, but by 1970 it accounted for 61 per cent of all ton-miles performed and over 80 per cent of all tonnage carried. Transport costs as a proportion of the total costs in industrial production amount to about 9 per cent, and road transport absorbs between 80 to 90 per cent of this expenditure.[47]

The trend in the distribution of road freight traffic as between professional hauliers and own account operations offers something of a contrast to that experienced on the passenger side. Apart from the early post-war years, when C licence vehicles probably improved their share of the market, own account operations have steadily diminished in importance. Traffic carried by public hauliers nearly quadrupled between 1952 and 1970 (as against a doubling of own account operations) and their share of the total road freight market rose from 46 to 61·4 per cent. However, this shift towards the public section was not reflected in the relative growth rates of vehicle numbers engaged in the two classes of work. The figures in table 17 demonstrate that the total of C licence vehicles has grown faster since the war than those in categories mainly licensed for hire or reward. (The B licence covers both categories but most of the work done by these vehicles is professional.) One reason for the slower growth in the fleets of professional hauliers was the movement towards the use of larger vehicles, but vehicle utilisation has also increased much more rapidly than in the private sector,[48] a factor which may account in part for the shift away from own account operations.

Table 17   Goods Vehicles by Licence Category, 1938–1968

	A licence	Contract A licence	B licence	C licence	Total
1938	83,700	9,500	54,900	365,000	513,100
1946	80,900	9,200	57,800	383,700	531,600
1952	93,000(1)	9,700	58,700	761,300	922,700
1958	88,500	20,400	64,700	1,049,100	1,222,700
1968	104,000	38,000	96,000	1,263,000	1,474,000

(1) Includes BTC vehicles not subject to carriers' licences.
Source: British Road Federation, Basic Road Statistics, 1971, 15.

Though own account operations account for the majority of the vehicles in the road haulage industry most of them are very small (less than three tons unladen weight). A large proportion are employed on local or regional delivery work of a kind which is hardly suited to contracting out to professional hauliers. The work-load performance is often very low; in 1962 C licensed vehicles of under one ton unladen weight performed on average, 1500 ton-miles per year, and were driven 140 miles per week; at the other extreme A licensed vehicles of over 5 tons did 293,000 ton-miles per year and were driven 700 miles a week.[49] Nevertheless, own account operators possess almost as many vehicles of over 3 tons as the total fleet of professional operators and much of the traffic they carry is competitive with the latter. There are various reasons why traders carry their own goods but relative cost is not generally one of them since many firms have only a vague idea of the cost of operating their own fleets. A survey of firms in Birmingham and the Black Country by Sharp found that about one half of all C licences operators had only a general idea of the costs involved.[50] This is perhaps not surprising since it is logical (though hardly rational) to expect firms to pay less attention to costs in circumstances where service and convenience factors tend to count more heavily. Reliability, availability, speed of transit and the nature of the traffic, among other things, may rank as more important than cost,[51] though it would be interesting to know whether firms would be ready to consider a switch to professional haulage if they were made aware of substantial cost differences. Own account operations may also have been favoured by the ease with which licences could be obtained.

COMPETITIVENESS OF PUBLIC ROAD HAULAGE

As far as professional haulage contractors are concerned their competitive power was certainly enhanced in the decade or so after the war by favourable trends in costs and productivity. Until the early 1960s haulage costs remained fairly stable and in real terms the price of road transport probably fell. Since then costs have escalated quite sharply due to large wage increases, increasing traffic congestion and various government enactments, including higher fuel and licence duties, selective employment tax and other measures, so that charges have risen quite rapidly in recent years. However, road haulage has been favoured by a high rate of productivity growth which enabled some of the increased costs to be absorbed. According to Deakin and Seward output per unit of input rose by 4·46 per cent per annum in the period 1952–1962, though the rate of progress slackened off in the 1960s.[52] Much of the improvement can be attributed to the use of larger and better designed vehicles, which are much more economical to run, and higher capacity utilisation. In the latter respect the professional haulier has outperformed his competitors, private haulage and the railways. The ton mileage performed per capacity ton mile available for service in road haulage contracting rose from 9988 in 1952 to 14,417 in 1962 whereas on the railways and in the non-contractual side of road haulage the improvement was only marginal (1523 to 1169 and 6961 to 7219 ton miles per capacity ton respectively). In effect the utilisation of road haulage carrying capacity was over 12 times greater than in rail freight transport in 1962 and the disparity is even more marked if gross output per capacity ton in service is used as a measure of assessment.[53]

The scope for further improvements in efficiency may however be limited unless capacity utilisation of road vehicles can be increased further, since technical changes in road haulage are somewhat limited. The most obvious possibility in the foreseeable future is the shift to larger lorries but this has raised severe environmental issues recently in this country. At present U.K. regulations limit the gross weight of vehicles to 32 tons with axle weights of 10 tons, which is very much lower than those currently in force within the EEC. Recently Dr Sharp in *Living with the Lorry* (1973) has argued the case for lifting the restrictions on lorry sizes on both economic and environmental grounds. By adopting the EEC 40 tonne (39·36 tons) lorry (which is likely to be raised in the near future), 100 lorries would be able to perform the same amount of work as 123, 32 ton vehicles, and this would generate cost savings in freight transport of £10 million a year. Secondly, since the number of lorries required in the future on the basis of projected growth rates is considerable, the shift to larger vehicles would contain the rise in numbers below that necessary if the 32 ton standard continued to be operative. It would seem preferable from an environmental point of view to have fewer but larger vehicles, though whether this will convince the environmental lobby, which is now quite strong, is to be doubted. In any case the actual savings derived from the shift are not particularly large in relation to the total expenditure on road haulage transport and it is therefore questionable whether the change-over is that worthwhile. Probably the chief gainers would be the road hauliers themselves who would internalise most of the benefits. However, the study does do much to dispel the often mistaken assumption that there are a set of 'environmental' costs falling on the community which vary inversely with another set of 'economic' costs which are borne by the road haulage operator. Furthermore, the oft-quoted solution to the problem, namely a transfer of freight from road to rail, is for the most part not feasible since either the costs of rail transport are too high or the rail facilities are either inadequate or nonexistent.

Translating past changes into price terms it would seem that road haulage rates remained comparatively stable through the 1950s and early 1960s whereas rail freight charges rose sharply. After this date the reverse was true: rail charges were reduced steadily from 1963 onwards, whereas pressure on costs and lower productivity gains forced road haulage charges upwards. It is difficult to make general comparisons between the absolute level of charges between road and rail partly because aggregate figures are not very meaningful given the wide variety of commodities transported, but also because the information on road haulage rates is very limited. However, studies which have been made on comparative charges would seem to indicate that road haulage rates are often higher than those of rail. A survey carried out by Deakin and Seward for 29 commodity groups in 1966 found that in only 5 groups was the rate per ton mile by road lower than the rail charge. In some cases the difference in favour of rail was very large and on average the cost to the customer of using the public haulier rather than the railways was substantial.[54] Such comparisons are subject to a number of reservations. The rail charges do not include the costs of collection and delivery services, while rail rates were obviously too low given the large losses being made on freight traffic, though this latter factor does not of course alter the competitive effect given that charges are established at a level below costs. Furthermore, road hauliers were able to discriminate more easily in pricing and thereby capture the most lucrative traffic.

Nevertheless, these findings seem to confirm the point made earlier that cost is not the only factor which is relevant to determine whether traffic goes by road or rail. Several studies have noted that many consignments go by road even though the cost by rail is cheaper. Walters, for example, found that about one third of the consignments by British Road Services' general haulage could have been transported more cheaply by rail.[55] The explanation for this would seem to be twofold: first, many traders are not sufficiently aware of the relative costs of consigning by road or rail; and secondly, non-cost factors such as speed, convenience and reliability worked in favour of road haulage. Of course, in the final analysis the transport decision is a complex matter and such generalisations as we have made tend to mask the many considerations which are taken into account when choosing between one mode and another. Even so, the fact that much of the survey work in this field points to a marked absence of knowledge about relative transport costs on the part of traders (often with the result that they consigned goods by a more costly mode) would seem to indicate some misallocation of resources. But until we have an adequate idea of the value traders place on service, speed, availability and other non-cost factors it is difficult to determine the extent of this misallocation, if any.

In theory one obvious area in which road hauliers score over the railways is on pricing. Though adequate information on this subject is lacking, the traditional notion, derived from Walker's pioneering study of experience before the war,[56] was that road hauliers were in a much better position to relate the price of a service to its cost and to discriminate between customers. There are various reasons why this should be so. There was no control over road haulage charges nationally and the industry had no common carrier or social service obligations which involved cross-subsidisation and hence average charging as in the case of the railways. Partly because of the small scale nature of operations costs are fairly easy to allocate between services and vehicles, there is no problem of track costs and the allocation of joint and overhead costs is a much less difficult problem than with the railways. Finally, the industry is a competitive one and legal restrictions against discriminatory pricing policies are non-existent. What this meant in practice was that road hauliers were able to base their prices on costs and discriminate among their customers in such a way as to capture the most profitable traffic and leave the railways with the traffic which was least attractive. Indeed, in the competitive climate of the prewar period many hauliers charged down to their short-run marginal costs, especially on back haul loads, in an effort to attract traffic.

The position since the war is more difficult to ascertain. Certainly most of the factors mentioned above are still relevant in

the context of pricing, but there is some doubt as to how far the
practice of pricing conformed to the pattern described in the last
paragraph, or even if it ever did. The more blatant forms of price
discrimination have disappeared largely because the Road Haulage
Association frowns on such practices. Moreover, up to 1965 the
latter body recommended changes in rates to its members, though
this was discontinued after the Prices and Incomes Board recommended its abolition on the grounds that since costs vary so
greatly throughout the industry, and in any case depended so
much on a wide variety of circumstances, a process by which
uniform rate increases were imposed would lead to a divergence
of prices from costs in many instances. One further important
piece of information also came to light: the board was informed by
the RHA that many small hauliers had 'neither the time nor the
wherewithal for detailed cost analysis',[57] which would lead one to
suspect that pricing on the basis of the cost of service was not
likely to be easily attained in practice. The only other concrete
information on this matter relates to the pricing procedures of
British Road Services. After a detailed study of rate structure of
the BRS Midlands Division in November 1953 Walters came to
the conclusion that relative rates had already begun to diverge
significantly from costs. 'The trend, even at this stage, is towards a
"railroadisation" of rates and charges, that excess of averaging the
good with the bad that has caused such inefficiency in the economics of railways.'[58] Some years later the Prices and Incomes
Board examined the question and found that the methods used for
measuring costs were inadequate. Special reference was made to the
BRS Parcels division where the board found great difficulty in
determining the criteria for pricing. It was clear however that
costs were not one of them: 'it is not known how far the tariff
structure reflects the cost structure since the company has not
hitherto considered it worth while to undertake the complex
studies necessary to determine the structure of costs in relation
to the volume, weight and distance of parcels. While we recognise
that in the short run costs are not the sole determinant of charges,
in the long run there should in our view be a definite relationship
between them. In any event it would seem desirable for the com-

pany to know with some precision the relative profitability of its different types of business'.[59]

How far the industry as a whole has diverged from a cost-based price structure is difficult to say. BRS is not exactly typical and there is always the danger with a larger organisation that some kind of averaging procedure will imperceptibly take over in time. However, BRS has also tended to act as price leader and given the limited knowledge about costs among small hauliers one suspects that pricing policy in the industry at large does not conform to the ideal. And if this suspicion is correct one might also hazard a guess that but for the marked quality and service premium which road haulage enjoys over rail transport the industry might find it much harder to compete in price terms with rail than formerly.

THE LICENSING SYSTEM

As in the case of road passenger transport, road haulage activities have been controlled by a licensing system since the early 1930s, though the extent of the control has been somewhat less than in the former case. Carrier licensing was based on the principle that a trader could carry his own goods without restriction, but public hauliers operating for hire or reward were controlled by the Traffic Commissioners, acting as licensing authorities, who were responsible for the issue of licences. All vehicle owners were required to hold a carrier's licence of which there were three main types. An A licence entitled the holder to carry for hire or reward,[60] while C licences were issued to traders solely for the carriage of their own goods. Once granted few restrictions could be placed on holders of these licences, but the B licence (for both own account operations and hire and reward) was subject to special conditions regarding the type of traffic carried and the area of operation. All applicants had to fulfil conditions relating to safety, wages, working conditions etc. Apart from the restrictions placed on public hauliers after nationalisation which were lifted in 1953, the system as devised in the 1930s remained in existence until the revisions under the Transport Act of 1968.

In practice what this meant was that C licences were granted automatically (that is as long as applicants could meet the provisions relating to safety etc), but that public hauliers could operate only if a need for their service could be proved, which existing operators and the railways could challenge on the grounds that sufficient capacity already existed. As in the case of passenger transport, the main effect was to freeze the status quo. The system favoured existing operators and made entry into the industry more difficult with the result that much of the growth in the industry occurred in own account vehicles.

The system has frequently come under fire on the grounds that it stifled change and enterprise in the industry, and the justification for its introduction has also been challenged.[61] Certainly it did little to protect the railways nor did it promote greater co-ordination between road and rail transport as had been originally hoped. Nevertheless, it did bring a greater degree of stability to the industry and made for considerable improvements in the standards of operation of most hauliers. Moreover, there is no evidence that it severely restricted the growth of capacity or created exclusive monopolies of certain routes or areas as in the case of passenger transport regulation. It is true that the number of A licences grew rather slowly after the war (see Table 17) but this provides only a limited guide to capacity because of the shift to larger vehicles and improved capacity utilisation. Certainly there is no firm indication that the implementation of licensing caused a real shortage of haulage capacity in the public sector, and the fact that professional hauliers increased their share of the market after the early 1950s would seem to confirm this point.[62]

Whatever the merits or otherwise of licensing the committee set up to review the system in 1963 was clearly not impressed with it. Indeed the committee could find little to commend it. Towards the possible objectives of policy it was designed to achieve, such as the promotion of safety, reduction of congestion, greater use of rail transport and improved efficiency, the committee considered it had made a negligible contribution, while in some respects the effects had been detrimental. 'Neither the present system of licensing nor any variant of it based on control of the number of lorries and restriction of what lorries may carry offers a useful way to achieve what we think might be the main aims of government policy in regulating carriage of goods by road. In three respects such licensing acts adversely. It reduces efficiency. It tends to confer positions of privilege. And it tends to add to congestion on the roads.'[63] Not surprisingly therefore, the committee recommended the abolition of all restrictions on road haulage except for the issue of entry permits which would be freely available subject to good behaviour as regards all aspects of safety.

The Labour Government supported the committee's condemnation of the existing framework of control but did not feel that it should be scrapped. Instead they proposed to revise the system in such a way as to make it an instrument of national freight policy, which would achieve their ideal of a co-ordinated and integrated pattern of freight movement.[64] The Transport Act of 1968 embodied these ideas by introducing quality and quantity licensing. In part the Geddes Committee's recommendations were implemented. All vehicles of $3\frac{1}{2}$ tons plated weight or less (about 900,000) were completely freed from any form of licensing, except for those imposed on private cars, and could henceforth carry any kind of traffic. For vehicles above this weight the carrier had to obtain a quality licence which would only be issued as long as the licensing authority was satisfied of professional competence and that adequate provision was made with regard to safety, maintenance, working conditions and financial resources. Quality licences could not be refused on the grounds that adequate services already existed, as was the case previously, while the former distinction between professional and own account vehicles was removed which meant that all licensed vehicles could carry any type of traffic.

The most controversial aspect of the new system was the proposed quantity licensing since it appeared to be designed to favour the railways, though the main objective behind it was to secure a greater degree of integration in freight transport. Vehicles of over 16 tons plated weight required a special authorisation for the carriage of any freight over a distance of 100 miles, and for certain types of bulk products, such as coal, iron ore and steel products for any distance. This form of licensing applied to all traffic including that carried for own account purposes. Applications for quantity licenses were to be made to the licensing authorities and only the National Freight Corporation and the British Railways Board had right of objection. For the latter to succeed the NFC or BRB had to show that the railways could offer the consignor a better deal in terms of speed, reliability, cost or in some other way, than road transport.

The relaxation of the licensing system will no doubt increase competition in the industry. This is not simply because entry into the industry has been eased; it also follows from the fact that own account operators now have freedom to carry for hire or reward. Public hauliers, and especially BRS, could face severe competition from firms using regular routes wishing to fill their lorries on the return haul. However, the infusion of greater competition into the industry is probably to be welcomed despite road hauliers' initial dismay at the prospect. With quantity licensing there is room for debate, though discussion at this stage is somewhat academic since it appears that plans to introduce it have been shelved for the time being. This is perhaps not surprising in view of the critical reception these proposals received, particularly from long distance hauliers who feared a loss of traffic to the railways. However, the provisions for quantity licensing have perhaps been criticised unduly. Certainly the administration of the new system would present great problems particularly over the interpretation of the criteria relating to costs and intangible factors of service etc. Moreover, it was not made clear what would happen in cases where there was no balance of advantage either way. On the other hand, it could conceivably have been an instrument to secure a more rational allocation of traffic between road and rail. A system which forced traders to consider more carefully the costs of carrying traffic, particularly own account operators who have rather vague notions in this matter, would be all to the good, especially if it involved the translation of various intangible factors into calculations of benefits and costs. If traders were forced to compare relative costs this would ensure that non-rational elements, including inertia and habit, and ignorance of the true costs would not predominate in the selection of transport modes. This could result in a shift to rail transport on economic grounds, but it could work in reverse since the provisions offered no special protection to the railways. Thus in effect quantity licensing could be the means to secure the benefits of competition and hence produce a more efficient allocation of freight traffic. There may in any case be grounds for shifting more freight onto the railways since, as Webb points out, all the evidence suggests that both the capital and operating costs of rail transport may be considerably lower than those of road providing that rail capacity utilisation is adequate.[65]

CHAPTER SEVEN

Civil Aviation

THE GROWTH OF TRAFFIC

AVIATION HAS BEEN undoubtedly the fastest growing sector of transport since the war both in this country and abroad. World air traffic on scheduled services (in terms of numbers of passengers carried) has increased on average by around 12–14 per cent per annum while air freight has expanded slightly more rapidly. An idea of the magnitudes involved can be derived from table 18 which gives data on the volume of passenger traffic; it does not include non-scheduled operations (charter work etc), a sector that has grown very rapidly in recent years. Despite the rapid growth of air freight, passenger traffic still accounts for the bulk of the airlines' revenue and it is in the field of passenger movement that aviation has had its most dramatic impact.[1] On long distance international and domestic routes air transport's penetration of the market has been very rapid indeed. For example, as early as 1957 as many passengers flew the North Atlantic as went by sea, while by the end of the decade US domestic airlines carried almost as many inter-city passengers as the railways and buses together.[2] By the early 1960s air travel dominated many long distance routes; in 1962, 75 per cent of all passengers on the North Atlantic went by air, 90 per cent on the Pacific, 70 per cent on the South Pacific, 70 per cent on the route from central America to Europe and 94 per cent on that from South America to the United States.[3] As far as outward passenger movement from the UK is concerned almost an equal number of passengers went by sea as by air in 1961. A decade later total air traffic was twice that by sea and on virtually all routes except that to the Irish Republic air transport predominated by a large margin. In fact, on most long distance routes (that is excluding the European Continent and Mediterranean Sea Area) sea travel is now virtually a thing of the past.[4] Thus within the matter of a couple of decades the mode of international passenger travel has undergone a complete revolution.

Table 18   The Growth of air traffic on scheduled services, 1946–1969

| | Passengers carried (millions) | | Freight carried (short tons) |
	World total	UK airlines	UK airlines
1946	18	0·4	6,773
1949	27	0·9	19,461
1959	99	4·7	206,424
1969	289	13·2	338,968

Note: UK airlines include the Airways Corporations and private companies but not the Corporations' associates and subsidiaries overseas.

Sources: International Civil Aviation Organisation, *The Development of Civil Air Transport: Traffic Statistics, 1945–1969* (1970, no 142); *Annual Abstract of Statistics* (HMSO); Ministry of Civil Aviation, *Report of the Ministry of Civil Aviation for 1948 and 1949* (1950)

Several factors can be put forward to explain this rapid change in the mode of travel: these include rising real incomes, reductions in air fares, a decrease in travel time, increasing comfort and convenience and a greater preference for air travel as a result of improved safety. All these forces operated more or less simultaneously during the 1950s and 1960s which makes any assessment of the impact of any particular one somewhat difficult. Moreover, the market is far from homogeneous so that the influence of any one factor will vary according to the type of traffic. Tourist or pleasure travel for example is generally more price elastic than business traffic where time savings count for more. Calculations made by Straszheim suggest that over half the growth in air travel can be explained in terms of price and income leaving an annual growth of 5·6 per cent to be accounted for independenly of these variables.[5]

Two very important determinants of air traffic growth have been price and travel time. This would seem to be a logical assumption for two reasons: first, because favourable changes in these variables would appeal to both the main types of air traffic (that is business and pleasure travel) and secondly, the post-war period has seen quite dramatic changes in the price and speed of air travel. Rapid progress in aircraft technology has produced larger, faster and more economical machines. The big break-through in this period came in the late 1950s and 1960s with the introduction of jet aircraft and subsequently very large jets (jumbos). By 1964 72 per cent of the capacity offered by world scheduled airlines was on jets. The impact in terms of size and speed can be seen from the details of typical aircraft given in table 19. Jets also brought a significant reduction in unit operating costs; the DC–8, for example, had a seat-mile cost some 50 per cent less than the DC–3, though the difference here may be somewhat exaggerated on account of the uneconomical nature of the latter aircraft.[6] Technology was not the only factor making for lower operating costs since these fell significantly in the decade 1948–58 when aircraft design remained relatively static. In these years the main gains were derived from improved management techniques (eg in the organisation and handling of traffic) and scale economies in a rapidly expanding market.[7]

Table 19   Technical development of aircraft

	Aircraft type	Maximum number of seats	cruising speed mph
1939	DC–3	28	180
1949	Boeing 377 Stratocruiser	60	300
1959	Boeing 707	144	545
1969	Boeing 747	490	585

Source: K. Hammarskjöld, 'The '70s—Challenging Years for the World Air Transport System', *Institute of Transport Journal*, 33 (1970), 444.

It is difficult to translate these changes into a meaningful cost index since the experience of airlines differs considerable. BOAC, for instance, achieved a reduction of 40 per cent or more in costs per capacity ton-mile[8] from the late 1940s through to 1970 whereas BEA's record was very much less impressive. On average it would probably be correct to say that the major long distance airlines of the world realised a reduction of around one third or more in their unit costs of operation during this period, much of which was passed on to the consumer. Again it is difficult to give an overall picture since there is no satisfactory index of air fares and even with respect to any one route the position is complicated by the increasing complexity of the price structure over time. But if the North Atlantic route is anywhere near typical then air fares by the early 1970s were up to 50 per cent below what they had been twenty years earlier.[9]

Though it has frequently been argued that price reductions could be even greater if some of the service frills were cut out and the industry was relieved of the IATA's stranglehold on pricing, there is no doubt that in monetary, and even more so in real, terms air travel became very much cheaper in this period. By the end of the 1960s it was generally cheaper to travel by air than by sea on long distance routes, and of course very much quicker. The fall in air fares has meant that air travel is increasingly chosen by people further down the income scale (the most price conscious group) and this has opened up the way for the penetration of the mass market. Moreover, consumers have enjoyed considerable improvements in comfort, speed, safety and in service scheduling. Even more important in the last decade or so has been the rapid development of non-scheduled services which has made available very much cheaper air travel for the lower income groups through charter and inclusive tour operations.

REGULATION OF THE INDUSTRY

Since the war aviation in this country has been dominated by two large public corporations though alongside which a vigorous band of independent operators has struggled gallantly to secure recognition. Throughout the period the industry has been rigidly controlled as regards entry, capacity and tariffs. The provision of new services on both domestic and international routes has been subject to rigorous control by UK licensing authorities and on international routes only one carrier has normally been allowed to operate. For every scheduled service a British operator must secure landing rights in the countries to which he wishes to fly; these international traffic rights are negotiated between governments on a bilateral basis and as a rule only one national flag operator is recognised per route. Domestic fares are fixed by the licensing authorities and since 1945 all international fares have been negotiated on a uniform basis through the periodic conference meetings of the International Air Transport Association. Hence there is virtually no price competition on scheduled services, and competition has been further restricted by pooling arrangements between airlines on specific routes with respect to the capacity each will offer and the division of the combined revenue of each route.

It is within this complex framework of control that British airlines have had to operate since the war. The system has frequently been criticised on the grounds that its excessive rigidity severely restricts the scope for competition and hence leaves the consumer with little choice but to accept a uniform and highly priced product.[10] In particular, the IATA monopoly over pricing has been severely attacked in recent years largely on the grounds of efficiency and consumer choice. 'A price system which depends on the good-will of the high-cost producer and which overlooks the demand characteristics of the market cannot be designated as efficient'.[11] Similarly, it can be argued that strict control over entry into the industry has restricted the growth of independent operators and thereby limited the range of consumer choice. Such criticisms are open to debate, as we shall later see in the case of the independents, but unfortunately limitations of space preclude a full discussion of this controversial issue. For the most part the remainder of this chapter will be devoted to examining the main developments and progress of British civil aviation since the war.

THE FORMATIVE YEARS

In 1946 the Labour Government partly reversed the policy of 1939–40 when it sliced BOAC into three groups each with a clearly defined geographical sphere of operation. BOAC itself was to concentrate on the main-haul routes, including the Commonwealth, the Far East and North Atlantic; British South American Airways Corporation (BSAAC) had the task of developing the South Atlantic market; while internal and European routes were entrusted to the third company, BEA. These three state corporations were given exclusive rights to fly scheduled services and in consequence many of the existing privately owned airlines operating scheduled services were taken over and integrated into the BEA network. These included some of the private airlines which had provided domestic and cross-channel services before the war—Scottish Airways, North Eastern Airways, Allied Airways, Railway Air Services and a host of others.[12] The white paper outlining the plans for civil aviation recognised air transport as a public service and thereby concluded that national ownership and control 'offers the best guarantee to the public of disinterested expansion of the nation's air services with economy and efficiency'.[13] It was also anticipated that for an interim period aviation would need to be subsidised and so provision was made, in the Civil Aviation Act of 1946, for deficiency grants to be paid to the corporations over a limited period.

In fact operations proved to be extremely unprofitable in the early post-war years and subsidy payments had to be made until well into the 1950s. Altogether some £51·5 million was paid to the airlines, and of this amount £35·1 million went to BOAC (including BSAAC which was merged with BOAC in 1949).[14] The main problem was lack of suitable aircraft. Initially the airlines had to make do with a motley collection of very uneconomic aircraft most of which had been converted from military use. In 1947 BOAC was running 175 aircraft of no fewer than 18 different types few of which were really suited to long haul operations. They were expensive to maintain and service partly because of their age and design characteristics, but the main reason why unit operating costs were so high was the very low carrying capacity. Early in 1948 the average seating capacity of BOAC's fleet was only 19; to have broken even in the years up to 1950 the Corporation would have required an average load factor of just over 100 per cent as against the 60 per cent actually achieved.[15] The other two airlines were in a similar position though BEA's problem was not quite so bad since ex-military aircraft could be adapted more readily to short haul operations and by 1948-9 this airline had relatively satisfactory stop-gap aircraft in the Vikings and Dakotas.

The situation was aggravated by the obligation placed on the state airlines to buy British aircraft—a policy harking back to the days of Imperial Airways. During the war the aircraft industry concentrated its efforts on fighter and bomber machines and therefore was not in a position to convert readily to making civil aircraft afterwards. As an interim measure it had been decided that a number of advanced airliners based on combat aircraft should be produced to fill the gap. In practice this meant the development of aircraft types which were out-of-date before they left the drawing board; worse still, they either arrived late, crashed in flight or flew at a loss. BOAC, which suffered most in this respect, had the choice of two evils: either to fly high-cost ex-military converteds or make do with obsolete and inefficient stop-gap types. Eventually the corporation was allowed to buy a limited number of American aircraft to tide it over until satisfactory British machines became available. British South American Airways faced similar problems. Delays occurred in the delivery of its new Tudor planes, based on bomber aircraft, and shortly after they were introduced two disappeared in flight. Whereupon they were withdrawn from service forcing BSAAC to fall back on the obsolete York aircraft. This had a crippling effect on the corporation and ultimately prompted the government to merge its interests with those of BOAC in 1949.[16]

The policy of equipping the airlines with British aircraft was clearly a mistake since it saddled the corporations with inefficient machines at a crucial stage in their career and at a time when their competitors abroad were buying modern American aircraft. In 1947 BSAAC complained bitterly about the policy which preempted the airline's right to buy what it wanted: 'One of the prerequisites of successful airline operation is that the right aircraft shall be available at the right price. Under the present system, the Corporation has no control over price, is in the hands of the Ministry of Supply as to priority of deliveries, and is subject to very considerable influence as to design'.[17] As a consequence it was not until the early 1950s that the airlines had a reasonably modern and efficient fleet of aircraft in service and even then the problems were not over as BOAC discovered to its dismay when the Comet met disaster.

Lack of suitable aircraft was the main reason for the poor performance in the early post-war years but it was not the only one. It took time to build up an efficient organisation and both BEA and BSAAC had to start more or less from scratch. BOAC also faced organisational problems. It had the difficult task of rationalising a structure which had been adapted to wartime conditions. It had a far-flung network of bases and stations, scattered and improvised maintenance sites, a motley collection of aircraft dotted all over the world, an administrative organisation that was badly in need of overhaul, as well as serious deficiencies in its route structure. On top of this the corporation had a programme of services in which commercial considerations were often subordinated to the national interest. Under these conditions it is not surprising that commerical thinking was ruled out of court. Here wartime experience left its mark. One official described the situation as follows: 'for year after year . . . we were simply drawing deficiency payments from the Government. There could be no real accounting. It must be admitted that there was uncontrolled expenditure. We drew spares and fuel from the RAF whenever and wherever they were needed . . . A real effort had to be made to get back to commercial thinking'.[18] It was not until the appointment of Sir Miles Thomas as chairman in 1949 that a thorough overhaul of the organisation was instituted, and this together with the arrival of more up-to-date aircraft marked the turning point in BOAC's fortunes.[19]

PROGRESS OF THE STATE AIRLINES

By the early 1950s both airlines were in much better shape than they had been a few years earlier. Many of the immediate post-war difficulties had been sorted out, the fleets had been modernised (in 1952 BOAC introduced the first jet service) and the administrative and organisational structures of the corporations had been considerably streamlined. Financially too things looked brighter.

BOAC made a profit for the first time in 1951–52 and in the following year was able to dispense with Exchequer subsidies altogether;
by 1954–55 BEA was also in the black and subsidy payments were
discontinued a year later. Traffic was growing rapidly and everything seemed set fair for a period of steady expansion.

Tables 20 and 21 give details of their progress from the early
1950s through to 1970–71. Both passenger and freight traffic grew
rapidly in almost every year though the latter still only accounts
for a small proportion of the total revenue of both airlines. On
average total traffic increased by about 14–15 per cent per annum
and this compares favourably with the average for world airline
activity as a whole.[20] One notable feature, common to both airlines,
has been the tendency, especially from the late 1950s, for capacity
to expand faster than demand with a consequent deterioration in
overall load factors. This is a perennial problem in airline operation
due largely to the difficulty of adjusting capacity to changes in

Table 20   Traffic and operating statistics: BOAC

Traffic	1952/3	1960/1	1970/1
Capacity ton miles offered (millions)	201·9	577·4	1,974·3
Load ton miles sold (millions)	130·4	321·7	974·8
Overall load factor (%)	62·1	55·7	49·4
Passengers (000s)	282·4	794·5	1,845·5
Passenger miles (millions)	907·6	2,445·5	6,616·6
Passenger load factor (%)	64·4	59·8	53·9
Tons of mail	3,116	5,647	9,630
Mail ton miles (millions)	16·1	30·1	53·6
Tons of freight	6,618	12,998	58,960
Freight ton-miles (millions)	24·3	47·1	258·8
Traffic derivative			
Total cost per CTM (p)	16·86	12·64	9·51
Utilisation of resources			
CTM per aircraft hour	1,447	3,612	9,045
CTM per employee	12,144	33,454	85,006
Number employed at end of year	17,798	20,787	24,128

Source: BOAC, *Annual Report and Accounts*.   Note: Traffic statistics
relate to scheduled operations only.

Table 21   Traffic and operating statistics: BEA

Traffic	1952/3	1960/1	1970/1
Capacity ton miles offered (millions)	69·2	237·4	699·0
Load ton miles sold (millions)	43·5	154·8	378·6
Overall load factor (%)	62·9	65·2	54·2
Passengers (millions)	1·4	4·0	8·7
Passenger miles (millions)	373·0	1,393·4	3,274·5
Passenger load factor (%)	64·5	66·7	60·4
Tons of mail	6,289	8,850	16,700
Mail ton miles (millions)	2·5	4·2	7·1
Tons of freight	14,300	42,000	110,600
Freight ton miles (millions)	5·3	16·6	45·9
Traffic derivatives			
Total cost per CTM (p)	21·1	18·0	20.3
Revenue per LTM (p)	30·2	28·1	35·2
Utilisation of resources			
CTM produced per aircraft	604,100	1,857,100	6,689,300
CTM per employee	8,128	15,750	28,110
Average number of employees	8,518	13,240	24,868

Source: BEA, *Annual Reports and Accounts*. Note: Traffic statistics relate to scheduled operations only.

demand, as in the early 1960s when traffic growth slumped sharply, and to the inherent lumpiness of technological innovation.

The data in the accompanying tables also illustrate clearly some of the contrasting features between the two airlines. BEA, for example, carried four to five times more passengers than BOAC but because of the latter's much longer hauls BOAC flew about twice the number of passenger miles than BEA. BOAC also had a much better record in terms of cost and productivity, partly reflecting the fact that long haul aircraft spend a far greater time in flight service than those of a short haul airline such as BEA. In fact, over the period as a whole BEA's costs per unit of output (capacity ton-miles flown) changed very little despite an initial reduction in the 1950s, whereas BOAC's unit costs declined steadily so that by 1970–71 they were about 40 per cent below the level of the early 1950s. Productivity-wise BOAC also did very much better. Output per employee increased about seven times over the whole period compared with 3½ times for BEA, and the latter's labour force grew very much more rapidly than that of BOAC. Aviation's productivity record as a whole has been very much better than that of any other branch of transport.[21]

A comparison with other international airlines reveals little that is 'fundamentally wrong with the industry' in the opinion of the Edwards Committee.[22] Traffic growth has generally kept pace with world traffic expansion and BOAC consistently maintained second place in the international air market rankings. Unit cost levels of both operators have compared favourably with those of European airlines and though productivity performance has shown up poorly against American companies it has generally been above European standards. Moreover, BEA and BOAC have had very creditable records as innovators. BOAC led the world in jet services when it introduced the Comet in 1952, and despite the subsequent disasters to this aircraft BOAC still managed to introduce the first jet service on the North Atlantic (in 1958). BEA's reputation stems partly from being the first to introduce turbo-prop aircraft, and more recently for the experimental work in automatic landing mechanisms. Indeed, the Edwards Committee drew particular attention to the fact that 'the two Corporations are held in high respect by their fellow operators across the world. They have their critics— but we have not felt that the criticisms pointed to any deep-seated and serious inefficiency. This is not to suggest that they are perfect, (but) . . . we think it is fair to say that both airlines are well established in the top league of international aviation'.[23] However, it is unlikely that such a favourable verdict would have been forthcoming ten years earlier when the efficiency of the corporations, especially of BOAC, gave the Select Committee on Nationalised Industries cause for some concern.[24] It is an indication no doubt of the progress achieved since that date.

Unfortunately this creditable performance was not reflected in the financial outturn of the two airlines. Though they moved into the black in the first half of the 1950s operating profits remained low and the return on capital was far from satisfactory. Moreover, if allowance is made for interest on capital and other deficit items (eg BOAC's overseas subsidiaries) then the rate of return on capital was often negligible. During the late 1950s and early 1960s BOAC had a disastrous episode when very large losses were made which eventually led to a substantial write-off of liabilities. Since then financial performance has been somewhat better. Between 1966–67 and 1970–71 the corporation managed to achieve a yield on net assets of 13·6 per cent, that is slightly above the target of 12½ per cent set by the Treasury in 1966–67. BEA's target rate of return for the five years to 1967–68 was set at 6 per cent and the eventual outturn was very close to this figure. The target rate of return was unduly low however, even allowing for BEA's unprofitable domestic routes, and for the period up to 1971–72 it was raised to 8 per cent.

Taking the period as a whole the financial results cannot be regarded as particularly satisfactory. BEA's performance was the more stable of the two but its rate of return was too low. By contrast, BOAC experienced wide fluctuations in profitability and it is only in the last few years that an acceptable rate of return has been earned. Admittedly the corporations had a better record than the independent operators and their results bear comparison with foreign airlines, but this does not alter the fact that rates of return have been too low on average. Indeed it only serves to open the question as to why airline profitability has been poor. And this can best be answered by examining some of the factors which had a direct bearing on the financial performance of the two corporations.

BEA's DOMESTIC SERVICES

BEA's main problem was, and still is, its grossly uneconomic domestic services. In the ten years to 1965–66 the airline lost no less than £16 million on its domestic routes against a profit of £25 million on its international services. The Highlands and Islands services, which the corporation regarded as something of a social obligation, was only a minor element in the deficit. In 1970–71 the far flung Scottish services entailed an operating loss of £459,000 compared with a £5·7 million deficit for all domestic routes.[25] In fact every domestic route has consistently made a loss since the war; in 1965–66, for example, the London–Manchester service incurred a deficit of £509,000, or more than twice as much as the whole Highlands and Islands network.[26] During the 1960s the

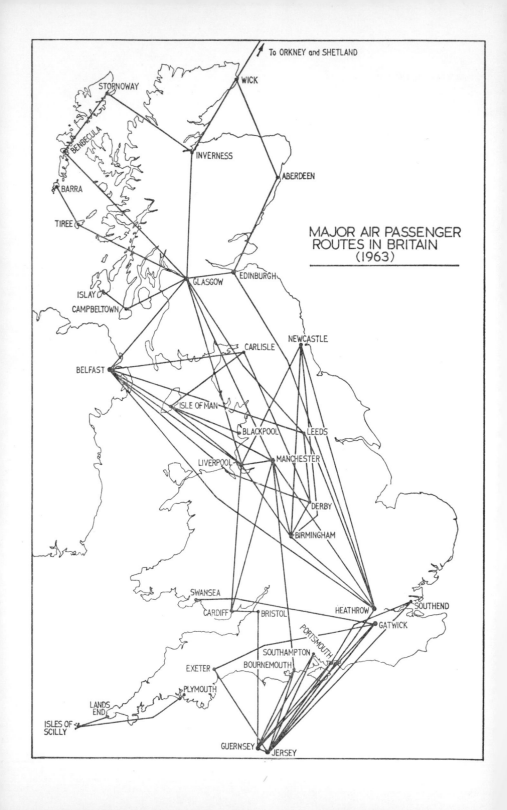

To ORKNEY and SHETLAND

MAJOR AIR PASSENGER
ROUTES IN BRITAIN
(1963)

position was made worse by increased competition from the independents and the railways.

There could be no justification whatsoever for this enormous degree of cross-subsidisation. Apart from the Highlands services, which should have been dealt with as a separate policy issue, most of the losses occurred on business or tourist traffic neither of which had any right to be subsidised. Yet little was done to rectify the matter. BEA frequently argued that the domestic services provided feeder traffic for its international flights but it provided very little proof of this fact, perhaps not surprisingly since it lacked any substance. Alternatively, BEA expressed the hope that they could be made profitable. The select committee of 1967 was informed that it would be possible to get the services to break-even point within two or three years by progressive fare adjustment, but this was obviously wishful thinking. In any case, there was little reason for retaining some services even on 'feeder' grounds. The London–Manchester route is a case in point for with the introduction of electric rail services in the mid 1960s the air route lost any advantage it once had, as shown by the rapid loss of traffic since 1965–6.

The equivocal attitude of the Air Transport Licensing Board, set up in 1960 to license routes and control domestic fares (see below), did not help matters in this respect. In its early reports the board expressed the view that losses on domestic routes should be minimised, that fares should be determined so as to allow operators to earn a reasonable profit, but that cross subsidisation was not a relevant issue with regard to the discharge of its duties. It also implied that competitive route licensing would be undesirable since 'in practice the actual and potential traffic on many domestic routes is so small as to make it difficult, often impossible, for even a single operator to break even'.[27] In fact its judgements turned out to be almost the reverse of these laudable principles. On the routes from London to Glasgow, Edinburgh and Belfast two independent operators, British United Airways and British Eagle (until its demise in November 1968), were granted licences to compete with BEA, and at one point the London–Glasgow route was serviced by three airlines. The upshot of this move was that BEA's traffic on these routes began to tail off, load factors deteriorated and as a result of competition the corporation was forced to introduce jet aircraft with higher operating costs per seat-mile than those of the Vanguard. What the customer may have gained in terms of service he lost elsewhere since fares on these routes were raised more sharply than would otherwise have been the case had BEA retained its monopoly. Even more disastrous was the licensing of a second operator (BUA) on the Channel Islands route since this simply resulted in both companies making heavy losses and eventually BUA was forced to cut back its operations drastically.

The Licensing Board's practice with regard to domestic air fares and the question of cross-subsidisation was a model of inconsistency and economic nonsense. Originally the board stated the case for minimising losses by charging what the traffic would bear. There was a good case for a sharp increase in domestic fares not only because of the heavy losses but also on the grounds that they were out of line with international tariffs despite the fact that domestic routes were more costly to operate. Yet in February 1965 the Board turned down a number of applications for tariff increases because it thought that there was a reasonable prospect of most domestic routes breaking even at existing fares.[28] How it came to this extraordinary conclusion one cannot imagine. The following year the board refused to take a stand against cross-subsidisation. Indeed it told BEA in no uncertain terms that the airline had an obligation to meet its deficits on domestic routes out of the surplus earned on its international activities. The board's judgement strains one's belief in economic rationality and for this reason it is worth quoting in full:[29]

We see no reason why this situation should not continue (on the unjustified grounds that) BEA for a long time enjoyed, among British operators, an almost complete monopoly of scheduled services between this country and Europe, a situation which remains largely undisturbed. We think it reasonable that BEA should set off the advantages they enjoy because of this position against the additional burdens they assume in the development of British air transport, and to make some contribution towards the cost of operating domestic services out of the profits earned on international operations.

The board did not care to speculate what would happen if there were no profits to draw upon in a bad year, nor did it offer any reasoned economic argument for such a pronouncement; it preferred instead to invoke a moral judgement which implied that the airline should not be allowed to make too much profit. At the same time it refused BEA permission to raise fares on the Highlands services for which it suggested a public grant would be appropriate. This was an even more curious decision in a way since if any services deserved a cross-subsidy these were surely the ones to qualify rather than those which catered for business and recreational traffic. Yet less than a year later (1967) the board allowed BEA to raise its Scottish tariffs since it felt that further cross-subsidising could not be justified.[30] But that was as far as the board were prepared to go in this matter since in December 1970 it refused BEA's application for adjustments to domestic tariffs, again on the grounds that they could be subsidised from more remunerative services.[31]

Quite clearly the ATLB followed an inconsistent and illogical policy with regard to domestic air transport and this tended to worsen rather than improve BEA's financial performance in this sector. Given the fact that in recent years about one half of BEA's operating profits on international routes has been absorbed by the losses on internal services the case for drastic action is obvious. Either fares should be raised sharply in the hope that this will secure profitability; failing that then all loss-making routes, apart from the social service ones, should be abandoned. A third alternative would be to hand all the routes over to the independent operators. But whatever course of action is to be adopted there is no justification for subsidising domestic air travellers and if the customers are not prepared to pay the true cost of the services then they must do without them. The recent withdrawal of first class accommodation on domestic flights may be a portent of things to come.

AIRCRAFT PROCUREMENT POLICIES

A major problem which has faced all airline operators is that of tailoring capacity to match demand. Although traffic has never declined in any one year there have been sharp fluctuations in the rate of growth. During the 1960s, for example, BEA's rate of traffic increase ranged from 16 per cent in 1963–64 to only one per cent in 1967–68 (in terms of passenger miles). When traffic expands less than projected forecasts it is difficult in the short run to adjust capacity for obvious reasons. The international pooling arrangements relating to capacity also inhibit quick adjustment since the capacity quotas are negotiated in advance and any one airline reducing its quota would leave that operator in a weakened position at the next round of negotiations. In any case, given the high proportion of fixed costs in airline operation withdrawal of capacity has only a limited effect in terms of cost saving.

The problem has been aggravated by the rapidity of technological change. 'The difficulty has been less the character of the technological changes than the speed with which they have succeeded each other. The pace has been embarrassing, for no sooner has a new aircraft been brought into service than its successor has followed hard behind'.[32] The absence of price competition in international air transport has placed a premium on new technical developments so that the introduction of better and less costly aircraft (that is in terms of unit operating costs) has featured prominently in the competitive strategy of airlines. Moreover, once one airline introduces a new model other airlines follow suit rapidly and this inevitably leads to overcapacity, premature financial write-offs of existing fleets, and financial deterioration in the accounts. This process has occurred frequently since the war but undoubtedly the classic example was the jet revolution.

The stampede into jets was occasioned by the surprise decision of Pan Am in 1955 to order 45 large jets. Very soon the race was on: in blind panic airlines the world over rushed to order the new machines irrespective of cost. 'I think', said the chairman of BEA in 1959, 'that the whole of the airline industry has gone crazy about jets', but added significantly, 'we cannot afford to be out of the race, but I am not sure that we have not all gone into the race

in too big a way too quickly'.[33] The Select Committee on Nationalised Industries of 1959 warned of the financial difficulties which
might ensue from too hasty a switch into jets but the warning went
unheeded.[34] By 1961 over half the international capacity offered
consisted of jet travel and already the world airline industry was
in financial difficulties. The greater speed and capacity of the new
aircraft brought forth an enormous rise in airline capacity in the
early 1960s at the very time when traffic growth was falling sharply.
Inevitably this led to excess capacity, a deterioration in load factors and heavy losses on the retirement of un-amortised propellor
aircraft. The financial consequences were disastrous and there
can be little doubt that these were largely occasioned by the
sudden introduction of jets from 1958 onwards.[35]

In this ordeal BOAC probably suffered more than its competitors
partly because of long-standing difficulties associated with its
aircraft procurement policies. Altogether cumulative losses after
interest on borrowings and taxation amounted to around £80
million between 1958 and 1963, over half of which was accounted
for by the accelerated depreciation of obsolete aircraft. The origin
of the Corporation's difficulties can be traced back to 1954 when the
first Comet was withdrawn from service following its unfortunate
mishaps. This led to a search for substitutes and plans for considerable capacity expansion in order to retrieve the airline's
lost share of the market on the North Atlantic. By 1957–58 this
policy was well under way and in the four years 1957–61 capacity
was increased by no less than 121 per cent against a traffic increase
of 90 per cent. But the worst was yet to come. For the fifth year
(1961–62) BOAC planned to increase its capacity by one third
which coincided with the first real check to world traffic expansion.
In the event BOAC 'were caught at the height of the storm carrying
every stitch of canvas'.[36] The load factor declined by more than
10 points and an operating loss of over £15 million was made in the
two years 1961–63.

However, BOAC's problem was more than one of sheer overcapacity arising from the scramble into jets. In the process of
building up the fleet after the Comet disasters BOAC saddled itself with too many different types of uneconomic aircraft involving

high introductory expenses and subsequently heavy write-off costs through premature obsolescence. The withdrawal of the Comet in 1954 left the airline short of long range aircraft and, while a new version of this aircraft was being developed, the corporation sought a substitute in the Britannia turbo-prop. Unfortunately both the medium and long range versions of this aircraft were late in arriving and technical snags developed when they were eventually introduced. Because of the delay BOAC was forced to purchase 10 DC-7Cs as a stop-gap measure which meant additional expense in flying another aircraft. By the time these aircraft were in service delivery of the new version of the Comet (IV) was being received. Thus by the end of the 1950s BOAC had three main types of aircraft all of which were uneconomic to fly in comparison with the American Boeing jets, a limited order for which had been placed in 1956 to service the North Atlantic route. Once the latter came into service in 1960–61 BOAC was forced to start an early retirement of the Britannias and DC-7Cs and subsequently the Comet IV. During 1961–62 the corporation suffered a large capital loss in providing for the extra depreciation; about £32 million was written off the value of the fleet, including £22·4 million on account of the Britannia, £4·6 million for the DC-7C and £4·7 million for the Comet. Altogether the total group loss for the year amounted to no less than £50 million. The upshot of this financial disaster was an investigation into the corporation's affairs, a shake-up of top management and eventually a financial reconstruction aimed at securing financial viability.[37]

Clearly a large part of the corporation's loss can be attributed to the commitment to buy British aircraft which were uneconomic and subject to delay. On this score the government was partly to blame since it exerted strong pressure on BOAC to buy British. Nor was the Atlantic replacement the end of the matter. A similar problem arose in connection with replacing the Comets and Britannias on the eastern and southern routes. The corporation was given to understand that, having been allowed to purchase 15 Boeings for the North Atlantic, any further orders would have to be placed with British manufacturers. The only suitable British aircraft then available was the VC 10 and in January 1958 a massive order for 35 was placed, about seven years in advance of delivery. Subsequently the order was modified several times, partly as a result of a new super version coming on offer, so that by 1964 it stood at 42 VC 10s (12 standard and 30 supers). By then however it had become obvious that BOAC had committed itself far too early and too heavily to the VC 10 for it turned out to be a very much less efficient aircraft than originally anticipated, with operating costs considerably above those of the Boeing. In 1964 therefore, the corporation proposed that all the super VC 10s should be cancelled and an order placed for a small number of Boeings instead. The government refused to sanction this and forced BOAC to accept 17. To offset the higher cost of these aircraft provision was made in the financial reconstruction carried out by the Air Corporations Act 1966. Accrued liabilities (including accumulated losses arising in the early 1960s) of £110 million were written off, while of the remaining capital liabilities amounting to £66 million, £31 million was treated as loan capital and the rest as exchequer dividend capital. This reconstruction and the subsequent rationalisation of activities brought an end to BOAC's period of financial distress. Henceforth the corporation's financial performance was to be very much better.

Problems associated with aircraft procurement were not of course unique to BOAC. With rapid technological obsolescence every airline has faced the difficulty of getting the right aircraft at the right time, and in the right quantity. BOAC clearly miscalculated in the 1950s and early 1960s with disastrous financial consequences. But the problem was also aggravated by persistent government interference with the airline's ordering policies which inhibited commercial initiative. During the later 1960s BEA, which normally bought British aircraft, was subjected to similar treatment when the government refused it permission to purchase American Boeings. The result was that BEA ended up with inferior aircraft the delivery of which was delayed, and eventually the government was forced to compensate the corporation.[38] Current and future procurement procedures are not likely to be any less problematical either. The introduction of jumbo jets is already giving rise to excess capacity, while the impending arrival of Concorde may pose difficult financial problems for BOAC.

THE ROLE OF THE INDEPENDENTS

Both corporations have faced growing competition throughout their careers. This has come mainly from two sources. On international services rapid expansion of capacity following technical breakthroughs has brought increasing competition from foreign airlines, more particularly on those routes not subject to pooling agreements. The most notable case is that of the North Atlantic route on which many different airlines compete. During the 1960s BOAC's share of this market declined sharply partly as a result of intensified competition especially from American operators, though the decline also reflected a deliberate policy of lower market shares following the shake-up arising out of the difficulties over aircraft procurement Secondly, competition from independent airlines has increased steadily since the early 1950s on both scheduled and non-scheduled services. The contribution of the independents is still fairly small but their growing participation in the air traffic market merits attention.

Under the Civil Aviation Act of 1946 the nationalised corporations were given monopoly rights to operate scheduled services which meant there was little left for private operators except for charter work and other fringe activities. Despite these limited prospects no fewer than 70 small companies were established shortly after the war;[39] many were owned by former wartime pilots and the life of some was extremely brief. They were forced to pick up business where they could and in 1946–7 carried about 119,000 passengers. A break came in 1949 with the Berlin Airlift when 23 independents participated in the operation under the general direction of BEA. This gave them valuable experience and convinced the government of their value as a military transport reserve. Subsequently therefore, air trooping contracts were awarded to the independents and this type of work became their chief activity in the 1950s accounting for two thirds of all passenger miles flown.[40] Later in the decade trooping began to decline in importance but by then the independents were gaining ground elsewhere.

During the late 1940s the independent operators pressed hard to be allowed to run scheduled services on routes not then being operated by the air corporations. This bore fruit in 1949 when a system was devised, without amending the 1946 legislation, by which private companies could legally operate services by becoming associates of the corporations. The minister used the Air Transport Advisory Council to advise him on the services which should be permitted and a number of associate agreements were subsequently concluded. In 1952 these airlines were given greater opportunities and the ATAC became a quasi-licensing authority with revised terms of reference. Henceforward the private airlines could apply for associate agreement rights to operate new routes and new types of services which would not seriously conflict with the established networks of the nationalised corporations. Under these somewhat informal licensing arrangements various new types of services were developed, including vehicle ferries, low fare colonial coach services, inclusive tours to the continent and a few scheduled services on domestic routes.

As a result of this greater freedom the independent airlines expanded rapidly during the 1950s. By 1960, the year in which the licensing arrangements were revised, there were 30 or so approved operators in existence.[41] Traffic growth on scheduled services was considerably more rapid than that of the state airlines and in 1960 the independents accounted for nearly one fifth of all passengers carried though their contribution in terms of passenger-miles

Table 22   Scheduled air traffic of private companies, 1950–1970

	Private companies		All U.K. Airlines	
	Passengers (000s)	Passenger-miles (millions)	Passengers (000s)	Passenger-miles (millions)
1950	73	9·7	1,156	794·0
1955	437	106·4	2,994	1,801·4
1960	1,275	272·3	5,875	3,957·1
1965	2,863	674·6	10,868	7,417·4
1970	3,283	844·2	13,874	10,832·1

Source: *Annual Abstract of Statistics*
Note: Excludes traffic of the Corporation's associates and subsidiaries overseas.

flown was less than 7 per cent (see table 22). However, the independents also carried out much non-scheduled work, including trooping, inclusive tours and charter and contract activities. The distribution of their traffic between different services is shown in table 23 for 1961–62. Though these figures are not complete they do indicate that the independents contribution to air transport was much greater than their scheduled operations would suggest. Moreover, though in terms of the number of passengers carried scheduled services predominated most of this activity consisted of short-haul operations and the bulk of the passenger-miles flown was derived from non-scheduled services. In terms of capacity supplied (that is capacity ton-miles offered) the Edwards Committee estimated that the independents' share of total UK capacity was about 25 per cent in 1961–62.[42] Ten years earlier it had probably been less than 10 per cent.[43]

Table 23   Traffic carried by independent operators by type of service, 1961–62

	Passengers	Passenger-miles (millions)
General scheduled services	1,660,901 (65%)	358·3 (26%)
Inclusive tours	273,210 (11%)	189·4 (13%)
Charter and contract work	301,181 (12%)	295·5 (21%)
Trooping	314,734 (12%)	564·4 (40%)
Total	2,550,026 (100%)	1,407·5 (100%)

Source: BIATA, *Annual Report, 1961–62*
Note: The data exclude traffic of some small companies which were not members of the Association.

However, it was scheduled traffic that really mattered to the independents since it was only on the basis of such operations that a stable and financially viable business could be developed. Most of the companies operated on a shoe-string and the seasonal and erratic nature of much of their business did not provide a very sound basis for stability.[44] Financial difficulties led to the disappearance of many small companies during the course of the 1950s. *The Aeroplane Directory* listed 93 companies in existence in 1949 but only 44 ten years later. In part this reduction was brought about by amalgamation and eventually five major operators emerged, the Airwork Group, Hunting-Clan Air Transport, British Aviation Services, Skyways and Eagle Aviation, all of which were backed or controlled by shipping interests.[45]

The prospects of the independent airlines appeared to brighten considerably in 1960 with the passing of the Civil Aviation (Licensing) Act which introduced fundamental changes in the system of regulation. It set up a formal licensing authority, the Air Transport Licensing Board (ATLB), which replaced the former Advisory Council. The monopoly right of the Air Corporations over scheduled services was abolished which meant that the independents could apply for licences to run scheduled services on their own account. Detailed guidance on the criteria to be used when considering applications was also laid down,[46] though the board was left with considerable discretion to formulate its own policy so long as in the process of so doing it furthered the development of British civil aviation. Finally, the board was empowered to fix domestic air fares.

The independents' expectations regarding the acquisition of scheduled routes as a result of the new policy were to be disappointed. The policy as formulated by the ATLB or through subsequent ministerial directives was such as to limit the number of new applications granted. The board was not prepared to permit any sudden or far-reaching changes in the current pattern of operations, which implied that licences would be granted sparingly to the independents. Even so, it was estimated that the licences granted in the first three years of the board's existence would divert from BEA some 47 per cent of its forecast traffic growth on international routes and 17·5 per cent of that on domestic routes. Secondly, independent airlines were only allowed limited services on those domestic routes operated by BEA. Thirdly, it was made clear by the minister in 1965 that on international routes only one British carrier would be permitted to operate scheduled services, with preference accorded to the nationalised corporations in the first instance. In other words, the independents' hope that they would be allowed to compete on an equal footing with the corporations was shattered and subsequent developments indicate that 'double designation' was only allowed on a small number of routes. Difficulties experienced in securing international traffic rights for a second British carrier were also relevant in this context. But there were sound economic reasons for rejecting applications. The Edwards Committee noted that the density of many European routes scarcely justified a second carrier,[47] while, as we saw earlier, domestic routes were unprofitable even with only one carrier and yet the board allowed some independents to participate. On the other hand, the North Atlantic presented a stronger case but in 1968 the ATLB rejected applications by British Eagle and Caledonian Airways to fly the Atlantic on the grounds that their resources were inadequate to service this route.[48]

The independents' growth of scheduled traffic in the 1960s was thus somewhat slower than in the previous decade though they were able to push up their share of the market slightly. Even so, in 1970 they accounted for less than 8 per cent of total passenger-miles flown on scheduled services, a slightly lower share than in 1965. In fact the main growth area was in non-scheduled traffic, particularly inclusive tour operations and charter activities.[49] Little restriction was placed on this area of activity by the ATLB so that the independents were able to benefit from the growth in demand for cheap travel. The most dramatic expansion was in inclusive tours. In 1960-1 the independents carried 200,000 passengers and performed 136 million passenger miles in this category; by 1967-8 the respective totals had jumped to 2·3 million and 1750 million, and at that date this traffic was twice as large (in terms of passenger-miles) as that carried on scheduled services. Thus though the independents made less headway in the scheduled traffic market than they originally expected the rapid expansion of non-scheduled activity served to raise their share of total UK capacity ton-miles supplied from 25 per cent in 1961-2 to 32 per cent in 1967-8.[50]

The Edwards Committee was happy to record the view that the independent airlines had played an invaluable role as commercial innovators and as a ginger group to spur the corporations. In particular, they expressed satisfaction with the contribution they had made in developing inclusive tour traffic to European holiday resorts. At the same time the committee was clearly concerned about the financial instability of the industry, especially since two companies, British Eagle and Transglobe, had gone into liquidation a few months before the report was completed. On average the private sector was not earning a commercial rate of return; between 1962–7 the average return on net assets of all the privately owned airlines was 5·2 per cent.[51] This average figure, moreover, conceals the fact that some of the independents earned very much less, and during the 1960s many went out of business or lost their separate identity because of financial difficulties. During these years at least 24 companies were actively in business at any one time and about 40 companies can be traced as having been in existence for part or all of the period.[52]

It is difficult not to conclude that far too many companies existed to ensure financial viability. The situation was curiously reminiscent of the 1930s and the Licensing Board, as its counterpart in 1938, must bear much of the responsibility for the outcome. Though the board complained frequently about the unsatisfactory financial position of the independents it appears to have done more to exacerbate the problem than to relieve it. By 1963 it had awarded licenses to 24 private airlines, fewer than half of which owned as many as four aircraft and some were in business with only one. In its third annual report the board reported that 10 had accumulated losses of £752,000 to the end of March 1963 and no fewer than 14 had gone out of business since 1961. Yet the board continued to license new companies which were no more soundly based than those that had folded up.[53] The board's policy earned a stern rebuke from *The Economist*:[54]

How can it believe that a country the size of Britain can provide work for 24 airlines in addition to the corporations, however good their costing? Applicants must prove their financial resources, but the Board in its charity ought to stop them from pouring these down the drain. If there are men anxious to invest in aviation, then introduce them to existing airlines that need an injection of new cash and new routes. The Board now knows small airlines make mistakes; it should not stand by, aimlessly wringing its hands, while a generation of investors repeats them.

But the board was not to be deterred by initial reversals and harsh criticism; throughout the 1960s it attempted to keep afloat a similar number of companies regardless of whether or not they could pay their way. The board hoped that one day they might do so but in some cases this was clearly out of the question given their inadequate resources and unsatisfactory accounting procedures. Moreover, heavy reliance on seasonal traffic and a limited amount of regular scheduled traffic were hardly conducive to sustained profitability. In any case, as already noted, domestic routes were highly unprofitable yet the board granted licenses to many independents to operate internal services which accounted for more than one half their total scheduled traffic. It appears that the licensing authority placed too much emphasis on the obligation to further the development of aviation and too little regard to some of the criteria which would have ensured a more stable and financially viable system. In fact, somewhat late in the day the board did wonder whether 'our absolute duty to further the development of British civil aviation is incompatible with an overriding government policy of ensuring that investments are made where the return to the country is greatest'.[55]

This is only one of many criticisms that can be made about the work of the ATLB. In addition, it failed to issue clear statements of intent and its policy, as in the case of domestic services, was anything but consistent or logical. On the economic side the board cannot be said to have achieved a resounding success partly because of its inadequate facilities. It did little to create viable route structures for private companies which usually ended up with a patchwork of unconnected routes. It failed to investigate properly the resources and financial strength of the airlines and simply proceeded to hand out licenses on a rather arbitrary basis to a multitude of small companies. The latter would argue that the board did not give them enough in the way of regular business, but it would be more correct to say that it gave to too many. The Edwards Committee felt that criticism of the board's work had been overdone but recognised that the licensing procedure contained deficiencies which required correction.[56]

REORGANISATION OF THE AIRLINE STRUCTURE

Increasing dissatisfaction with the licensing procedure was one of the factors which prompted a fairly radical change in civil aviation policy in the early 1970s. In 1969 a white paper, outlining a proposed new structure for the industry, emphasised the weakness of the system: 'The air service licensing system has not worked as well as was hoped when it was set up in 1960. . . . The basic weakness has been a lack of clarity about the objectives of civil aviation policy and a lack of suitable machinery for acting positively in their pursuit'.[57] The document also embodied many of the proposals made by the Edwards Committee which had been set up in 1967 to review the industry. After a long and exhaustive study the committee came to the conclusion that certain institutional and structural changes were required in the interests of long-term development. They proposed that the ATLB's functions be taken over by a new Civil Aviation Authority which would also be responsible for airport planning, air traffic control and the negotiation of international traffic rights. The long debated issue of whether BEA and BOAC should be merged into one concern was settled by a compromise;[58] each corporation should be allowed to retain its separate identity but the capital of both would be owned by a National Air Holdings Board which would act as 'a cementing device for ensuring that common problems and common interests were fully taken into account in the individual airlines and their decisions optimised for the whole group',[59] whatever that might mean. Radical changes were envisaged for the private sector. These included the creation of a second force airline, operating both long and short haul scheduled services, by amalgamating the main private operators, and a consortium of mainly internal feeder services (non-trunk) formed round the nucleus of British Air Services[60] in which the Holdings Board was to have a financial stake. In addition, there would still be room for a number of privately owned inclusive tour and charter operators.

The basic proposals of the committee were accepted in principle by both political parties, though with differences in emphasis, but because of the impending general election action to implement them did not begin until late in 1970. The first stage involved the creation of a second force airline, British Caledonian Airways, a government approved merger of two of the largest private operators, British United Airways and Caledonian Airways. The new company received some lucrative business to start it off by way of a compulsory transfer from the state airlines of routes yielding £6 million of revenue per annum. BEA lost £2 million of business on the London–Paris route as a result of this policy, while BOAC was forced to relinquish its services to West Africa and Tripoli. The corporations complained bitterly about these transfers and demanded financial compensation.[61] But given the decision to create a second force (which can be questioned) they made sense since there was little point in lumbering a new company with a hotchpotch of disconnected and unprofitable services at the start of its career. Whether the basic policy was a wise one remains to be seen.

The Civil Aviation Act of 1971 introduced the second stage of the reorganisation. It established a Civil Aviation Authority and a British Airways Board, much along the lines advocated by the Edwards Committee. The former Authority was to take over the licensing functions of the ATLB and assume responsibility for certain other matters such as air navigation services, safety and registration of aircraft, but it was not to be directly involved in the negotiation of tariffs or air traffic rights. It was also given powers to manage aerodromes and the Board of Trade's Scottish airports were to be transferred to it. As with the ATLB, the authority's main task was to implement policy rather than to initiate it, but in this respect it was allowed considerable discretion subject to any ministerial directive. It was also a more powerful body whose duties were to be carried out in such a way as to ensure that all substantial categories of public demand for air transport were provided with services 'at the lowest charges consistent with a high standard of safety . . . and an economic return to efficient operators'; that at least one major British airline, not controlled by the Airways Board, was given opportunities to provide charter and other services; and to secure the sound development of the industry and encourage its contribution to the balance of payments. These provisions seem to imply that the new authority will become much more concerned with the economics of the industry than

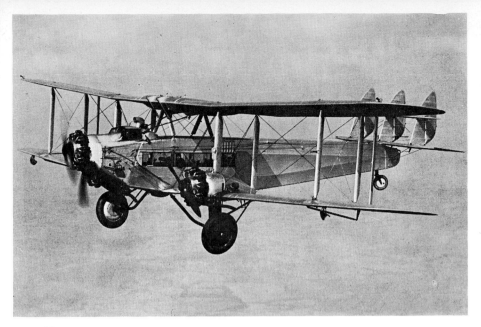

Page 229

Above: Imperial Airways commissioned the DH 66 *Hercules* in 1926 and inaugurated in the following year the first stage of the airline's trunk route between Basra and Cairo via Baghdad with this aircraft. Eventually nine were owned.

Below: Another, though later, aeroplane of Imperial Airways was the Armstrong Whitworth XV, *Atalanta*, here photographed in 1933. At the beginning of that year this particular aircraft flew from Croydon to Cape Town and, soon after, *Atalantas* were commonly employed on the last stage of the Cape Town route.

Page 230

Above: The jet age: a BOAC VC10 in flight. The airline introduced these aircraft in April 1964. The standard VC10 carries up to 151 passengers, though the Super version has accommodation for 174.

Below: The age of the common man and (in real terms) cheaper flight demanded ever bigger aircraft. Boeing's 747 has been the initial 'jumbo jet'. It began operation with Pan American in January 1970 and was quickly ordered by the world's great airlines.

ever the ATLB did, though there is a danger that the airlines may be subjected to investigation and control both by the authority and through departmental channels. Moreover, its relations with the British Airways Board are left somewhat obscure.

The British Airways Board became in effect a holding company since it was to control and direct all the activities of the two state corporations, and it could promote or acquire other airline undertakings as it saw fit. The board however was to be made subject to ministerial directives of a general or specific nature.[62] In other words, the government stopped short of a formal merger in the anticipation that most of the benefits could be obtained from a holding operation. However the logical conclusion was not long in coming. One of the board's first duties was to review the group's activities to see whether they were being carried on in the most efficient manner, and to report thereon to the Secretary of State. The results of this inquiry prompted the government recently to announce the merger of BEA and BOAC with effect from 1973.

This provides a fitting conclusion to our survey of air transport development since, with respect to its structural format, the wheel has turned full circle twice. To all intents and purposes British civil aviation began with one monopoly company, Imperial Airways; in 1935 it was joined by another designated company (British Airways) primarily engaged in short haul operations. The two were merged to form BOAC at the outbreak of war, but then split again in 1946. Since 1949 two state corporations have dominated the air transport market, though with a growing independent sector. The impending merger takes us almost back to square one, though with a slight difference in that there is now a second force operator and a larger independent component.

CHAPTER EIGHT

Shipping

IN TERMS OF SHEER SIZE shipping dwarfs all other forms of freight transport. On the basis of load ton-miles performed British merchant ships carried about 94 per cent of the traffic of all British transport or more than 15 times as much as trains, road haulage vehicles and aircraft added together.[1] Throughout the post-war period shipping has retained its monopoly in the movement of international freight. Of the world's international trade 78 per cent by weight went by sea, and 68 per cent in terms of value; most of the remainder was transported over land since air cargo accounted for less than one per cent in value, and even less in volume, of total international freight traffic.[2] On the passenger side the story was different for air transport rapidly whittled away the monopoly of the liner trade. By the early 1960s air passenger traffic to and from the UK had already overhauled that by sea and in 1970 it was nearly twice as large as the latter. Ocean passenger traffic as a whole continued to expand slowly but all the increase occurred on the short-sea routes. Many of the remaining long distance passenger vessels now concentrate on offering luxurious and expensive accommodation for cruising purposes.

Despite the check to passenger traffic the international maritime industry has been anything but stagnant. In contrast to the inter-war years the volume of international seaborne trade grew rapidly in the post-war period. Between 1950 and 1969 world seaborne trade increased on average by no less than 8·6 per cent per annum, with the fastest rate of expansion taking place in oil products. Moreover, if allowance is made for the increased length of haul of ocean shipments the rate of expansion would be even greater.

However, this secular upward trend masks the sharp fluctuations in the demand for ocean transport from year to year, with extremes ranging from a growth of 17 per cent in 1950–51 to —1 per cent in the depressed year of 1957–58.[3] In fact no other branch of transport faced such a volatile demand schedule. The growth in traffic was not reflected fully in fleet size; world tonnage growth was around 5 per cent per annum, that is considerably less than the rate of expansion in demand. This would seem to indicate considerable productivity gains arising from rapid technical innovation, notably in the form of massive tankers and bulk carriers, and to a lesser extent from container and other unitised services, improved cargo handling techniques, faster ships and more efficient port operations.[4]

PROGRESS OF THE UK FLEET

The history of Britain's merchant marine makes sad reading against this background of vigorous growth. The UK fleet expanded by a mere 1·7 per cent per annum between 1950 and 1970 and most of this growth came in the last two years. In fact, for nearly the entire post-war period the British fleet was, on average, no larger than it had been in 1930, whereas in the intervening period world tonnage had expanded no less than three times (1930–1970).[5] Consequently Britain's share of world shipping declined steadily and continuously from around 30 per cent in 1930 to a little over 11 per cent by the late 1960s (see table 24). The fleet of nearly every maritime nation of any substance expanded more rapidly than that of the British,[6] and by 1970 this country no longer held the position of chief maritime power having been superseded by Liberia and Japan.

The obvious question is why did British shipping, which had once held a semi-monopoly in ocean transportation, perform so miserably in the post-war years? After decades of relative decline, and given the buoyant trading conditions after 1945, one might have expected the industry to have put up a better showing. Could it be that factors outside the industry's control inhibited revival? The shipping community frequently maintained that the industry's efficiency left little to question but that this was no match against

Table 24   UK and world fleets, 1930–1970 (million gross tons)
(ships of 100 grt and over)

	UK(1)	World	UK as a % of World Fleet
1930	20·3	68·0	29·9
1938	17·7	66·9	26·5
1948	18·0	80·3	22·4
1950	18.2	84·6	21·5
1955	19·4	100·6	19·3
1960	21·1	129·8	16·3
1965	21·5	160·4	13·4
1968	21·9	194·2	11·3
1970	25·8	227·5	11·3

(1) The figures refer to tonnage registered in the UK; the figures for tonnage registered and owned in the UK are slightly lower.
Source: Lloyd's Register of Shipping, *Statistical Tables, 1970*, table 15.

unfair commercial practices—subsidies, flag discrimination etc—practised by shipowners abroad. 'It can fairly be claimed', stated the Chamber of Shipping at the end of the 1950s, 'that the British Merchant Navy is as efficient as ever it has been and the many modern ships which have come into service in recent years are evidence of this. But other countries are more and more supporting their shipping by artificial stimulants against which sheer efficient operation by itself cannot in the long run prevail'.[7]

Independent observers took quite a different view. One of the industry's most severe critics has been Professor Sturmey who launched a severe attack on the industry in 1962. He maintained that the industry's relative decline could be written almost solely in terms of internal constraints: that is, the decline was largely self-generated through the unenterprising internal structure of the shipping companies.[8] Similar criticisms had in fact already been expressed by Political and Economic Planning in its broadsheet published in 1959. It drew attention to the domination of family control which had not maintained the standards of efficiency once practised by the pioneer members, and then listed the many ways in which British shipowners had failed to keep abreast of the times. But the report concluded that 'Perhaps the greatest danger lies in the industry's readiness to confuse the avoidable with the unavoidable causes of its relative decline. The besetting sin of industries in decline is to defend inaction and brush aside constructive suggestions on the grounds that their problems are unique'.[9] A decade later the Rochdale Inquiry into Shipping expressed misgivings about the industry's performance, but the tone of their criticisms was tempered by the fact that during the course of their investigations they had detected 'a new spirit of enterprise evident in the management of many shipping companies, which is leading to greater efficiency in operation and a greater awareness of, and willingness to exploit, the opportunities offered by recent technological developments'.[10] Whether this revival augurs better prospects for the future only time will tell, but our main concern here is to attempt an explanation of the depressing record through to the end of the 1960s.

EXTERNAL CONSTRAINTS ON GROWTH

Basically an answer to the question depends on two sets of factors: whether the industry's performance was determined largely by forces outside its immediate control, or whether the decline was a symptom of the industry's lack of enterprise. In general, shipowners have argued that it was the former which were mainly responsible for the failure to expand. They have drawn attention in particular to the rapid growth of foreign maritime fleets under the stimulus of governmental aid in one form or another, to the slower growth in the home trades compared with world trade as a whole together with the decline in some traditional activities, and to the impact of war. Most of these factors tended to affect British shipowners adversely but it is doubtful whether they add up to a convincing explanation of stagnation.

As far as the shock of war is concerned, no other industry suffered such heavy losses. About one half the UK fleet was lost through enemy action, and though a large proportion of the loss was made good by replacement the fleet was still 25 per cent down on the pre-war level by the end of hostilities.[11] However, most other maritime powers, especially those engaged in combat, suffered even sharper reverses so that by 1946 their fleets showed substantially greater declines than the British. The world fleet as a whole increased over the period 1939–46 but this was largely due to the enormous expansion of shipping activity in the United States, the one country with a post-war performance less enviable than Britain's. Thus in purely physical terms British shipping did not emerge from the war under a severe handicap. Indeed, if the large American Reserve Fleet is excluded from the world tonnage figures then the British fleet at the end of the war was as strongly placed as in 1938, which makes the subsequent decline appear all the more disastrous.

From the financial standpoint the matter is a little more complicated. Most vessels sunk were eventually replaced but often at prices considerably above their historic cost since the price of new ships doubled during the course of the war and continued to rise rapidly thereafter.[12] Kendall calculated that the cost of replacing war losses ran to about £600 million, of which £287 million was covered by insurance claims and £210 million by depreciation reserves, leaving £103 million to be met from general reserves. This, he argued, placed a serious financial burden on British shipping.[13] However, these figures probably overstate the amount involved since many ships were replaced before costs had escalated too far. After a detailed if somewhat diffuse analysis of this issue Sturmey came to the conclusion that most of the shipowners' wartime gains were used in restoring the fleet to pre-war strength, but that on balance British shipowners were no worse off than their competitors, with the exception of America and Sweden,[14] Perhaps more to the point was the fact that some of the ships bought for replacement were not of a type most suited to post-war needs.[15]

The war cannot therefore be regarded as more than a short-term setback and Britain came out of it as well placed, if not better, than most of her chief competitors. More relevant for the long-term was the slow growth of the home trades in comparison with world seaborne trade and the decline of some traditional shipping outlets. In the latter context the two most notable were the erosion of long-distance passenger traffic and the collapse of the coal export trade, both of which had provided important sources of employment for British vessels in the past. Ocean passenger traffic increased throughout the post-war period but all the growth took place in the short-sea routes which were operated mostly by nationalised shipping services.[16] The mainstay of the liner trade, long-distance ocean travel, succumbed under the impact of air competition. By the end of the 1960s little was left of what was once a flourishing and profitable trade and passenger liner tonnage had been reduced to one third its pre-war level with much of it engaged on cruising activities. In the same way the contraction of the coal export trade hit the traditional tramp owner. Coal exports had been in decline since 1914 but during the second world war they vanished altogether and throughout the 1950s and 1960s they were but a fraction of the 1938 volume.[17] But there were no lack of opportunities for the employment of tramp vessels of the right kind as the growth of tramp fleets abroad demonstrated.

Overall the UK domestic trade grew less rapidly than world seaborne trade and this would seem to offer at least a partial explanation for the limited expansion of the British fleet. Between 1950 and 1970 the weight of imports and exports combined increased by more than 150 per cent, or at the rate of 5·0 per cent per annum (much of the growth coming from oil imports) as against 8·6 for world seaborne trade. Even if we take 1938 as the base year (when the coal export trade was very much larger than in 1950) the aggregate volume of all UK trade had more than doubled by 1970.[18] Such a rate of expansion, though lower than international standards, does not square with the virtual stagnation of the UK fleet. The discrepancy can be partly explained by increased capacity utilisation of shipping space, but even allowing for this it is clear that the home trades still offered considerable opportunities for shipowners to expand their activities in this period. That British owners neglected their own waters is evident from the increasing proportion of foreign entrances and clearances (with cargo) at British ports. By the 1960s one half or more of the entrances and clearances consisted of foreign ships whereas they had constituted only about one third in the immediate post-war period. The diminishing importance of British shipping in the home trades (see table 25) indicates the extent to which British owners were losing out to their competitors. There is little wonder that UK shipowners complained bitterly about foreign competition and it is to this problem that we now turn.

Table 25   Share of British tonnage in the entrances and clearances (with cargo) at UK ports (%)

	Tonnage entrances	Tonnage clearances
1913	65	59
1938	57	59
1947	70	78
1950	63	70
1955	55	62
1960	49	60
1965	46	54
1970	39	48

Source: *Annual Abstract of Statistics* and *Annual Reports of* the Liverpool Steam Ship Owners' Association

FOREIGN COMPETITION

Foreign competition in the maritime trades generally increased considerably in the decades after the war. Not only was there a big expansion in the size of the world fleet but there was also a significant increase in the number of maritime nations as a number of newly independent countries established fleets of their own. In 1949 there were 46 maritime nations of any importance but by 1963 this number had risen to 66, and at least half of the new national flag lines organised since 1949 were initially financed and largely controlled by governments, as they still are in many cases.[19] Inevitably therefore British shipowners were likely to find the going more difficult given this expansion in foreign maritime activity. Yet it was not so much the expansion of world tonnage capacity as such that alarmed British shipowners but rather the alleged unfair commercial practices adopted by foreign countries in an effort to boost their maritime activities. These took a variety of forms including financial subsidies, flag discrimination, flags of convenience, the development of state fleets and reservation of the coastal trades to ships of the national flag.[20]

The subsidy question is perhaps the most complex since such a variety of practices were adopted to assist the maritime industries. The main ones include operating and construction subsidies, indirect financial benefits through the taxation system and the operation of state-owned fleets on non-commercial lines. The paucity of really reliable factual data makes it difficult to evaluate the impact of all these policies precisely. Moreover, definitional difficulties complicate the problem of interpretation. British shipowners received no operating subsidies but they benefited considerably from tax relief on investment. The Rochdale Committee chose to regard tax benefits as a separate issue from the question of subsidisation, but as Sturmey noted in 1962, the total amount then paid in aid to French shipping was less than the tax relief derived from investment allowances by British shipowners.[21] However, since most countries provided some relief through the taxation system, and the British Government has been more than generous in this matter, we can count this as a factor common to all.

If we adopt this more limited definition then the most subsidised maritime fleets were those of Australia, France, Italy, the United States, Japan and Spain. The first three employed both operating and construction subsidies as well as operating state-owned fleets; the United States had both operating and construction subsidies, while Spain and Japan concentrated mainly on operating subsidies, though backed up by liberal credit assistance from time to time in the case of Japan. Experience in terms of fleet growth varied. The fleets of Italy, Spain and Japan expanded at a faster rate than world tonnage between 1950 and 1970, especially the Japanese which increased from just under two million tons gross to no less than 27 million tons in 1970. Undoubtedly generous financial aid was of some importance in boosting the growth of the latter, but given Japan's outstanding performance in other fields it seems plausible to assume that her maritime activities would have responded without assistance, though perhaps not quite so spectacularly. On the other hand, Australia, France and the United States did not match world growth, while a number of other subsidised fleets did badly, notably the Canadian which hardly grew at all. The evidence would appear somewhat inconclusive were it not for the fact that many European and Scandinavian countries managed to expand their fleets rapidly without the aid of protection to any significant degree. Thus Norway, Greece and Germany easily outpaced the world fleet, while Sweden, Denmark, Finland, Portugal, the Netherlands and Belgium did very much better than Britain; in most cases the fleets of these countries more than doubled. In the light of these findings it is difficult to conclude that subsidies were a crucial factor in the growth of foreign fleets in general. Moreover, many of the opportunities open to non-subsidised operators were also available to British shipping.

Flag discrimination embraces a wide variety of measures and pressures exerted by governments which are designed to direct trade to ships of the national flag. In its most stringent forms it effectively prevents the foreigner from competing for available business. The most common form is the reservation of certain proportions or types of cargo to national ships, applied either unilaterally or through bilateral trade agreements. But there are a host of measures designed to achieve similar ends, including the reservation to national ships of imports qualifying for preferential credit facilities, special tariff concessions, preferential fiscal treatment, exchange control preference and port concessions. In addition, military cargoes are often reserved for national ships, while unofficial policies are sometimes practised which in turn lead to official retaliation.

The British shipping industry has always regarded discriminatory practices of this sort as particularly damaging to its interests because of its world-wide services. Certainly discrimination in one form or another became more widespread after the war; of the 64 countries to which British ships traded in 1957 no fewer than 40 had practised flag discrimination in one form or another within the previous five years, while trade treaties known to include discriminatory shipping clauses were concluded by some 35 countries.[22] In terms of the amount of cargo involved the most important flag discriminators were the United States, the Latin American countries, and one or two other countries, notably Egypt and India. It is unlikely however that the proportion of total world trade involved was ever very large; Sturmey doubted whether more than

5 per cent of world seaborne trade was removed from free competition by official discriminatory practices in 1957,[23] while the Rochdale Committee estimated that for 1966 only about 50 million metric tons, or 3 per cent of the non-communist world's seaborne trade, was diverted from normal commercial channels by flag discrimination.[24] The committee did not reckon that the impact on British shipping had been particularly serious—a rough estimate of the loss of carryings was put at 5 million metric tons—though discrimination did bear more heavily on the liner and cross trades, areas in which the UK had large interests. On individual routes the effect could be quite severe. The proportion of liner traffic carried by UK operators on the UK to Uruguay service almost halved between 1962 and 1967, while on the Brazilian run it declined by nearly one quarter between 1958 and 1967. In the case of the Calcutta to US North Atlantic ports route, the trade of which had been monopolised by British liners before the war, the indirect effects of flag discrimination eventually forced the British companies to abandon operations altogether because of indequate returns.[25] Thus UK shipping certainly lost trade on specific routes as a result of flag discrimination but the total losses were not large and other countries suffered too, especially Norway with its extensive interests in the cross trades. Moreover, the main countries indulging in flag discrimination, the United States and many Latin American countries, did not have particularly good records as regards fleet growth; in fact in the last decade or so their share of the world fleet has been declining.

The practice of registering shipping under flags outside the owner's country of residence began before the first world war but the really sustained growth in flags of convenience fleets took place after 1948. Between that date and 1968 the tonnage so registered rose from 3 to 33 million tons gross, most of which consisted of dry bulk and tanker vessels. The principal fleets are those of Panama and Liberia, especially the latter which by 1966 became the largest fleet in the world, and Greek and American owners predominate. Legal impediments, among other things, have discouraged British owners from registering under these flags. The main attractions of registering with such states have been the low tax rates, cheaper crew costs and freedom from many operating restrictions imposed by governments in other countries, though some of these advantages diminished over time. It is unlikely however that shipping under these flags seriously damaged British shipping interests, and certainly it cannot be used as an explanation of the decline. For one thing, it scarcely affected the liner trades, while opportunities for expansion in tramp and tanker shipping were fairly good. Secondly, though ships registered in this way had considerable advantages in the past *vis-à-vis* British shipping because of the tax benefits, the tax arrangements for UK shipping were improved to such an extent after 1954 that by the end of the 1960s public companies probably found the UK fiscal benefits preferable to registration under a flag of convenience. Finally, in the absence of these flags most of the tonnage would still probably have existed, though under another registration; it is unlikely that much of it would have been registered in Britain, but even if it had this would not have increased the size of the fleet owned by British residents.

A final factor to contend with was the expansion in the fleets of communist countries and of those countries formerly dependent on others for shipping services. Both these could be a source of danger because of State backing and the attendant possibility of non-commercial operation. Communist fleets expanded their share of world tonnage in this period but by and large they were used to carry the trade of these countries and there was no significant participation in the cross trades. The newly developing maritime nations were a different matter since many had depended heavily on British shipping services in the past. Many of the fleets remained very small by international standards but in aggregate the tonnage of these countries increased from 1·7 million tons gross in 1939 to 14·3 million in 1968, and as a share of the world total from 3 to 8 per cent. In some instances British shipping was affected severely by such developments. On the trades between the UK and India and Pakistan British owners lost heavily and by the late 1960s Indian liner operators had obtained about 50 per cent of the trade.[26] British liners also lost about one third of the traffic between this country and West African ports, a trade which they had monopolised in 1952. But in this case only part of the loss can be attributed to competition from new national fleets; far more important was the slice captured by third flag operators.[27]

One may conclude, therefore, that foreign competition in its various forms did reduce the trading opportunities open to the UK fleet on certain routes and services, more especially on those in which Britain had held a predominant share of the traffic before 1939. Britain probably suffered more so in this respect than other countries partly because she had more to lose at the beginning of the period. Though it is impossible to provide any precise quantification, the overall impact of foreign competition does not appear to have been very significant.[28] As for the other external constraints already considered, neither war nor the slower growth of the home trades can be regarded as agents of the relative fleet decline. In total therefore, purely external constraints can explain very little of the UK setback, certainly they cannot explain the near stagnation of the British fleet. Moreover, when account is taken of the rapid expansion of free market trading opportunities since the war, which were exploited vigorously by unassisted European and Scandinavian maritime powers, then the performance of the UK shipping industry appears all the more discreditable.

At this point it would be tempting to launch an attack on the industry's failure to exploit the opportunities available, both trade and technological, and thereby derive an internally generated explanation of the decline of the UK fleet since it is clear that external constraints cannot serve this purpose. On both counts there was no lack of opportunities; seaborne trade grew very rapidly after the war and the pace of technological change has rarely been more active. But this line of attack might serve no useful purpose if it turned out that shipowners' reluctance to expand their fleets simply reflected a rational reaction to the rate of return that could be earned on shipping operations. In other words, we ought first to examine the record of profitability.

THE PROFITABILITY GAP

Rates of return have been historically mediocre in the maritime trades, and shipowners generally, it would seem, worked to lower rates of return than companies engaged in other spheres of economic activity. The Assistant Manager of the Shaw Savill and Albion Line (part of the Furness Withy group) observed that a company producing a 6 per cent profit after depreciation would be doing 'remarkably well' and even 3 per cent could be regarded as a fair average rate.[29] The post-war record has been dismal to say the least. An independent survey carried out for the Rochdale inquiry found that the average return (after depreciation but before tax) on capital employed for the years 1958–69 was as low as 3·6 per cent, that is less than one third the average for all companies. For the period 1950–57 data compiled by *The Economist* produced a somewhat higher return, 10·3 per cent, though even this was little more than half the rate of industry as a whole and it included two boom periods for shipping, the Korean War and the Suez Canal closure. Such low rates of return could hardly have given shipowners much incentive to invest in new tonnage. Indeed, as the committee was quick to observe: 'In view of their experience it is not surprising that they did not extend their fleets more in the period under review; rather it may be considered surprising that they continued to invest in new vessels as much as they did. . . . Indeed, unless a shipping company is able in future to achieve a much higher rate on its capital assets than have most over the last 20 years, it would only be acting in the best interests of its shareholders if it decided to run down its investment in shipping activities'.[30]

On this evidence there would seem to be a case for arguing that British shipowners were acting rationally in not investing extensively in new tonnage. But the matter is not quite so simple as this. It could have been the case that returns were low because of bad investment decisions and poor management. Unfortunately the data we require at this point are not available, namely figures for the profitability of foreign fleets, though there is enough indirect evidence to suggest that it was somewhat better than the returns earned by UK shipowners.[31] Assuming this to be the case then it would be reasonable to argue that the responsibility lay with the internal management of British companies. In any case, the absence of a cross-country comparison of rates of return does not preclude an investigation into the allocation of British shipping investment to ascertain whether it was employed in the most profitable way. There are several possible routes by which defective management could lead to low rates of return. Investment might be made in the wrong technology and trades, operating costs may be higher than they should be because of poor capacity utilisation and low levels of productivity, or the pricing system may be at fault. An examination of these points in turn should prove instructive.

TECHNICAL CHANGES

The post-war period has seen a massive technological revolution in ocean shipping comparable to anything that took place in the nineteenth century.[32] The enormous growth in commodity trade, especially oil shipments, and the dwindling importance of passenger traffic exerted a significant impact on the composition of fleets. The majestic passenger liners of the nineteenth and early twentieth centuries have all but disappeared, the days of the small general purpose tramp are now numbered and the traditional cargo liner is steadily becoming outdated. In their place have appeared giant tankers, ore and other bulk carriers, and more recently container and other unitised services. The most dramatic change has been in the size of vessels. The size of tanker vessels in particular increased very rapidly, especially after the closure of the Suez Canal which boosted the demand for ships of large dimensions. By the early 1970s tankers of 200,000 tons deadweight were becoming typical[33] whereas twenty years earlier the standard had been 20,000 tons or less. The size of dry bulk carriers has grown almost as rapidly though in absolute terms they are still trailing behind tankers. As one writer observed at the end of the 1960s: 'the time during which two thirds of all seaborne cargo passed through ports capable of receiving ships of up to 14,000 tons only has definitely gone'.[34] These changes brought significant cost reductions mainly through savings on capital and crew. A 200,000 ton vessel has a similar crew to that of 20,000 tons and its capital costs are about one third per deadweight ton; the effect is to reduce the ton-mile cost to about one third that of the 20,000 ton vessel.[35] Or to take a specific example: a British ore shipping agency acquired in 1969 one large bulk carrier of 120,000 deadweight tons with a carrying capacity equivalent to 12 of its 1947 vessels at a cost of one quarter of the latter in real terms and requiring only one twentieth of the manning[36]. Similar cost reductions will probably be achieved with container services, which by the later 1960s had begun to revolutionise the general cargo trade.[37]

British shipowners certainly displayed some reluctance in exploiting the new developments. One of the fastest growing sectors was the shipment of oil yet shipowners in this country neglected the tanker market for much of the period. Between 1939 and 1968 the world tanker fleet increased nearly six-fold whereas the UK tanker fleet barely trebled, with the result that Britain's share of total world tanker tonnage declined from 25·5 to 12·1 per cent.[38] This was during a period moreover when our oil imports rose no less than nine times so that opportunities were being lost in the home as well as the cross trades. Furthermore, had it not been for the oil companies own operations in this field, which accounted for no less than three quarters of the UK owned and registered tanker fleet in 1968, the record in this sector would have been very much worse. Since liner and tramp companies virtually ignored the tanker market until well into the 1960s the oil companies, which normally serviced between one third and two thirds of their tanker requirements, were forced to look outside Britain for long-term charters. UK shipping companies would undoubtedly have enjoyed a higher return on their assets had they invested more heavily in tankers and less in other types of vessel. The tanker market was relatively profitable—indeed a few individuals managed to become millionaires from their activities in this field— and given the right ships and efficient management a rate of return of 8 per cent or more was possible, that is twice the rate earned on the UK fleet as a whole in the 1960s. The financial record of British independent tanker owners fell considerably short of this rate but largely because, until recently, they invested in sub-optimal size vessels. Sturmey suggests that by the early 1960s, 85 per cent of the tanker fleet was below the optimum economic size commensurate with the level of British crew costs.[39]

Page 247
Above: The 10,762 ton tanker *British Aviator* was built at Yarrow in 1924 and scrapped in 1953. It belonged to the British Petroleum Company.

Below: BP's *British Endeavour* of 12,250 tons and built in 1949 shows the 'small' size of tanker persisting. This vessel was sold for scrap in 1962.

Page 248

Above: Since the Suez Crisis of 1956 tankers have grown steadily larger. *British Queen*, built for BP in 1959, was then at 50,000 tons considered big.

Below: Today tankers of a quarter of a million tons—or even more—are no longer rare. This is BP's *British Inventor* of 215,000 tons on trial off Nagasaki, Japan.

One possible constraint initially was the size of the UK oil terminals though since the oil market is international this did not preclude chartering for the cross trades.

Another area of neglect was in the bulk carrier trades. Here profits were fairly high, especially in bulk ore carriers which netted returns of 10 per cent or more on average during the 1960s. Until 1958 most bulk cargo moved in general purpose tramps after which large bulk carriers quickly began to oust the latter in the carriage of dry bulk cargo. By 1969 over 75 per cent of the seaborne trade of five major bulk commodities was carried in bulk carriers of over 18,000 deadweight tons.[40] The British tramp trade was not well placed to exploit these opportunities at the beginning of the bulk carrier revolution. UK owners had not anticipated profitable conditions to continue after a short-lived post-war boom and allowed the tramp fleet to decline through to 1956 when conditions were fairly prosperous. Then as the freight index was about to reach its peak UK owners placed substantial orders for many ships of the wrong type, moderately sized general purpose tramps which came into service just at the time when other maritime powers were beginning to move into large specialised bulk carriers. At the end of 1960 the world tramp fleet included 229 bulk carriers of over 14,000 deadweight tons, a size virtually without represent-ation in the UK fleet. Given the UK cost structure tramps of less than about 15,000 tons were uneconomic to operate, yet by the early 1960s the bulk of the British tramp tonnage was below this despite the fact that one third of the total had been built in the previous five years. The effect of the size structure was reflected in the very low returns and the high proportion of ships laid up.[41] After this mistiming it is perhaps not surprising that tramp owners then delayed switching to large bulk carriers. Thus between 1958 and 1968 the world bulk carrier fleet rose more than eight-fold, while that of the UK increased by a factor of less than four. By the latter date the UK accounted for less than one tenth of the world bulk carrier fleet, that is some way behind the major participants in this sector, Liberia, Norway and Japan.[42]

Conventional liner operators also had a dismal financial record after the mid 1950s. The worst section was of course the passenger trade for obvious reasons, but cargo liner operators also had to face competition from bulk carriers in some trades and from air transport and newly established fleets abroad. Yet UK owners continued for many years to build conventional liners even though prospective profits were minimal. They failed or somehow were unable to adapt to changing conditions. They ordered ships designed to be efficient for the 40 per cent of the time spent at sea, rather than for the 60 per cent which they spent in port. Only towards the end of the period, under the impact of cumulative technological changes culminating in the introduction of container services and unitised load systems, did a radical reappraisal of investments prospects occur. UK shipowners then showed considerable initiative in this respect both in forming national consortia and in joining international consortia for the development of container services. After 1965 container traffic grew rapidly though much of the initial expansion was in the near and short-sea trades, and even here some doubt has recently been expressed as to whether British owners have adequately exploited new and developing trades.[43] Nevertheless, by the late 1960s the transformation of the traditional cargo liner trades had at least begun though it will be some time before the process is complete and the financial implications of the new developments become apparent.

There seems little doubt, therefore, that British shipowners neglected the faster growing and more profitable sectors of the market for much of the post-war period. Until recently a large part of the investment in shipping went into the traditional type of ship. Between 1958 and 1967 over 40 per cent of total investment (excluding that of the oil companies) was absorbed by the relatively small traditional cargo liner vessel and over 22 per cent went into general purpose tramps, both areas of low return. Yet in the branches of activity where returns were relatively high, that is bulk carriers of one form or another, the proportion of investment was very low, under 10 per cent of the total. Tankers also offered better prospects yet shipping companies virtually ignored this sector; only about 12 per cent of the investment programme was devoted to tankers between 1958 and 1967.[44]

Despite low returns a shortage of finance cannot be held responsible for the failure to exploit the new opportunities properly. Much of the past investment was internally financed and the resources could just as easily have been switched into the newer sectors. In any case, shipowners both at home and abroad had access to readily available supplies of cheap credit and tax incentive schemes to encourage investment. Indeed, the facilities available in this respect during the 1960s were generous to a degree and it could be argued that this favoured treatment tended to channel resources into shipping to an uneconomic extent in that it allowed the industry to operate on considerably lower margins than other commercial activities which were less favoured. Even worse in this context was the fact that cheap credit facilities and tax allowances on investment were granted rather indiscriminately, to efficient and inefficient firms alike, and regardless of the desirability of distinguishing between sound and unsound investment projects. Despite the obvious misallocation of resources in the past the Rochdale Committee were reluctant to recommend any significant reduction in the financial facilities available to shipping.

Lack of finance cannot then be regarded as the main barrier to innovation. In which case the relative neglect of new fields must be attributed to the failure of management to recognise the importance of the new opportunities offered. In this respect as in others, eg research and development in which the past record has been poor, management was not in a position, partly because of a lack of qualified personnel both on the technical and economic side, to appreciate the importance of new changes and the alternative investment choices thereby presented. Many companies, for example, failed to follow through the full financial implications of their investment proposals, and there was a marked reluctance to employ modern methods of investment appraisal using discounted cash flow techniques. Sturmey's explanation for unenterprising management runs in terms of the innate conservatism of shipping groups long dominated by family control and the conference system.[45] This pattern was breaking down in the 1960s but it still had some force.

Some outstanding points still require clarification however. Assuming that the bulk of past investment in shipping had been switched from traditional fields into bulk carriers, tankers etc, then the rate of return on capital would have improved. But it would still have been considerably lower than that earned in industry as a whole. In general shipowners have been prepared to work to lower rates of return though quite why this should be so is not clear. However, the crucial question is how these potential returns would have compared with those earned by foreign shipping companies. Other factors could intervene to reduce the profitability of British shipping even though operating under a common technology. Crew costs might be higher or the management of shipping operations may be inefficient leading to lower levels of productivity and higher operating costs *vis-à-vis* those abroad.

Satisfactory information on these matters is not readily available so that it is not easy to say whether shipping operations, even on the basis of the chosen technology, were grossly mismanaged. As far as labour costs are concerned the industry suffered little disadvantage on this score during the 1950s and early 1960s. In fact, British owners probably had crew costs somewhat lower than those of several other maritime countries partly because of the large proportion (35-40 per cent) of low wage non-European labour employed, though this advantage was sometimes offset by higher manning ratios.[46] But the productivity record was very poor in this period, a reflection no doubt of the slow rate of innovation. Subsequently productivity growth improved considerably with a consequent sharp reduction in the required labour force.[47] Part of this decline was the result of the reduction in the number of deep sea passenger ships which are labour intensive, but it also reflected the effects of an increase in average ship size and the more efficient use of manpower arising from automation and improved manning arrangements.[48] Thus for a decade or more after the war low productivity growth contributed to the low returns earned in shipping, though in the absence of data for other countries an international comparison is not possible.

THE PRICING SYSTEM
.A further possible source of shipowners' difficulties may lie with

the pricing system for shipping services. Even if investment decisions are correct and shipping operations are efficiently managed low returns might still result if charges for services supplied are fixed at such a level that prevent normal profits from being made. The assumption that an optimal pricing system can be pursued depends very much on the extent of cross subsidisation and the degree of competition. We know very little about the extent of the former but it almost certainly existed and this inevitably led to excess capacity. Price structures varied according to the type of market served. In the case of general purpose tramps rates were determined in a free market according to demand and supply relationships so that shipowners had little leeway in which to manoeuvre and any single shipowner could do little to influence the market trend set by the market. However, since tramp owners missed several profitable opportunities after the war it is not necessary to look to the erratic freight movements under a free market system to explain the low returns of UK owners. With bulk carriers and tankers (excluding those owned by the oil companies) contract rates were usually fixed for lengthy periods of time and since average returns in these sectors were reasonable there is no pressing need to probe deeply into the pricing structure. But in 1968 a third or more of the UK fleet still consisted of multi-deck dry cargo vessels of the traditional type most of which were employed on liner services the freight rates for which were fixed by the shipping conferences.

The negotiation of conference rates has always been shrouded in secrecy so that it is difficult to arrive at definite conclusions on this point. Though rates are cost orientated, rather than demand determined as in the case of tramp freights, it is difficult to believe that the rates charged for particular services are related to costs in any meaningful way since, as Goss has observed, it is not immediately obvious how the costs of carrying any particular commodity are to be identified.[49] Moreover, the use of a value system of classification and the power of the conference to discriminate between shippers makes it even less likely that individual rates are based on the true costs of the service performed. Inevitably, therefore, the system leads to an averaging of charges, though not to the same extent as in other transport sectors because of the readiness of conference members to discriminate.[50] Not a great deal of empirical study has been made of this subject but McLachlan's useful investigation for the period 1948 to 1961 shows that liner rates moved closely with aggregate shipping costs and this helped to stabilise the level of profits of liner companies compared with those of tramps. But since the conferences did not generally use their power to obtain abnormal profits in boom periods the rewards of restraint were limited. The annual average gross profits per ton of a sample of liner companies turned out to be little better than the corresponding returns for a sample of tramp companies.[51] It would seem, therefore, that cargo liner companies paid a high price for relative stability in freights and that these on average were fixed at too low a level.[52] Furthermore, the element of cross-subsidisation, a failure to allow adequately for inflation and the subsequent competition from bulk carriers in certain trades all helped to restrain margins in this sector.[53]

THE END OF STAGNATION?

Whatever measurement of assessment is adopted the post-war record of British shipping has been poor. External constraints, mainly foreign competition and protection, cannot be considered as a major causal factor of this performance since unassisted fleets managed to grow rapidly and some increased their share of the world fleet. Low profits no doubt reduced the incentive to invest, but since these in turn stemmed partly from a misallocation of investment resources, with a predilection, at least until well into the 1960s, to invest in traditional techniques, low profits can be regarded as both cause and effect. Profits were also probably depressed by relatively high operating costs which can be explained by the slow rate of productivity growth up to the early 1960s. The small productivity gains were in turn the product of the slowness to innovate and the failure to improve significantly the efficiency of existing shipping operations. To a certain extent defective pricing policies may have contributed to lowering returns, more especially in the case of cargo liners, though given the competition from more efficient operators there may have been a limit to which a high cost operator could adjust freights within the conference structure. In short therefore, the management of British shipping has a lot to answer for. Broadly speaking, the management structure was unsuited to grasping new opportunities, and it is significant, as the Rochdale Committee pointed out, that 'higher financial returns have been achieved by those companies with good management as reflected by an ability to take prompt advantage of opportunities which have presented themselves'.[54]

Fortunately we do not need to end this survey of shipping on a wholly pessimistic note. As mentioned earlier, the Rochdale Committee, during the course of its deliberations, detected a new spirit of enterprise among shipowners the beginnings of which can probably be traced back to the early 1960s when productivity began to accelerate smartly. The full force of this wind of change came in the big spending spree at the end of the 1960s and it was almost certainly encouraged by a rising trend in profits and a new and even more generous system of investment grants introduced in 1966. Towards the end of 1969 British owners had nearly eight million tons gross of shipping on order, the most significant feature of which was that nearly all of it comprised orders for bulk carriers, tankers or cellular container vessels. Much of this tonnage has come on stream during the last two or three years with the result that since 1968 the British fleet, after decades of imperceptible growth, increased by nearly a fifth. The fleet also now has a much more modern appearance and the future prospects of British shipping depend on the extent to which management continues to respond to new developments.

CHAPTER NINE

Adapting the Infrastructure

INTRODUCTION

THE INFRASTRUCTURE, in the form of track and terminals, forms an integral part of the transport system without which it would not be possible to carry on operations. One of the main problems in the past has been that the provision of such facilities—roads, ports and airports—has not kept pace with the rate of progress in the field of locomotion. This was certainly the case in the nineteenth century —witness the constant pressure to enlarge and improve dock facilities—but it has become even more of a problem in the twentieth century. Most people today are aware, from practical experience, of the shortage of road space and the pressure on air terminal capacity, though probably less so of the apparent need for more and better dock accommodation. There are several general and fairly obvious reasons for this current deficiency in facilities.[1] For one thing the lag is of long standing and has been aggravated by economic circumstances. A period of economic uncertainty (1919–39) bounded by two world wars and their aftermath was hardly conducive to building new infrastructures and what investment there was tended to be of the make-do-and-mend variety. Moreover, the fact that a large part of the expenditure emanated from public funds also tended to damp down investment since for much of the time the prevailing economic philosophy scarcely imparted a spirit of enthusiasm for large scale public spending on works of this nature.

These specific circumstances apart, there are features inherent in the system which make for delay. Some lagged reaction in the provision of facilities is almost inevitable since the justification for

256

their construction depends upon the demand generated from transport operators. Thus to take a specific example: one is hardly likely to contemplate providing dock facilities to accommodate large tankers of between 200–300,000 tons if the feasible state of technology only permits the production of tankers one quarter this size. Only when large tankers become a commercial possibility does the pressure on terminals begin to produce a reaction. However, as long as technical developments in the means of locomotion are gradual and steady and are of a type which can be readily adapted to the existing infrastructural framework no serious problems need arise. But in practice technology does not choose to oblige us in this way. It tends to erupt in sudden bursts and is subject to lumpiness, which means that infrastructures are unable to cope with the sudden changes in the scale or pattern of the new demands and hence they become inadequate or prematurely obsolete. In the post-war period evidence of this process at work is not difficult to find. The dramatic technical advances in aviation and shipping (eg much larger craft, containers etc), plus volume growth in both cases and in road transport have put enormous pressures on track and terminal facilities, resulting in a never ending battle to try and keep pace with requirements.

The problem is complicated by the fact that the transport operators and the owners and providers of infrastructures are not identical even though state participation at some level is prevalent in both cases. In this context it might be noted that the railways have been, and still are, unique in that the traction, terminals and track have always been under one and the same management, so that by and large the provision of all three has tended to keep in step.[2] This has never been the case with other forms of transport, road, air and sea transport, and their respective facilities, with the result that conflicting and disintegrated interests have inevitably led to reaction lags in infrastructure development. For example, most shipping is owned by private enterprise but the port and dock services are not; they are owned by a number of different bodies including the state. Airports are owned both by the state and by municipal authorities but not by the airlines. The administration of the roads is in the hands of the central government and a multiplicity of local authorities, and road users have little control over their track. Moreover, the disintegration and separation of control makes it difficult to plan and meet requirements on a national basis.

A further complication is that the market mechanism is not fully operative in this sector; therefore investment needs are not easily or readily reflected through the price/profit mechanism. Either the prices charged for the services offered do not fully reflect true resource costs, as in the case of airport and dock facilities, or the price mechanism is non-existent as in the case of the roads. Moreover, the construction of these facilities often gives rise to large externalities (costs and benefits though more often the latter) which need to be taken into consideration. In effect, this means that investment cannot be determined solely by the operation of market forces. In the absence of what might be regarded as normal criteria a more sophisticated approach to investment in infrastructures needs to be employed, though until recently much of the investment proceeded on a rather hit or miss basis.

Most people would probably readily agree that both in the recent past and at the present time there is a pressing need for more and better infrastructure facilities. Motorists point to increasing road congestion and severe bottlenecks to prove their case, air travellers are conscious of delays at air terminals, while shipowners and traders are finding that it is sometimes cheaper and more convenient to use near continental ports because of inadequate facilities in this country. The physical needs appear obvious but whether all the demands can be justified on economic grounds is quite another matter. The post-war problem has arisen basically as a result of two main factors: the rapid growth in the volume of transport and travel, especially on the roads and in the air, which has created a physical capacity shortage in terms of track and terminals; and secondly, rapid technical change, especially in sea and air transport, has rendered many existing terminal installations obsolete or at least partly inadequate.

Attempts to meet the growing requirements of the post-war period varied considerably. For a decade or more after the war only a half-hearted effort was made to adapt the infrastructure to the new requirements. In fact investment was very low in the early post-war years, and even in the late 1950s and early 1960s, when more resources were devoted to this sector, progress was probably little more than sufficient to recoup part of the backlog. Moreover, the allocation of investment funds to this sector, though modest, had little economic rationale behind it; investment projects went forward on an *ad hoc* or piecemeal basis according to apparent priority, rather than on the basis of an economic analysis of their viability. During the 1960s, however, a much more serious and sustained attempt was made to step up the rate of investment and this was accompanied by the increasing application of more sophisticated economic analysis designed to determine the feasibility of major investment projects. The rest of this chapter is therefore devoted to examining the main developments relating to roads, airports and docks and the extent to which the demands were met.

THE ROADS

The key to the road building programme depends very much on the level of government spending since a large part of the finance is derived from central sources. The government is directly responsible for all trunk roads (which includes motorways) including their maintenance, though it may appoint local authorities as agents. Classified roads were the responsibility of local authorities but a large slice of the expenditure on these came in the form of grants from the Exchequer. Local authorities were also entirely responsible for the planning, construction and financing of unclassified roads. In April 1967 the system of classification was changed for purposes of finance. A new category of principal roads, roughly equivalent to the former class I roads, was created, while class II and III roads were combined with unclassified roads. For improvements on principal roads a government grant of 75 per cent was allowed, while various types of rate support grants were available for local authority expenditure on other roads. Apart from the early post-war years, the major source of finance has been the motor fuel tax which in 1971 produced a revenue almost twice as large as that derived from vehicle and licence duties and purchase tax receipts on vehicles combined. Total motor taxation as a proportion of national revenue was nearly 12 per cent in 1971 compared with around 3 per cent in the late 1940s.[3]

Since the main burden of demand for road space has fallen on inter-city trunk routes and the principal roadways in urban areas it is obvious that these should have been accorded priority. And given the nature of financial control it is clear that progress in these sectors would depend very much on the importance which the central government attached to the roadbuilding programme.

Shortly after the end of the war the Labour Government announced an ambitious road programme aimed at improving through communications, reducing traffic congestion, assisting industrial and urban development and promoting road safety. A period of ten years was envisaged for the programme during which time the main national routes would undergo comprehensive reconstruction and a start would be made on building motorways. Expenditure in the first two years alone was planned to run at the rate of £80 million per annum. However the programme never got off the ground since the economic difficulties of these years led to drastic cuts in planned road expenditure. In fact few major improvements or new constructions were made in the period 1946–53 and expenditure on these two items was little more than £5 million per annum. Even disregarding price changes this rate of spending was very much lower than in the later 1930s and, when allowance is made for depreciation, net capital formation in road building must have been negative.[4]

It was not until the mid 1950s that the roads were accorded greater priority in government budgets. In December 1953 the Minister of Transport announced a three year investment plan amounting to £50 million for new construction and major improvements authorised between 1954–57. Further successive increases in the road investment programme were authorised in subsequent years with priority being given to projects of national importance including the first sections of motorway, the Preston by-pass and the London–Birmingham Motorway, both of which were open to traffic by the end of 1959. In 1960 road spending plans were again revised upwards to reach a level of £88 million in 1962–63; emphasis was to be on schemes to relieve urban congestion, though five major projects for through routes, which had been in the pipeline for some time, were also put high on the list. These were the improvement of the Great North Road, a motorway from London to the North West, the Medway Motorway, the Midlands–South Wales route and a road from London to South Wales, including the Severn Bridge. It was anticipated that these projects would be completed by the middle of the decade. At the same time long-term rolling plans were started. Local authorities were to prepare plans on a three year basis with guaranteed grants, while in 1961 the first five year road programme was announced by the Chancellor of the Exchequer. This covered the years 1962–67 when it was envisaged that £607·5 million would be spent on new roads and major improvements in Great Britain. By the mid-1960s reappraisals of projected expenditure had almost doubled this figure for the period 1965–70. It included several new motorway projects and it was anticipated that a 1000 miles of motorway would be in use by the early 1970s.[5]

The increased activity was reflected in the level of spending on roads after 1955. Total road expenditure rose from £137·2 million in 1955 to £301·2 million in 1962, but the amount spent on major improvements and new construction increased much more rapidly, from £14 million to £125·5 million.[6] However, initially there was not much to show for it and it is doubtful whether the increased level of spending up to the early 1960s even managed to make good the original backlog. As Day observed in 1963: 'there is no period since the late twenties when it can possibly be claimed that the road programme has begun to approach requirements. The programme started in the mid-fifties has to try to deal with twenty-five years of neglect as well as with the current and prospective growth of traffic'.[7] By 1962 there were but a mere 151 miles of motorway open to traffic and the increase in road mileage since 1946 amounted to about 12,000 miles most of which was accounted for by unclassified roads. As against a 7 per cent increase in road mileage the number of vehicles on Britain's roads had more than trebled over the period, while total vehicle mileage run rose even faster. As a consequence the number of vehicles per mile of road increased from 17 in 1946 to nearly 54 in 1962. These figures of course tend to give an exaggerated impression of the relationship between the demand for, and supply of, road space since they make no allowance for relief afforded by minor improvements, eg road widening, nor do they take account of variations in the intensity of use of different classes of roads. But few would deny that both visibly and statistically the traffic problem had got worse.

Reasons for the slowness in tackling the road problem are not difficult to find. For a decade or more after the war roads were given a low priority in the budgetary allocations partly because of severe pressures on resources in the reconstruction period, and in times of difficulty this was found to be a fairly easy item to sacrifice. Secondly, neither the Treasury nor the Ministry of Transport were keen to press the case for road expenditure. The Treasury still held the view that public expenditure should be restrained as far as possible and in 1952 it informed the Select Committee on Estimates that as long as road expenditure remained below the pre-war level it was satisfied that no undue extravagance was being incurred. For its part the Ministry of Transport seemed scarcely aware of the pressing need to spend large sums on new roads, and in part this reflected the fact that for some 15 years or more after the war the ministry's estimates of future traffic growth were far too low.[8] Moreover, the ministry was still under the impression that traffic problems could be solved largely by patchwork improvements and judicious control of traffic at crucial points. As late as 1960 the minister had optimistically informed the House of Commons that 'the problem of getting from city to city will not be a problem in about five years' time'. The ministry certainly did not fully appreciate the enormous, and ever increasing, costs arising from congestion, nor was it in a position to carry out the sort of analysis which would have determined whether road projects were viable from social cost-benefit point of view.

By the early 1960s forces and pressures were strong enough to ensure that the decade would witness greater progress. The traffic problem, especially in large urban areas, was already very acute, and it was apparent, from projected estimates of car ownership, that it was going to get very much worse in the future. Current estimates of the cost of congestion indicated that they were already high and that they tended to increase about twice as fast as the growth in traffic.[9] The worst black spots were the urban areas where little major development work had taken place since the war, though various minor improvements and traffic engineering devices had helped to alleviate the problem in the short term. The magnitude and implications of the problem in the cities were brought home clearly by the publication in 1963 of the Buchanan Report on *Traffic in Towns*, which warned of the environmental dangers of allowing uncontrolled access of vehicles to towns. By implication, any attempt to try and accommodate traffic in towns would involve very expensive physical reconstruction of cities in order to avoid a deterioration in the quality of urban environment.

The cost of the whole exercise and the benefits flowing therefrom were not easy to estimate. One made in 1961 suggested that over £3000 million would be needed during the 1960s to make reasonable provision for traffic, on the assumption that it grew at a rate similar to that in the previous decade.[10] But such calculations tended to assume that reasonable accommodation should be made for all traffic which offered itself regardless of whether or not it could be justified on strict economic criteria. Since there was no pricing mechanism for the use of roads the problem was one of finding suitable criteria for assessing road projects. The answer to this difficulty appeared to lie in the application of cost-benefit analysis which would identify all the costs and benefits likely to arise from any projected scheme, convert these to a common monetary standard (by imputing values to items where necessary) and the net annual savings arising could then be expressed as a return on the anticipated capital outlay. Whether the project went forward or not would depend on how the rate of return compared with the current rate of interest or some such acceptable yardstick. This type of analysis was first applied to the London–Birmingham Motorway, the M1, though after the decision had been taken to build it. It concluded in favour of the scheme, though it was suggested that other alternative projects might have been more rewarding.[11] The details of the analysis may be criticised and many of the techniques used have since been improved upon. The methods of measuring the various benefits in monetary terms have been refined and later studies adopted a more sophisticated approach than the crude rate of return on capital, by discounting all benefits and costs to their present value using a selected rate of discount.[12] However the important point is that this marked the beginning of a move towards a more rigorous approach to assessing projects of this sort and during the 1960s the Ministry of Transport became firmly convinced of the utility of appraising major transport projects in this way, including those relating to the roads. This is not to say that the new methods were without defects, but at least it led to a more scientific analysis of investment projects than had been the case in the 1950s. And it could be argued that some of the returns derived from these investigations prompted the need for greater action.

It would be tedious to consider in detail all the many changes in the road programme during the 1960s. As already noted, the Ministry of Transport, in the early 1960s, began to plan expenditure on a rolling five year basis and in most years the projected expenditure was revised upwards throughout the decade, though cuts were made in 1965 and 1968. Primary emphasis was given to the development of trunk routes, including the motorway programme, and the improvement of road communications in large urban areas. The effect in terms of actual spending on roads was dramatic. Total expenditure rose from £238 million in 1960 to £663·7 million in 1969 and the bulk of this increase was absorbed by outlay on new construction and major improvements, which advanced from £81·7 to £392·5 million. Although the total road mileage increased by only a little more than in the previous decade, by the end of 1971 approximately 800 miles of motorway were in service and a start had been made on the reconstruction of many trunk routes. Moreover, by this time further massive programmes, extending through the 1970s and beyond, had already been announced. These entailed the completion of a network of 3500 miles of high quality strategic trunk routes of which about 2000 miles would be motorways. The main aims of the policy were to achieve environmental improvements by diverting traffic from many towns

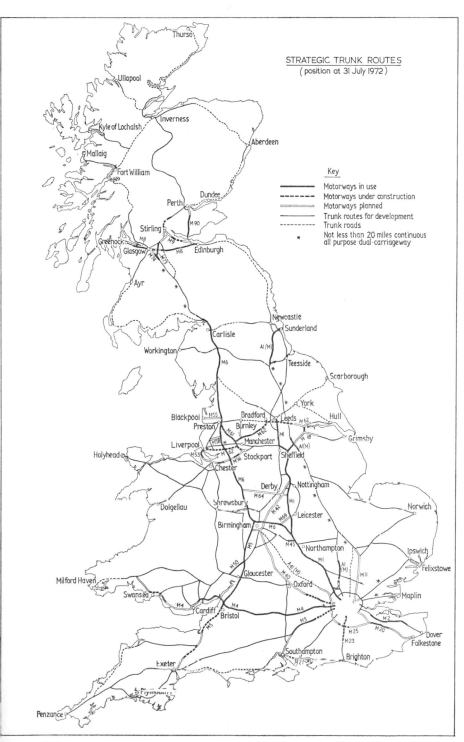

STRATEGIC TRUNK ROUTES
(position at 31 July 1972)

Key

Motorways in use
Motorways under construction
Motorways planned
Trunk routes for development
Trunk roads
Not less than 20 miles continuous
all purpose dual-carriageway

and villages and to connect all major cities, towns, ports and airports to the national network.[13]

At the same time various attempts were made to improve traffic flows, especially in large cities. To further this end many minor road improvement schemes were carried out, as well as the building of by-passes and fly-overs, but principally resort was had to a variety of traffic engineering devices designed largely to reduce impediments to movement, but also in some cases to restrict the right of entry to traffic. These included the use of one-way streets, prohibition of entry into certain streets, parking meters, clearways and linked traffic lights. Most cities have now introduced some or all of these measures and in some cases traffic is actually prohibited from using certain sectors of the city. Moreover, the building of ring-roads or urban motorways also eased the problem of through traffic in some cities. Many of the measures represent no more than temporary expedients though in the short-term they have produced some improvement. In 1964 the London Traffic Management Unit of the Ministry of Transport reported that overall journey speeds had actually improved despite an increase in the volume of traffic, and this could no doubt be attributed to the conversion of central London streets to one-way working and to other improvements designed to ease the traffic flow.[14]

Despite the progress made in the 1960s it was not enough to satisfy the insatiable appetite of the motorist. By 1970 the number of motor vehicles per mile of road had advanced to nearly 72 (as against 48·6 in 1960), a higher average than in almost any other country. Though some improvement had probably taken place on trunk routes, especially where new motorways were in operation, the situation in urban areas seemed to have deteriorated further. In 1968 the Brookings Institute study of Britain's economy was highly critical of the lack of achievement in this respect: 'road congestion in urban centres in Britain is widely acknowledged to be about the most severe in the world and is increasing. In most cities physical capacity of both road and public transport is inadequate. The basic problems are those common to all advanced countries; as in almost all of them, the British attempts at a solution have been belated, piece-meal and inadequate. The result has been a deterioration of urban amenities; the worst of both worlds. These problems stem partly from past transport policies, but they are unlikely to be alleviated by present policies'.[15] Calculations made by Smeed show that between 1956 and 1966 traffic mileage by motor vehicles increased at a much faster rate than the capacity of the road system in urban areas and he estimated that the then current rate of road construction and improvement was only sufficient to provide capacity for about one quarter of the annual increase in traffic. The volume of traffic in urban areas was almost at saturation point. Even to keep pace with the future growth of traffic would require an increase in expenditure of about 70 per cent, and by very much more if any material improvement were to be effected.[16]

Estimates of the cost caused by congestion vary a great deal depending upon the value one attaches to leisure time etc, but there seems little doubt that it has been increasing since the early 1950s. The Road Research Laboratory's revised calculations suggest that congestion costs were rising at the rate of about 5·2 per cent per annum with the total approaching £1000 million in the early 1970s, equivalent to over 2 per cent of Britain's gross domestic product. Even to hold the congestion costs at this level would require an enormous investment in roads during the next couple of decades. Estimates prepared by the Ministry of Transport suggest that between £10,000 and £18,000 million would be required simply to equip urban areas fully to handle the projected forecasts in traffic. This may be compared with a figure of around £2000 million spent on all new construction and major improvements between 1950 and 1969 and with the projected expenditure plans of some £3000 to £4000 million over the next decade or so. On the other hand, the estimated annual savings from containing congestion costs at the present levels would rise progressively from £35 million in 1968 to around £650 million in 1981 (including both economic and social savings), giving an average rate of return on capital invested of approximately 7½ per cent.[17]

The above data would seem to present an incontrovertible case for much more spending on roads in the future. It also makes clear the degree of neglect since the war and how difficult it is to catch up once a significant backlog develops at a time when demand is expanding rapidly. However, the issue itself is not so straight-forward as it appears at first glance. The statistical case for more roads may at first sight seem compelling but when one probes a little more deeply the matter is much less clear cut.

We must first ask whether congestion can be relieved in other ways. Public transport offers an alternative both within cities and on inter-urban routes and it is a well-known fact that buses cause much less congestion per passenger than cars, while railways create none at all. The costs and savings arising from the transfer of traffic to public services must be compared with those to be derived from more road construction if we are to get the right answer. Secondly, there is a danger that the cost-benefit studies of road projects tend to exaggerate the net savings since they often under-estimate the costs and over-value the benefits. For example, no proper allowance is usually made for loss of amenity and com-pensation required by those whose residential facilities are affected adversely as a result of new road schemes;[18] whereas the benefits of road improvement are conferred on those who would probably not be prepared to pay the price for the road space they require. Several writers have argued the case for introducing some kind of pricing system for the roads to overcome this difficulty but there are severe practical difficulties involved in its application. Motorists would argue of course that they are already paying far more to the Exchequer, by way of fuel tax, purchase tax and vehicle and licence duties, than they receive in terms of road expenditure. However, when allowance is made for the fact that part of these taxes is for general revenue purposes, as in the case of imposts on many other commodities for which the consumer receives no return benefit, then the difference is quite small; certainly not sufficient to finance road expenditure on the scale required to relieve congestion fully. Finally, it should be pointed out that many new road improve-ments are designed to relieve congestion at peak periods but for much of the day the assets are relatively underutilised. This could be justified if peak users were prepared to pay the full economic cost (including a going rate of return on capital invested) of providing the additional facilities, but in practice this is unlikely to be the case.

In physical terms there is no question that road capacity has not kept pace with requirements since the war. The visible effects of this are plain for all to see and they do not require spelling out in detail. But it does not automatically follow that large scale spending on roads should ensue. The issues involved in this problem are complex and have only been considered very briefly here. We must first know the cost of alternatives, the full costs and benefits of new road schemes, and how far the motorist is prepared to pay for the burdens he imposes on the community. It is also important to bear in mind that the ultimate cost might be the destruction of the city as we know it if the motor vehicle is allowed to have free and unlimited access. This raises much wider issues regarding urban planning as a whole and in recent years nearly every major town and many smaller ones have been busy producing large scale plans designed to adapt city structures to cope with the changing pattern of transport demand. If this is an indication that city planners are becoming slaves of the motor car then we may have to resign ourselves to the fact that city structures will be quite different in the future.

A POLICY FOR THE AIRPORTS

The enormous growth in air travel since the war has necessitated substantial investment in airport facilities. It was not simply a question of accommodating the growing demand; airport facilities also had to be adapted to meet the requirements of bigger and faster aircraft as a result of rapid changes in technology. The landing and terminal facilities required by today's jumbo jets are vastly different from those used by even the most advanced aircraft of the 1930s. Such developments posed a particularly acute problem for the main international airports, especially those in London since the bulk of the overseas traffic passed through this centre. The smaller provincial airports were also forced to improve their facilities to meet changing patterns of demand though here the question was more one of locational need rather than a problem of capacity restraint.

Before the war airport development had taken place in a most haphazard manner. A large number of sites were established all over the country, the majority owned by municipal authorities. Most were small and unsuited to post-war requirements and it is doubtful whether many of them were financially solvent. During the war many new aerodromes and landing fields were brought into use some of which had hard concrete runways as opposed to grass landing strips. By the end of the war about 700 airfields of one sort or another were in existence some of which could be adapted for civil aviation. The fact that the government already controlled many of the sites seemed to present an ideal opportunity to press forward a co-ordinated plan of airport development to meet the future needs of aviation.

The Labour Government was clearly anxious that its plans for air transport should not be hindered by lack of suitable airports. Accordingly, the white paper on air services envisaged that airfields required for scheduled operations would be owned and managed by the Ministry of Civil Aviation.[19] The need for a co-ordinated plan was emphasised by the Parliamentary Secretary to the Ministry early in 1946: 'if we are to secure the orderly development of transport aerodromes in the right place and up to the right standards, it is necessary to have a central plan'.[20] It was not expected that airports would be able to pay their way in which case the resources for development would have to come from the state. To implement the policy the minister was given wide powers to obtain land which would be required for development.

Good intentions were not translated into effective policy however. No airport plan materialised and the government simply announced in 1947 that the ministry would acquire 44 airports. Reasons for the choice of sites were not given and the distribution of airports between regions was very uneven. Yorkshire and Lancashire were to have four each, but only two were designated for the entire Midlands area. The acquisition policy itself did not get very far. Many of the airports in the programme had not been taken over by the time the Labour Government's term of office came to an end, and even before then the original policy was showing signs of crumbling. In 1950 Manchester Corporation was allowed to retain ownership of Ringway Airport with the ministry agreeing to contribute towards the costs of capital projects. Thereafter the policy became one of disposing of State airports wherever possible and during the 1950s the ministry surrendered several more, mostly to local authorities. By 1961, when this policy of devolution was formally acknowledged in a white paper on civil aerodromes,[21] the state owned 22 airports (including London's airports and several in the remote parts of Scotland), 25 were controlled by local authorities, while 48 private aerodromes were licensed for public transport, most of which were very small and not equipped to deal with regular scheduled flights.

The prime reason for the shift in policy was financial. Ownership of airports proved more costly than originally anticipated. The Select Committee on Estimates reporting in the mid-1950s found that no state-owned airport made a profit and when all operating costs were taken into account it turned out that the ministry was losing about £6 million per annum on the deal. The committee felt that the best course was to encourage the municipal authorities to take over the airports in their areas, and apparently the Treasury was already exerting pressure on the Ministry in this direction in an attempt to relieve the Exchequer of the financial burden. It was also considered that local ownership would lead to a more commercial approach and at the same time serve the needs of particular areas better.[22] The white paper of 1961 played down the financial motive somewhat, no doubt partly because some local authorities, notably Birmingham and Liverpool, were reluctant to take up control through fear of the burden on the rates. Instead it argued that the circumstances which had originally led the state to assume responsibility for the airport programme were fast disappearing. Much of the basic investment had been carried out and financial prospects were changing for the better; airports were approaching a self-supporting basis, Heathrow being quoted as a case in point. Consequently 'there is now less need for assistance from the Government, or for direct Ministerial responsibility and supervision over day-to-day matters in what is largely a business enterprise'. Moreover, the government could see no valid reason why taxpayers in general should foot the bill for airports which served

the inhabitants of particular areas, and in any case local management was probably better adapted to cater for user needs.[23] Apart
from these considerations, the greater degree of freedom given
to private airlines to operate scheduled services also encouraged
the move towards decentralised airport control. Approval for new
flights was more easily obtained if they did not encroach on the
traffic of the air corporations. This meant using airports not served
by the latter, and since the ministry was reluctant to establish
any more, new airports were created by local authorities, eg
Southend and Newcastle, and by private firms, notably Exeter, to
cater for the needs of the independent airlines.

Although the white paper of 1961 envisaged the disposal of most
of the remaining state airports, apart from several serving the
remote parts of Scotland which would require subsidies indefinitely,
it did accept the recommendation of the Select Committee on
Estimates that the main international airports should be retained
and managed by a separate Airports Authority,[24] which would also
plan, build and manage any new airports eventually required.
Legislation to this effect was passed in 1965 and the new British
Airports Authority assumed control of Heathrow, Gatwick,
Stansted and Prestwick on 1 April 1966. The Authority was
expected to pay its way in accordance with the new financial
provisions relating to nationalised industries laid down in 1961

Thus by the end of the 1960s 44 airports were suitable for
scheduled air transport services by aircraft of HS 748 size and
upwards. On the basis of ownership and management they could
be classified into four groups. The British Airports Authority
owned the four main international airports which accounted for
60 per cent of all UK traffic.[25] Municipal authorities owned 19 and
accounted for about 30 per cent of all traffic; the largest airports in
this group were at Manchester, Glasgow, Birmingham, Liverpool
and Southend. The state still owned 12 airports virtually all of
which served the remote parts of Scotland, while the remainder
were operated by private enterprise though one or two of which
were actually owned by the government. Apart from these regular
facilities arrangements were made from time to time for civil
aircraft to use Ministry of Defence airfields.[26]

The absence of any clearly defined policy with regard to airport planning led to an extraordinary fragmented pattern of ownership. This resulted in local rivalries between neighbouring airports, an uneven distribution of facilities with overinvestment in some areas, and the lack of any attempt to co-ordinate regional facilities. For example, in the Midlands rivalry developed between Birmingham and Coventry, while further east, at Castle Donington, yet another airport was established by a consortium of local authorities. There would appear to be little justification for either Coventry or Castle Donington. Coventry Corporation hangs on to its airport, despite the fact that hardly anyone uses it, in the hope that it might be designated as the West Midlands airport. Castle Donington has more traffic but it is badly sited and in any case Birmingham is within easy reach. Similarly, Liverpool and Manchester airports, within 35 miles of each other, spent large sums on developing competing facilities while at the same time Lancashire County Council was advocating the creation of a regional airport between the two at Burtonwood.[27] In the North East there was little attempt at regional co-operation between Newcastle (Woolsington) and the consortium of local authorities which ran Teesside Airport. Altogether £4 million was spent on developing these airports situated roughly 35 miles apart.[28] Again, bitter rivalry developed in the late 1960s between Abbotsinch, the new Glasgow airport, and Prestwick yet the latter could have been linked quite easily with Glasgow for about one half the cost spent in developing Abbotsinch.[29] An even more wasteful allocation of resources developed in the Southampton-Portsmouth conurbation in the 1960s. Within a distance of 50 miles there were no fewer than three airports under different ownership, national, municipal and private, with no attempt whatever at co-operation. They were located at Bournemouth (Hurn), Southampton (Eastleigh, sold to private owners in 1961) and Portsmouth, the old municipal airport established before the war. One regional airport would have sufficed in this area and until 1965 Hurn was the major site handling over 200,000 passengers a year. Subsequently Eastleigh was extensively modernised with the result that most of the traffic transferred from Hurn leaving the latter with a mere 20,000 passengers by

1967. Portsmouth, never a very active airport at the best of times, catered for fewer than 50,000 passengers in 1967. Thus as Hurn and Portsmouth declined Southampton assumed the role of an expanding regional airport. But this was far from ideal. Southampton's airport had obvious drawbacks, notably limitations on further expansion and a noise problem which affects a wide area of population. Hurn would be a far better site for a regional airport since it had sufficient facilities to cope with expanding traffic, good access to London and the noise problem was less acute. Even Portsmouth would be preferable but this airport was recently closed. The Buchanan proposals for South Hampshire also indicated that Eastleigh was unsuitable as a regional airport and it seems quite possible that much of the investment will be wasted if an alternative site is adopted.[30]

The absence of any proper national or even regional planning with regard to airport location undoubtedly led to a serious waste of resources. Far too many airports were developed in close proximity with a consequent duplication of facilities. Many were too small and uneconomic and they often competed with each other in the same catchment area. At the other extreme some regions were inadequately served, if at all. North Wales had no airport while East Anglia fared little better. Excluding London and the remote Scottish airports about 12 regional airports would have been more than sufficient to serve the whole country.[31] In this context it is interesting to note that the Maybury Committee in their plan to rationalise the domestic route structure of the 1930s recommended that activity should be concentrated on a similar number of key centres.[32]

If provincial airport develoment lacked a guiding hand from the centre the same cannot be said for London's airports. The attention lavished on these, both in the past and currently, may have been disproportional to the results achieved. There can be no doubt that they received their fare share of debate and scrutiny, probably not without due cause since London has been by far the major traffic centre and the problems of coping with both volume growth and technological change have been on a vastly different scale from those experienced by any of the provincial airports, even including Manchester, Glasgow and Prestwick. For many years now well over one half of all air travellers have passed through London's terminals and the majority through Heathrow. The history of Britain's airport development since the war would not be complete without some consideration of the changes in the metropolis.

For a time after the war London was served by no fewer than seven airports—Heathrow, Croydon, Northolt, Bovingdon, Gatwick, Blackbushe and Stansted. In 1946 most of the traffic went through Croydon and Northholt, while the others came into operation as reserve airports from 1949 onwards. This was a temporary measure while Heathrow, which had served as a satellite for Northolt during the war, was being developed as London's chief airport. During the course of the 1950s about £28 million was spent on making Heathrow one of the finest international airports in the world and by the end of the decade it was already dealing with 90 per cent of London's passenger traffic. At the same time most of the other airports were abandoned: Northolt was closed to civil flying in October 1954, Bovingdon in April 1956, Croydon, one of the oldest airports, in September 1959 and Blackbushe in May 1960. Of these only Northolt continued to handle significant amounts of traffic until its closure.[33]

This left Gatwick and Stansted and the question of London's second and third airports. In the early 1950s, when the government announced the impending closure of the subsidiary London airports, it was stated that Gatwick would be reconstructed as a second airport with Stansted held in reserve. The expectation was that Heathrow would, by the early 1960s, reach its capacity limits and that a major alternative airport would be required to cope with the expansion of traffic. Though several possible sites were examined Gatwick was considered to be the best and, after a public inquiry, the government announced its intention in 1954 to press forward with the project.[34] Four years later the first stage of the reconstruction of Gatwick was complete and the new airport was officially opened in June 1958.

It soon became apparent however that Gatwick was a costly experiment which was unlikely to provide an adequate solution to

Heathrow's capacity problem. Much of the traffic was seasonal and of short or medium haul since many airlines were reluctant to use Gatwick because of its limitations (it was not suitable for the bigger jets). Consequently it remained badly underutilised. By the early 1960s official doubts were being expressed as to its future role. The original intention had been that Gatwick would serve as a second major airport but it was later stated by the Minister of Aviation that its main functions were to act as a diversionary airport for Heathrow, particularly for short haul and domestic services, and as a base for independent operators, but that it was not intended that it should be a replica of Heathrow as an airport for regular long-haul operators because of its runway limitations. There were certain physical difficulties involved in extending the facilities and the minister felt that the high cost and social disturbances entailed in providing Gatwick with a runway big enough for long range jets to take off fully loaded would not be justified in view of the limited demand and the facilities available at Heathrow.[35]

This clearly suggests that the government was having second thoughts about the viability of Gatwick as a major international airport and in fact, though extensions were subsequently made to the existing runway, plans for further stages of development were quietly shelved. By this time attention was already being focussed on other alternatives, notably Stansted, and the further expansion of facilities at Heathrow.

During the 1950s it became apparent that Heathrow's capacity limits would not be reached as early as originally anticipated since there was still further potential to be exploited. The Millbourne Committee reporting in 1957 was convinced that the airport could be developed to handle (by 1970) up to 80 aircraft movements in the peak hour and up to 64 movements an hour over a continuous three hour stretch, with a maximum annual passenger flow of around 13 million, but beyond that it would not be possible to go without straining the air traffic control capacity of the airport. In view of the fact that the traffic offering was likely to exceed these limits by that date the committee urged that immediate consideration should be given to further stages of development at

Gatwick.[36] The committee's recommendations relating to Heathrow were accepted and during the 1960s the airport's facilities were extended to the extent that by 1970–71 it was handling more than double the number of passengers of a decade earlier (15·7 as against 6·3 million) with the prospect of more to come. In terms of aircraft movements it was operating at about 80 per cent capacity with 75 movements in the peak hour.[37] The second suggestion was not taken up however; instead Stansted was rescued from oblivion to become the subject of study as a possible third London airport, and in the process the subject of a fierce public controversy.

The Stansted episode is a curious affair. In 1953 the white paper on London's airports had concluded that Stansted, originally established as a US Air Force base in 1942, was unsuitable as a site for a major London airport for several reasons: it was on the wrong side of London for most aircraft, access to London by surface transport was poor, it would interefere with military flying in the area and there were problems with regard to air traffic control. Nevertheless, it was decided to retain the airport on a care and maintenance basis as a standby for Heathrow and Gatwick and for training purposes. In practice what this meant was that Stansted saw very little activity and by 1957 most of its traffic consisted of training flights. Nothing more happened until 1961 when the Estimates Committee queried the cost of retaining the site for what seemed to be very little purpose and suggested that an immediate assessment be made to see whether it would be suitable for development as a third London airport. The Committee was anxious lest the vacillation and delay over the development of Gatwick be repeated and intimated that, in view of the money already spent on Stansted, it would be expedient to proceed further with its development.[38]

This rekindled interest in the possibilities of Stansted and within a short space of time it was virtually on the drawing board as the third airport. An inter-departmental committee (the Hole Committee) was set up to inquire into the matter and came out in favour of Stansted. The government accepted its decision, whereupon it conducted a hasty public inquiry into local objections (December 1965 to February 1966) and, upon the recommendation of the inspector, an almost equally hasty review of alternative sites and other complex issues was carried out. By early 1967 the whole exercise was complete and the government announced that after thorough scrutiny the best of all possible sites was Stansted.[39]

It is difficult to believe that Stansted could have become such an attractive proposition in view of its known drawbacks in the early 1950s. In fact it is doubtful whether it had; it still suffered many defects and probably the reason why it came out best was simply because no proper examination or costing of either Stansted or alternative sites were ever made. The Hole Committee had very limited terms of reference which precluded it from examining the wider implications of airport development such as the effect on regional planning, the question of noise and other environmental aspects. The committee, only two members of which had any professional connection with aviation, met 18 times, reviewed 18 sites but visited only one, Stansted. No costs comparisons were made and 'from the start this important decision was governed by expediency and was pushed with a marked lack of other considerations'.[40] It is clear that the Public Inspector was none too happy with the situation since he made no firm recommendation one way or another. In fact he actually stated that a major airport at Stansted 'would be a calamity for the neighbourhood', and that it could only be justified on grounds of national necessity which 'was not proved by evidence of this inquiry'. In view of these misgivings it is not surprising that he recommended a further review. The latter suggestion was accepted but it fell far short of a thorough investigation; it was conducted in secret by government officials intent on producing ammunition for the forthcoming white paper. Only a cursory survey of other sites was conducted; 11 sites were examined but no proper calculation of the costs and benefits was made. Only for the Isle of Sheppey and Stansted were approximate costs prepared and these related simply to the costs of building the airport and its facilities. These came out in favour of Stansted by a large margin. The investigation of prospective noise levels left much to be desired, while the assumption that the third airport should be located in London was never questioned.

It is obvious, therefore, that the choice of Stansted was derived in a very unsatisfactory manner. It was a contrived decision based on the belief that after years of delay Stansted should be utilised regardless of its suitability. Fortunately the saga of Stansted did not end here, for a highly successful lobby forced the government to reconsider the decision and as a consequence a commission was set up to inquire into the matter once again. This proved to be the largest and most sophisticated investigation ever carried out on a public project of this type. The Roskill Commission drew evidence from a galaxy of experts; it held lengthy public hearings, and made extensive use of cost-benefit analysis as a means of assessing the merits of particular sites. The results of its labours appeared in 1970 in nine large and closely written volumes.

Space does not permit a detailed review and critique of the commission's findings. Though it was a far more thorough and sophisticated survey than anything previously attempted, the final results left plenty of scope for doubt and debate.[41] Working on the assumption that the third airport should be located near London, which in itself leaves much room for discussion, the inquiry team eventually short-listed four sites: Cublington (Buckinghamshire), Thurleigh (Bedfordshire), Nuthampstead (Essex) and Foulness (near Southend). The least cost site was found to be Cublington but the margin in its favour over the other sites was very small with the exception of Foulness. Despite the recommendation of Cublington by the commission the government, in April 1971, decided to locate the new airport at Foulness, a decision determined largely by environmental considerations and the force of public opinion. As the *Financial Times* remarked: 'after all the cost-benefit analysis possible is brought to bear, the final choice must be a political one based on hunch. The Government's hunch has led it to support the popular preference for Foulness'.[42]

Whether a *right* decision can ever be reached in such complex matters is to be doubted. The fact the commission chose Cublington did not indicate that it was the best possible of all sites;[43] it was the best of the four investigated in depth and then only in terms of the valuation yardsticks used for measuring the intangibles in this particular instance. Had these been weighted in another way the result might have been quite different. After this expensive exercise the government finally selected the costliest location, a choice which seems to accord more closely with popular opinion, but one which could have been made without mounting such a massive inquiry. It was, moreover, a decision that could have been made a lot sooner had there been a more concerted effort to plan airport development in the post-war period.

Apart from the planning aspect the financial management of airports in the post-war period left much to be desired. Few airports managed to make profits consistently and most of them incurred large losses. The net cumulative losses on the four airports taken over by the Airports Authority for the period 1947–66 amounted to no less than £17·26 million. Not only have most airports failed to pay their way on current account but they have been subsidised heavily on capital account and through the provision of safety and air navigation services by the Board of Trade at far below true cost.

From 1947 onwards several policy statements were made to the effect that it was intended to make airports self-supporting in the long-run, and the move towards decentralised control was aimed in this direction. But by the mid 1950s the Select Committee on Estimates found that the ministry had done little to rectify the situation. Indeed, airport landing charges were virtually the same as in 1948 and little attempt had been made to increase revenue from other sources such as rentals and trading concessions. The committee were annoyed to find that the ministry lacked commercial drive being told that 'the object is not to make as much money as we can on the aerodromes, or even to make them pay'. Apparently the ministry optimistically hoped that as traffic increased losses would be reduced; but in fact this did not happen and the only conclusion to be drawn was that 'the operation of the aerodromes is either so inefficient or so financially insolvent that the more traffic there is ... the greater the loss becomes.'

For their part the ministry put forward several reasons why

charges should not be raised. It was claimed that they were already high by international standards, that any increase would divert traffic to other countries, and that it would force the airlines to raise their fares. These arguments did not convince the committee. Quite rightly, they could see no reason why air travellers should be subsidised at the expense of public funds. 'Direct subsidies may be justified for unremunerative services or specialised development, but the industry is now established and Your Committee can see no justification for such a large indirect subsidy to public and private airways, corporations or companies, both British and foreign, as this enables them to charge fares which, because they do not cover their true cost, are inadequate. Your Committee consider that speed and comfort are important luxuries which should be paid for by those enjoying the amenities and not by the taxpayer at large'. Immediate action to reduce the losses was recommended and failing that the committee suggested that urgent consideration be given to the Vote for Civil Aviation by the Committee of Supply.[44]

Subsequently some progress was made in the direction of financial solvency, particularly at the London airports. Here landing fees were doubled between 1955–6 and 1961–2 and by the latter date Heathrow was making a modest surplus, though state airports as a whole were still losing about £2 million a year.[45] The Estimates Committee were still not happy with the progress achieved. They stressed once again that airport costs must be reflected in the charges made and urged a much more rigorous control of airport financial management.[46] Yet when the Edwards Committee analysed airport returns for 1967–8 it was found that, apart from Heathrow, Manchester and Glasgow, nearly all airports were losing money. Moreover, when account was taken of the cost of air navigation and other services provided by the Board of Trade only a small part of which was recouped, the overall deficit amounted to over £12 million.[47] In a few cases deficits could be justified in that airports served a social need for people living in remote areas, but in most other instances there was no adequate justification for subsidising air travellers. There was no reason at all, for instance, why ratepayers should have subsidised each air passenger using Coventry airport by more than £3·50 or each one using Castle Donington by £1·80.[48]

The improvement in the financial outturn of London's airports during the 1960s is to be welcomed. By 1970–71 all three London airports and Prestwick were profitable and the Airports Authority made a total profit of nearly £23 million over the period 1966–71 as against the cumulative losses of more than £17 million before it took control.[49] The improvement can be attributed to the authority's rigorous financial management and the firm guidlines under which it operates. It is expected to pay its way and self-finance a substantial part of its capital expenditure. It was set a financial target of 14 per cent on average net assets and in the last three years the results have approximated very closely to this rate of return. The recent report by the Select Committee on Nationalised Industries expressed some doubt about the way the level of profits was determined but was satisfied that the BAA was 'as efficient as any airport authority in the world, and to its being in the van of airport research and design'.[50]

PROBLEMS IN THE PORTS

The ports have several features in common with roads and airports. For one thing investment in port and dock facilities lagged seriously behind requirements, especially up to the early 1960s. Secondly, there has been an enormous growth in traffic at UK ports since the war together with a significant change in the composition of trade. Between 1948 and 1970 the quantum of exports doubled while imports expanded more than threefold. As table 26 below shows, the most important structural change on the import side was the rapid growth in petroleum which, by 1970, accounted for well over one half the total. Raw materials and manufactured goods also experienced significant growth but in terms of physical volume they are now easily surpassed by petroleum products. The slowest growing sector was that of food, wine and tobacco which increased by less than one third but remained at slightly less than the 1938 level. As far as exports are concerned, the most notable change was the almost complete disappearance of the coal trade which in 1938 had accounted for the bulk of

Britain's exports in terms of weight. Most of the decline had already taken place by the early post-war years, and though non-coal exports advanced rapidly these were not sufficient to replace the loss of coal. Thus by 1970 the volume of exports was no greater than in 1938 and considerably less than in 1929 and 1939.

Table 26   Estimated weight of UK foreign trade 1938–1970 (million tons)

Imports	1938	1948	1960	1970
Food, tobacco, wine etc	22·0	16·0	20·3	21·4
Raw materials (excluding crude petroleum)	26·3	24·0	38·3	41·8
Mineral fuels and lubricants	11·7	17·2	60·2	125·7
Manufactures (excluding refined petroleum)	7·3	4·7	9·4	14·1
Total	67·3	61·9	128·2	203·0
Exports and re-exports				
Coal	38·2	11·6	6·8	4·6
All other exports	11·5	11·6	25·7	43·9
Total	49·7	23·2	32·5	48·5

Source: Liverpool Steam Ship Owners' Association, *Annual Reports*

A third significant feature, and one that has parallels on the airport side, was the rapid pace of change in ocean transport technology. The late 1950s and 1960s in particular saw a spate of new developments including container ships, giant tankers and ore carriers, hovercraft, LASH (lighter-aboard-ship) vessels, roll-on/roll-off ships and unit load systems of cargo handling. Some of the changes were quite spectacular. For example, in the early post-war years the typical tanker was no more than 20,000 deadweight tons if that, and even by the mid 1950s the first tankers in the 50,000 range were only just on delivery. The closing of the Suez Canal in 1956 gave an immediate boost to the construction of much bigger vessels and by the early 1960s tankers of 100,000 tons or more were on delivery with plans for much larger ships in preparation. By the end of the decade tankers of 200,000 tons and upwards were becoming common and vessels approaching 400,000 tons and even above were on order. The container revolution, regarded by some as of equivalent importance to the changeover from sail to steam in the nineteenth century, has been equally dramatic. In 1962 there were very few containership operators but by the end of the decade about 88 lines offered container services to 200 or so ports throughout the world, though few ships were designed exclusively to carry containers.[51]

Taken together these changes—new transport modes, a rapid expansion in port traffic, the shift in the composition and structure of the import trades, a switch to road access to the ports, and above all the significant increase in ship dimensions in the 1950s and 1960s—were sufficient to call for dock developments on a sweeping scale. They not only necessitated a substantial increase in new facilities but they affected the fundamental design of ports and the procedures required to control their development at the national level.[52] Despite these pressures the ownership and control of ports remained fragmented, as in the case of the airports, though in the 1960s there was some attempt to co-ordinate investment plans at the major ports.[53] Oram identified no fewer than six different types of port management, namely port authorities or statutory bodies, commercial undertakings, municipal control, the British Transport Docks Board, the British Railways Board and the British Waterways Board; and even within these types there was little attempt at standard management practices.[54] Many of the 300 or so port and harbour authorities in Great Britain are very small and for practical purposes the number can be reduced considerably. At the end of the 1960s 17 major ports accounted for 86 per cent of the nation's total trade, while most of the remainder passed through 35 secondary ports.[55] Of the former eight were owned by public trusts,[56] seven by the British Transport Docks Board,[57] while the other two were owned by a local authority (Bristol) and a public limited company (the Manchester Ship Canal Company).[58]

Ownership of the thirty-five secondary ports was even more fragmented: twelve belonged to the state, another twelve were owned by public trusts, five by local authorities, while the remaining six were in private hands. Some were small specialised ports catering for one type of traffic or engaged almost exclusively with coastal shipping. Thus 85 per cent of the trade of Blyth, Sunderland, Poole and Ayr was coastal, while the traffic of Heysham, Par, Fowey and Penarth was concentrated on one commodity. However, the bulk of the traffic of the secondary ports passed through 19 general ports, the most important of which were Dover, Felixstowe, Preston, Harwich, Grimsby, Ipswich and Poole. In recent years they have made good progress in attracting traffic partly as a result of expansion in their unit load services.[59] The privately owned port of Felixstowe has been particularly successful in this respect. Dover and Harwich are also important passenger ports and, together with Folkestone and Newhaven, account for much of the passenger traffic at Britain's ports.[60] The success of some of the smaller ports stems from a variety of factors but it is quite probable that they have gained traffic as a result of deterioration in facilities at some of the major ports. However, it is with the latter that we shall be mainly concerned in this section.

Until well into the 1960s most of the major ports relied heavily on past investment to service the growing requirements of the post-war period. Though they coped reasonably well with traffic expansion it was becoming clear that a policy of make-do and mend on a system whose basic fabric had been laid down in the Victorian era could not continue indefinitely. The Rochdale inquiry into the major ports in the early 1960s drew attention to the low level of investment in Britain's ports compared with that in other transport undertakings and noted that most of the capital expenditure since the war had been in minor works. Total port investment up to 1960 added up to little more than *one* year's investment by the railways or shipping industry. Apart from the Langton/Canada Dock scheme at Liverpool and the provision of the major oil terminals (much of the investment in the latter being provided by the oil companies) no single scheme had cost more than £10 million. Furthermore, no new deep water berths for dry cargo had been constructed since the 1930s, with the exception of Lackenby Dock at Teesport then still incomplete. The absence of deep water berths placed a serious limitation on the size of ships which could be accommodated and in this respect Britain's ports compared unfavourably with those in the United States and on the Continent.

In fact the inability of Britain's major ports to accommodate properly the much larger vessels then coming onto the market was the main factor which eventually forced port authorities and the government into action. Finally, the committee also noted that in many cases there was excessive obsolescent capacity, that there had been little evaluation of investment projects and almost a complete absence of any co-ordination between ports as regards investment.[61]

This sorry state of affairs was perhaps little more than might be expected given the circumstances. The docks had suffered extensive damage during the war so that for a decade or more the authorities were occupied with the work of reconstruction and repair. There was scarcely a major port, with the possible exception of Bristol, which did not require extensive repair work after the war. Total war damage for 33 ports has been estimated at over £28 million and by far the worst hit were Liverpool and London.[62] In Liverpool over one third of the dockside sheds and warehouses were completely destroyed and another third were severely damaged with the result that many berths were put out of action. A major programme of reconstruction, costing some £25 million, was carried out by the Mersey Docks and Harbour Board but it was not until the end of the 1950s that most of the damage had been made good. The Port of London Authority faced a similar situation. About one third of its facilities were destroyed and much of the authority's energy and finance were devoted to reconstruction and repair work in this period. Moreover, in the early years after the war the low priorities assigned to raw material allocations and construction permits for dock work inevitably slowed down the task.[63] Thus for a decade or more after the war port authorities were occupied either with repair work and catching up with the backlog of maintenance caused by the war, or with the problem of trying to adapt their structures in an attempt to meet expanding requirements.

A second factor which militated against investment in large scale projects was the unsatisfactory financial state of many ports. The Rochdale Committee found that no major port succeeded in earning sufficient revenue to meet working expenses, interest on loans, taxation and depreciation of assets on a replacement cost basis. Any further replacement of assets or new development would require borrowing on an increasing scale with the result that the financial position would likely worsen unless remedial action were taken.[64] The main factor behind the financial difficulties was the unsatisfactory pricing system, a problem common to many transport undertakings in this period especially those in the nationalised sector. It would take far too long to unravel in detail the complexities of port charging procedures, but briefly stated port charges had in the past lagged behind costs, while inadequate accounting systems had made the proper costing (and hence pricing) of port facilities and services impossible. That charges at British ports were sometimes higher than those at continental ports begs several questions including that of comparative efficiency, but the fact remains that the level of charges was frequently too low to cover costs and provide resources for investment. Statutory control of charges had not made it easy for the ports to adjust their charges when the need arose, while the predominance of user elements on the Boards of the major ports had led to artificially low charges being maintained, and also to some confusion as to what the operating criteria of a port should be. In short therefore, it could be argued that had the price mechanism been allowed to operate freely the true cost of inadequate or inefficient port facilities would have been demonstrated together with the benefit to be had from greater investment.[65]

In any event there is some doubt as to whether the limited investment made in the fifteen years or so after the war was in fact allocated in the most efficient manner. Certainly there was little in the way of rigorous evaluation of specific investment projects and no means existed by which to co-ordinate the investment plans of the ports as a whole. Indeed, as one paper commented, the system of port administration 'could hardly be further removed from any kind of co-ordinated, overall plan; on the contrary, every one of Britain's scores of ports has pursued its own individual development'.[66] The fact that many estuaries had a number of competing ports inevitably gave rise to wasteful duplication of facilities and an inherent reluctance to abandon obsolete capacity.

The rivalry between Bristol and the South Wales ports is a good case in point. And even in the case of the latter ports, which were under the same management (the BTC and then the British Transport Docks Board), not much progress was made in rationalising facilities and reducing excess capacity.[67] In the absence of any directional guidance it was perhaps only to be expected that not all investment expenditure embarked upon would yield a satisfactory return.

Given the unsatisfactory state of the port industry it was obvious that unless drastic action was taken quickly the ports would be unable to meet anticipated future requirements. Not surprisingly therefore the Rochdale Committee recommended fairly sweeping changes. The committee stressed the prime need for a properly planned programme of port development. For this purpose it proposed the creation of a National Ports Authority whose 'most vital function would be to supervise the development of ports in accordance with a national plan'. The authority would assess all schemes put forward by the individual ports and all projects above a minimum figure should be made subject to its approval. In this way the authority could evaluate all schemes and rank them in order of priority; it could then reject schemes which it felt to be undesirable and propose new schemes considered essential to the national interest. The committee also felt that co-ordinated investment planning would be achieved more easily within a system of estuarial authorities. Hence it recommended that the NPA should submit to the minister schemes for the creation of new estuarial authorities incorporating a number of docks. Specifically it listed the ports of the Bristol Channel, the Clyde, the Forth, the Tyne and the Tees, the Humber and Southampton for treatment in this way.

As regards new developments the most pressing problem was the need for more deep water berths. The committee felt that high priority should be given to developing those at Tilbury, Southampton, Leith and the Tees. Urgent consideration should also be given to the provision of better ore importing facilities on the South Wales coast. These of course were only the basic priorities designed to provide a rapid increase in port capacity and the committee was fully aware that further schemes would have to be considered at an early stage, notably for the Humber ports, the Upper Bristol Channel and the Clyde, and for more ore terminals. Moreover, expenditure on modernisation and improvement of existing facilities and the need to improve efficiency, especially by way of greater mechanisation, were no less urgently required.

Finally the Rochdale Committee had clear and specific proposals relating to financial matters. The unsatisfactory financial condition of the major ports had caused the committee some concern since it rejected the notion that ports should be run as a public service. They should be regarded as commercial undertakings and if this were to be achieved a thorough overhaul of their financial and accounting machinery was imperative. A more realistic pricing policy, including the abandonment of statutory control over port charges, would be required if the ports were to become financially viable undertakings. Limited supervision over port charges should be undertaken by the National Ports Council which would take steps to simplify the complicated system of charging and make it more scientific. The committee firmly rejected the case for subsidising port developments—ports should finance their own schemes either by loans or internally—though it recognised that in certain cases government loans or grants might be justified.

Many of the recommendations[68] were accepted by the government though they did not always materialise in the form envisaged by the committee. In July 1963 the National Ports Council (with Lord Rochdale as chairman) was established and given statutory backing by the Harbours Act of 1964. However, it was a somewhat weaker body than that envisaged by the inquiry. It had no direct executive powers (except to collect statistical data and initiate research) and it could only advise or recommend policies to the Minister of Transport who was given wide powers over ports and their organisation and who in the final analysis took the decisions.[69] Though the council had no power to initiate schemes of development it was entrusted with most of the functions of planning and reviewing future developments. In particular, it was to formulate a comprehensive plan for the development of harbours in Britain which meant in practice considering all the plans put forward by the individual ports, and assessing and co-ordinating these proposals to secure maximum benefit. It could also submit schemes to the Minister relating to the amalgamation of ports on an estuarial basis, advise on procedures designed to simplify charging policies, assist port authorities in the execution of their projects (after they had been approved by the minister) and encourage them to perform their duties as efficiently as possible.

The Act also included a number of important financial provisions. Investment control was exercised by the minister in that all schemes costing £500,000 or more had to be submitted for his approval after consultation with the council. Projects below this amount and maintenance and routine repair work were excluded from control. Approved harbour schemes could qualify for assistance in the form of loans and grants (20 per cent modernisation grants) up to a maximum aggregate of £50 million at any one time (this could be raised to £100 million subject to House of Commons' consent). Finally, most of the existing statutory controls over charges were abolished and it was expected that port authorities should so conduct their affairs as to ensure financial viability.[70]

What then was achieved by the introduction of a more vigorous policy for the ports? There can be little doubt that it provided a considerable stimulus to investment. By 1966 investment was running at twice the rate of the early 1960s and over the period 1966–70 total investment in docks and harbours amounted to £230 million (of which about £30 million was in the form of grants), which was greater than the total amount spent in the period from the end of the war to 1960. The bulk of the expenditure went on new works at the major ports. Almost from the beginning the National Ports Council was literally deluged with proposals for large scale projects from most of the chief ports and a number of lesser ones, and under the impression that there was no time to be lost it hurriedly prepared an interim plan. Most of the proposals submitted were accepted and in all the plan recommended development schemes at 14 ports involving the construction of 70 new berths and the renovation of about 46 existing ones. The total cost would be in the region of £150–155 million; major works at

London, Southampton, Bristol, Liverpool and Hull would absorb about £115 million, while the remainder was to be spent at Newport, Swansea, Manchester, Glasgow, Greenock, Grangemouth, Leith, Immingham and the Tees. The Council emphasised that the proposals only represented a minimum to deal with expected traffic by the early 1970s and hinted that much more would be forthcoming in due course. It also took some pains to stress the urgency of prompt action: 'The arrears are serious and the prospective growth of traffic considerable; the schemes are urgently necessary, and should go ahead as quickly as possible'.[71] In fact most of them did except the Portbury project at Bristol which was turned down by the minister.

Before discussing the wisdom of the council's zealous haste it might be convenient to review briefly some of its other activities. In the interim plan reference was made to two important long-term tasks, that of effecting amalgamation of ports by estuary and reforming the constitutions of port authorities, and the need to bring about improvements in port finances which involved the overhaul of charging systems. Progress with schemes of reorganisation was somewhat slower than anticipated but by 1970 new estuarial authorities had been established for the Tyne, Tees Forth and Clyde, while at Southampton and the Humber the British Transport Docks Board had taken over as the estuarial authority. Only the ports in the Bristol Channel had not been dealt with in the manner suggested by the Rochdale Committee. The process of reorganisation and amalgamation was accompanied by a much overdue streamlining of the constitutions and boards of the relevant port authorities. For example, one board composed of about 15 members replaced three with a total of 79 members on the Clyde, while reconstitution orders for slimming the boards at other ports were promulgated.[72]

On the financial side the council was less successful. The task of overhauling the accounting systems of the ports and their charging policies proved far from easy. In fact the financial position got worse during the later 1960s; many port authorities were sliding into deficit the culmination of which came with the dramatic financial crisis of the Mersey Docks and Harbour Board in the latter half of 1970 after the government refused to come to its rescue. After this event the government reaffirmed its faith in the principle of securing financial viability but offered to assist port authorities to put their house in order by providing loans to authorities encountering difficulties over the renewal of their debt. Part of the problem could be attributed to the fact that little had been done to rationalise or adapt the system of port charging. It is true that some charges had been raised but at the end of the 1960s the council was still pondering over the question of restructuring the charging system in a way (presumably) that would reflect costs more accurately. The delay may have been caused partly by the Labour Government's proposals for nationalising all the principal ports, but it certainly proved a costly one.

Although a considerable programme of new work had been carried out at the ports by the early 1970s reservations have been expressed about the allocation of the investment. It has been argued, for example, that a co-ordinated investment programme such that the most profitable use is made of available resources, has not been possible in practice due to the competing claims of rival ports and the lack of effective central control over investment programmes. There is some basis for this contention though the extent to which it led to a misallocation of resources or to over-investment in port facilities is difficult to establish precisely. It is a known fact that when the new policies were introduced the authorities were anxious to ensure that all the major ports should make up for past neglect and that they should be equipped to cope with the anticipated growth of traffic and the latest vessels. We noted earlier that the National Ports Council rather hurriedly prepared its interim plan containing large schemes for most of the main ports; these it had little time to check in detail but it was convinced that they were desirable in view of the urgency of the situation. Moreover, the council was notably reluctant initially to use the recommended investment appraisal techniques (discounted cash flow rate of return) partly because of difficulties over port pricing procedure which had still not been solved. The result was 'an inbuilt tendency to encourage any port investment without the realisation that this may result in wasteful competition . . .'.

But so long as the individual ports were able to present viable schemes (that is properly appraised) and the ministry had the power to check and ultimately veto any project that did not measure up to the stipulated criteria, there would seem to be little reason for doubts on this score. However, the matter was not quite so straightforward as it may seem at first sight. Though many of the projects appear to have satisfied the 8 per cent rate recommended, at least as far as we can tell from the limited information released on the projects, this does not mean that the appraisal procedures used were well-founded, or even in fact the right ones (see below). Secondly, the fact that the NPC and the ministry had to rely on proposals thrown up by the individual ports working independently of one another could lead to undesirable consequences. The tendency was to consider each plan separately rather than as part of a national programme. Feasible alternatives were never considered since the main force behind the control and vetting procedure was essentially negative, that of withholding approval from schemes rather than determining the best alternative. Finally, it was possible for each port authority to present its claim in the most favourable way possible but only at the expense of other ports, and unless there was proper cross-checking and co-ordination this could lead to overinvestment in facilities.

With reference to the last point the classic case in question was the £27 million project of the Port of Bristol Authority for Port-bury. The claim was based on the assumption that 2 million tons of cargo would be exported through the port by 1980, that is a ten-fold increase in traffic on 1963–4. The National Ports Council favoured the project even though recognising it to be risky, but the ministry was far less happy about it and proceeded to mount a fuller appraisal of the scheme. This showed that Bristol's traffic projections were wildly optimistic, being based on the diversion of unrealistic amounts of cargo from other ports (mainly London and Liverpool), and even on the original estimates the return was somewhat less than the minimum normally required. Fortunately in this case the scheme was turned down and one wonders whether a more intensive reassessment of other projects would have put a different complexion on their viability in some cases.

With regard to container berth planning there was certainly an over-inflation of claims as a result of competitive bidding. Greenock and Liverpool, for instance, justified their claims to construct container berths for transatlantic traffic partly on the grounds that each would capture the traffic of the North of England. Eventually no fewer than six ports submitted plans for container berths to serve this route despite the fact that the number required was four at the most and they could probably have been concentrated at one deep water port. But many port authorities, realising the opportunities offered by containers and anxious not to lose out on the deal, desperately sought to back their claims by overestimating their traffic potential through diversion, a practice which would clearly produce an aggregate estimate greater than the total traffic realisable. As the report on container transport commissioned by the NPC pointed out, 'many ports give the impression of planning facilities on the basis of hope, rather than on any rational prediction of the future'. No doubt the council and the ministry subsequently evaluated the proposals, but they appear either not to have appreciated the economics of the situation or else they were powerless to effect a more rational allocation of facilities. For, despite the monopoly approved for container traffic on the Australian route (all through Tilbury), the ministry conceded the claims of a number of ports to construct container terminals for the transatlantic trade.

The inherent weakness in planning procedure was not the only problem. Doubts have been cast on the methods used for investment appraisal. The ministry was clearly anxious to impose greater financial discipline on investment decision-making and during the 1960s port projects were subject to much more sophisticated analysis than they had been in the past. Unfortunately no generally accepted method of appraising port investment had been devised. The ministry and the NPC (the latter rather reluctantly), following the guidelines laid down by the Treasury, utilised the discounted cash flow approach for appraising port investments. But, as Goss has pointed out, this type of analysis is not altogether satisfactory when applied to the ports since their charges bear little relationship to long or short-run average or marginal costs. A pricing system unrelated to costs will not only tend to understate the level of investment required in some cases and overstate it in others thereby distorting its allocation, but it will fail to reflect fully the social costs involved. Given the defects of the pricing system Goss suggests the use of an overall cost-benefit approach though the valuation of the benefits poses a difficult problem in this particular case. This approach has so far not been used to evaluate specific port projects hough it will no doubt be increasingly employed as the question of port investment becomes more closely associated with regional planning and with the council's proposed maritime industrial development areas.

Whatever criticisms might be levelled at the investment and planning procedures of the 1960s the ports do appear to have undergone considerable improvement. Not only was there a significant expansion in facilities and new dock accommodation but methods of handling cargo and conditions of work were being radically transformed, so much so that 'the modern port is almost unrecognisable to pre-war eyes'. By the turn of the decade the ports were no longer lagging behind events, or so it would seem. The Rochdale Committee on Shipping reporting in 1970 stated that 'it can no longer be said that, in the matter of port facilities and relative to the country's needs, UK ports are today really behind events'. The Government too was happy with the progress achieved: 'the ports have been substantially modernised and equipped with facilities which compare favourably with those in other countries. Far-reaching improvements have been made in operating methods and in working conditions'. Even the high level of UK port charges compared with those at continental ports could be explained away by the more lavish government assistance given to ports abroad. One suspects that these comments were a little on the optimistic side, but they do indicate some measure of improvement had taken place during the 1960s.

Select Bibliography

The following bibliography only provides a select number of writings on British transport to assist those readers who wish to inquire further into particular topics. A comprehensive bibliography was out of the question since for the post-1945 period alone the author's card index runs to well over 1500 items. Most of the entries refer to the post-war period since a comprehensive bibliography on the pre-1939 period can be found in H. J. Dyos and D. H. Aldcroft, *British Transport* (1969). Reference is given for only a few key official publications since a complete list would fill nearly a chapter.

BOOKS

D. H. Aldcroft	*British Railways in Transition: The Economic Problems of Britain's Railways since 1914* (1968)
G. F. Allen	*British Railways after Beeching* (1966)
J. H. Appleton	*Geography of Communications in Great Britain* (1962)
C. K. Atkins	*People and the Motor Car* (1964)
A. G. Bain and S. T. Bonnington	*The Hydraulic Transport of Solids by Pipeline* (1970)
B. T. Bayliss and S. L. Edwards	*Transport for Industry* (1968 HMSO)
B. T. Bayliss and S. L. Edwards	*Industrial Demand for Transport* (1970 HMSO)
E. Bennathan and A. A. Walters	*The Economics of Ocean Freight Rates* (1969 New York)
J. Bird	*Major Seaports of the United Kingdom* (1963)
M. R. Bonavia	*The Organisation of British Railways* (1971)
A. H. J. Bown and W. A. Fleve	*Port Economics* (1967, 2nd edn)
G. W. Briggs	*Road Haulage Management* (1965, 2nd edn)

P. W. Brooks   *The Modern Airliner: Its origins and develop-*
                        ment (1961)
R. Y. Chuang   *The International Air Transport Association*
                        (1972, Leiden)
G. Clayton and   *The Economic Problems of Rural Transport in*
J. H. Rees   *Wales* (1967)
W. P. Clegg and   *British Nationalised Shipping, 1947–1968* (1969)
J. S. Styring
M. H. Cooper and   *The Price of Air Travel* (1971, Hobart Paper 53)
A. K. Maynard
D. Corbett   *Politics and the Airlines* (1965)
A. D. Couper   *The Geography of Sea Transport* (1972)
A. G. Course   *Docks and Harbours of Britain* (1964)
R. E. G. Davies   *History of the World's Airlines* (1964)
A. C. L. Day   *Roads* (1963)
B. M. Deakin and   *Productivity in Transport: A Study of Employ-*
T. Seward   *ment, Capital, Output, Productivity and*
                        Technical Change (1969)
R. S. Doganis   *A National Airport Plan* (1967, Fabian Tract
                        377)
J. Drake et alia   *Motorways* (1969)
H. J. Dyos and   *British Transport: An Economic Survey from*
D. H. Aldcroft   *the Seventeenth Century to the Twentieth*
                        (1969)
S. L. Edwards and   *Operating Costs in Road Freight Transport*
B. T. Bayliss   (1971, HMSO)
A. A. Evans   *Technical and Social Changes in the World's*
                        Ports (1969, Geneva)
P. Ford and   *Coastwise Shipping and the Smaller Ports* (1951)
J. A. Bound
C. D. Foster   *The Transport Problem* (1963)
C. W. Glover   *Urban Traffic Congestion* (1966)
R. O. Goss   *Studies in Maritime Economics* (1968)
H. Gripaios   *Tramp Shipping* (1959)
K. M. Gwilliam   *Transport and Public Policy* (1964)
G. Hallett and   *Maritime Industry and Port Development in*
P. Randall   *South Wales* (1970)
J. Hibbs   *The History of British Bus Services* (1968)
J. Hibbs   *Transport for Passengers* (1971 2nd edn, Hobart
                        Paper 23)

M. Hubbard   *The Economics of Transporting Oil to and Within Europe* (1967)

International Civil   *A Review of the Economic Situation of Air Aviation Organisation   Transport 1957–1967* (1968, Montreal)

K. M. Johnson and   *The Economics of Containerisation* (1971)
H. C. Garnett

S. Joy   *The Train that Ran Away* (1973)

A. L. King et al. (eds) *Proceedings of Hydrotransport: The First International Conference on Hydraulic Transport of Solids in Pipes* (1970)

A. G. M. Koch   *Current Pricing Behaviour in Liner Shipping* (1965, Bergen)

H. M. Kolsen   *The Economics and Control of Road-Rail Competition* (1969, Sydney)

J. Longhurst   *Nationalisation in Practice: The Civil Aviation Experiment* (1950)

B. N. Metaxas   *The Economics of Tramp Shipping* (1971)

R. Miller and   *The Technical Development of Modern Aviation*
D. Sawers   (1968)

E. V. Morgan   *Economic and Financial Aspects of Road Improvements* (1965)

R. S. Nielson   *Oil Tanker Economics* (1959, Bergen)

C. O'Loughlin   *The Economics of Sea Transport* (1967)

R. B. Oram   *The Story of Our Ports* (1969)

R. B. Oram and   *The Efficient Port* (1971)
C. C. R. Baker

OECD   *Maritime Transport 1970 and a Review of the '60s* (1971)

G. H. Peters   *Cost Benefit Analysis and Public Expenditure* (1968 2nd edn, Eaton Paper 8)

K. G. J. Pillai   *The Air Net: The Case Against the World Aviation Cartel* (1969)

W. Plowden   *The Motor Car and Politics 1896–1970* (1971)

G. Polanyi   *Comparative Returns from Investment in Nationalised Industries* (1968)

G. Polanyi   *Contrasts in Nationalised Transport Since 1947* (1968. Background Memoranda 2, IEA)

H. Pollins   *Britain's Railways: An Industrial History* (1971)

G. J. Ponsonby   *Transport Policy: Co-ordination Through Competition* (1969, Hobart Paper 49)

R. Pryke   *Public Enterprise in Practice: the British Ex-*
                    perience of Nationalization over Two Decades
                    (1971)
J. Pudney   *The Seven Skies: A Study of BOAC and its*
                    Forerunners Since 1919 (1959)
H. Rees   *British Ports and Shipping* (1958)
G. L. Reid and   *Nationalised Industries* (1970)
    K. Allen
D. J. Reynolds   *Economics, Town Planning and Traffic* (1966)
H. W. Richardson   *Urban Economics* (1971)
P. Ritter   *Planning for Man and Motor* (1964)
W. Robson   *Nationalised Industry and Public Ownership*
                    (1960)
A. Rosenberg   *Air Travel Within Europe* (1970, Stockholm)
G. Roth   *Paying for Roads: The Economics of Traffic*
                    Congestion (1967)
J. R. Sargent   *British Transport Policy* (1958)
C. I. Savage   *Inland Transport* (1957)
C. I. Savage   *An Economic History of Transport* (1966, rev
                    edn)
K. Sealy   *The Geography of Air Transport* (1966)
C. Sharp   *The Problem of Transport* (1965)
C. Sharp   *Problems of Urban Passenger Transport* (1967)
C. Sharp   *Transport Economics* (1973)
C. Sharp   *Living with the Lorry* (1973)
J. M. W. Stewart   *A Pricing System for Roads* (1965)
M. R. Straszheim   *The International Airline Industry* (1969)
A. H. Stratford   *Air Transport Economics in the Supersonic Era*
                    (1967)
S. G. Sturmey   *British Shipping and World Competition* (1962)
S. G. Sturmey   *On the Pricing of Tramp Ship Freight Service*
                    (1965, Bergen)
S. G. Sturmey   *Consideration of the Ends and Means of National*
                    Shipping Policy (1965, Bergen)
A. S. Svendsen   *Trends in World Seaborne Shipping* (1965,
                    Bergen)
J. C. Tanner   *Factors Affecting the Amount of Travel* (1961,
                    HMSO)
J. Tetlow and A. Goss *Homes, Towns and Traffic* (1968, 2nd edn)

A. W. J. Thomson and   *The Nationalised Transport Industries* (1972)
L. C. Hunter
R. F. Trillo   *Marine Hovercraft Technology* (1971)
A. A. Walters   *Integration in Freight Transport* (1968)
A. A. Walters   *The Economics of Road User Changes* (1968)
M. Webb   *Transporting Goods by Road* (1972)
S. Wheatcroft   *Economics of European Air Transport* (1956)
S. Wheatcroft   *Air Transport Policy* (1964)
G. L. Wilson   *Nationalisation of Transport in Great Britain*
                       (1949, Washington)
R. Worcester   *Roots of British Air Policy* (1966)

ARTICLES

M. E. Beesley and   'The Victoria Line: Social Benefits and
C. D. Foster   Finances', Journal of the Royal Statistical
                       Society, A128 (1965)
M. E. Beesley and   'Urban Form, Car Ownership and Public
J. F. Kain   Policy: An Appraisal of Traffic in Towns',
                       Urban Studies, 1 (1964)
M. E. Beesley and   'A Study of the Profits of Bus Companies,
J. Politi   1960–1966', *Economica*, 36 (1969)
D. Bejakovic   'The Share of Transport and Communications
                       in Total Investment', *Journal of Transport
                       Economics and Policy*, 4 (1970)
J. W. S. Brancker   'The Effect of Nationalisation on Air Trans-
                       port', *Journal of the Institute of Transport*, 23
                       (1949)
J. W. S. Brancker   'Air and Sea Competition on the North
                       Atlantic', Institute of Transport Journal, 29
                       (1962)
P. Brooks   'Development of Air Transport', *Journal of
                       Transport Economics and Policy*, 1 (1967)
R. H. Brown and   'Cost Savings from One-Man Operation of
C. A. Nash   Buses', *Journal of Transport Economics and
                       Policy*, 6 (September 1972)
A. F. R. Carling   'Control in Passenger Road Transport: A
                       View of Service Licensing after 35 years',
                       Institute of Transport Journal, 31 (1966)

J. L. Carr 'The Case for Discriminatory Rail Charges', *Journal of the Institute of Transport*, 28 (1960)

W. F. Cassie 'Roads in the British Economy', *Institute of Transport Journal*, 33 (1970)

M. Chisholm 'Economics of Scale in Road Goods Transport? Off-Farm Milk Collection in England and Wales', *Oxford Economic Papers*, 11 (1959)

C. M. Cunningham 'The Dock Industry in Merseyside', in R. Lawton and C. M. Cunningham (ed.), Merseyside; *Social and Economic Studies* (1970)

D. M. Dear 'Some Thoughts on the Comparative Costs of Road and Rail Transport', Bulletin of the Oxford University Institute of Statistics, 24 (1962)

R. S. Doganis 'Airport Planning and Administration: A Critique', *The Political Quarterly* (1966)

P. Donaldson 'Transport and Public Policy in the U.K.', *Applied Economic Papers*, 3 (1963)

A. C. Durie 'The Road Programme', *National Westminster Bank Review*, 68 (1964)

S. L. Edwards 'Transport Costs in British Industry', *Journal of Transport Economics and Policy*, 4 (1970)

P. K. Else and M. Howe 'Cost Benefit Analysis and Railway Services', *Journal of Transport Economics and Policy*, 3 (1969)

A. W. Evans 'Inter-City Travel and the London Midland Electrification', *Journal of Transport Economics and Policy*, 3 (1969)

S. A. Finnis 'Progress in the Ports', *Institute of Transport Journal*, 32 (1969)

L. Foides 'Domestic Air Transport Policy', *Economica*, 28 (1961)

R. C. Fordham 'Airport Planning in the Context of the Third London Airport', *Economic Journal*, 80 (1970)

R. T. Foster 'Pipeline Development in the United Kingdom', *Geography*, 54 (1969)

A. H. Fox 'Fare Fixing in Air Transport', *Three Banks Review*, 35 (1957)

H. C. Garnett — 'Competition Between Ports and Investment Planning', *Scottish Journal of Political Economy*, 17 (1970)

J. M. Gifford — 'Rochdale 1962 and 1967', *Institute of Transport Journal*, 32 (1967)

R. O. Goss — 'Towards an Economic Appraisal of Port Investments', *Journal of Transport Economics and Policy*, 1 (1967)

R. O. Goss — 'Some Financial Aspects of Shipping Companies', *Journal of Transport Economics and Policy*, 5 (1967)

K. M. Gwilliam — 'The Regulation of Air Transport', *Yorkshire Bulletin of Economic and Social Research*, 18 (1966)

K. M. Gwilliam — 'Domestic Air Transport Fares', *Journal of Transport Economics and Policy*, 2 (1968)

P. Hall — 'Transportation', *Urban Studies*, 6 (1969)

K. Hammarskjöld — 'The 70s—Challenging Years for the World Air Transport System', *Institute of Transport Journal*, 33 (1970)

A. J. Harrison — 'Economies of Scale and the Structure of the Road Haulage Industry', *Oxford Economic Papers*, 15 (1963)

P. E. Hart — 'The Efficiency of the Road Haulage Industry under Nationalization', *Journal of Industrial Economics*, 2 (1953–54)

P. E. Hart — 'The Quality of Nationalised Road Haulage', *Journal of Industrial Economics*, 6 (1957–58)

E. K. Hawkins — 'The Political Economy of British Transport', *Annals of Collective Economy*, 33 (1962)

W. P. Hildred — 'From Subsonic to Supersonic', *Journal of the Royal Society of Arts* (1965)

R. Holloway — 'The Problems of the Ports', *Lloyds Bank Review*, 99 (1971)

M. Howe and P. K. Else — 'Railway Closures: Recent Changes in Machinery and Policy', *Public Administration* (1968)

H. C. Johnson — 'Twenty Years of Nationalised Railways', *National Provincial Bank Review*, 83 (1968)

J. Johnston   'Scale, Costs and Profitability in Road Passenger Transport', *Journal of Industrial Economics*, 4 (1956)

C. D. Jones   'The Performance of British Railways, 1962 to 1968', *Journal of Transport Economics and Policy*, 4 (1970)

M. G. Kendall   'Losses of U.K. Merchant Ships in World War II', *Economica*, 15 (1948)

R. M. Kirwan   'Economics and Methodology in Urban Transport Planning', in J. B. Cullingworth and S. C. Orr (eds.), *Regional and Urban Studies: A Social Science Approach* (1969)

G. H. C. Lee   'The New Mass Market in Air Travel', *Institute of Transport Journal*, 31 (1965)

N. Lee   'A Review of the Transport Bill', *District Bank Review*, 165 (1968)

N. Lee and I. Steedman   'Economies of Scale in Bus Transport I. Some British Municipal Results', *Journal of Transport Economics and Policy*, 4 (1970)

D. L. McLachlan   'The Price Policy of Liner Companies', *Scottish Journal of Political Economy*, 10 (1963)

D. Marx Jr.,   'Regulation of International Liner Shipping and Freedom of the Seas', *Journal of Industrial Economics*, 16 (1967–68).

P. G. Masefield   'Some Economic Factors in Air Transport Operation', *Journal of the Institute of Transport*, 24 (1951)

P. G. Masefield   'Air Transport: A Statistical and General Review of its Economic Problems', *Manchester Statistical Society*, (1953–54)

P. Masefield   'The Modern Airport and its Future', *Journal of the Royal Society of Arts*, 116 (1968)

G. Mills   'Investment Planning for British Ports', *Journal of Transport Economics and Policy*, 5 (1971)

Ministry of Transport   'Motor Car Ownership and Use', *Economic Trends*, 116 (1963)

E. J. Mishan   'What is Wrong with Roskill?' *Journal of Transport Economics and Policy*, 4 (1970)

D. L. Munby   'Economic Problems of British Railways',
                      Bulletin of the Oxford University Institute of
                      Statistics, 24 (1962)
D. L. Munby   'The Economics of City Traffic', in T. E. H.
                      Williams (ed), Urban Survival and Traffic
                      (1962)
D. L. Munby   'The Reshaping of British Railways', Journal of
                      Industrial Economics, 11 (1962–63)
D. L. Munby   'British Industry Today. 7. Inland Transport',
                      Journal of the Institute of Bankers, 85 (1964)
D. L. Munby   'The Economics of Road Haulage Licensing',
                      Oxford Economic Papers, 17 (1965)
D. L. Munby   'Mrs Castle's Transport Policy', Journal of
                      Transport Economics and Policy, 2 (1968)
H. E. Osborn   'Road Haulage and Roads', Institute of Trans-
                      port Journal, 31 (1966)
D. W. Pearce   'The Roskill Commission and the Location of
                      the Third London Airport', Three Banks
                      Review, 87 (1970)
Political and   'The Birtish Shipping Industry', Planning, 25
  Economic Planning   (1959) 437
M. V. Posner   'Pricing and Investment in Nationalised In-
                      dustries', in A. Cairncross (ed), The Man-
                      aged Economy (1970)
A. R. Prest   'Some Aspects of Road Finance in the U.K.',
                      The Manchester School (1963)
D. A. Quarmby   'Choice of Travel Mode for the Journey to
                      Work: Some Findings', Journal of Transport
                      Economics and Policy, 1 (1967)
W. F. Quin   'The Functions of the Traffic Commissioners',
                      Journal of The Institute of Transport, 28
                      (1959)
G. F. Ray   'Transport Notes and Comments', National
                      Institute Economic Review, 24 (1963)
G. F. Ray and   'Problems and Policies for Inland Transport',
  C. T. Saunders   in W. Beckerman et alia, The British
                      Economy in 1975 (1965)
P. W. Reed   'The 1968 Transport Act—A Triumph for
                      Commonsense', The Bankers' Magazine, 209
                      (1970)

C. I. Savage   'Problem of Uneconomic Public Transport in
                      Scotland', *Scottish Journal of Political
                      Economy*, 10 (1963)
E. Schenker   'Nationalization and Denationalization of
                      Motor Carriers in Great Britain', *Land
                      Economics*, 39 (1963)
K. R. Sealy   'The Siting and Development of British Air-
                      ports', *Geographical Journal*, 133 (1967)
C. Sharp   'The Allocation of Goods Traffic between
                      Road and Rail', *Journal of Industrial
                      Economics*, 7 (1958–59)
C. Sharp   'The Economics of Super-Heavies', *Motor
                      Transport* (March 12 1971)
C. H. Sharp and   'More Powerful Engines for Lorries: An Exer-
    A. Jennings   cise in Cost-Benefit Analysis', *Journal of
                      Transport Economics and Policy*, 6 May (1972)
J. Sleeman   'The Rise and Decline of Municipal Transport',
                      Scottish Journal of Political Economy, 9 (1962)
J. F. Sleeman   'A New Look at the Distribution of Private
                      Cars in Britain', *Scottish Journal of Political
                      Economy*, 16 (1969)
R. J. Smeed   'Traffic Problems in Towns', *The Manchester
                      Statistical Society* (1961)
R. J. Smeed   'Traffic Studies and Urban Congestion',
                      Journal of Transport Economics and Policy, 2
                      (1968)
J. M. A. Smith   'The Impact of the Motor Car on Public
                      Transport', *Journal of the Institute of Trans-
                      port*, 29 (1961)
S. G. Sturmey   'Some Aspects of Ocean Liner Economics',
                      Manchester Statistical Society (1963–64)
S. G. Sturmey   'British Industry Today. 6. Merchant Ship-
                      ping', *Journal of the Institute of Bankers*, 85
                      (1964)
S. G. Sturmey   'Economics and International Liner Services',
                      Journal of Transport Economics and Policy, 1
                      (1967)
M. F. Tanner and   'Port Development and National Planning
    A. F. Williams   Strategy', *Journal of Transport Economics
                      and Policy*, 1 (1967)

D. R. Thomas	'Cost-Benefit Analysis of Railway Closures', *Institute of Transport Journal*, 34 (1971)
M. Topham	'Road Passenger Transport in Unremunerative Areas', *Yorkshire Bulletin of Economic and Social Research*, 20 (1968).
G. J. Walker	'The Transport Act 1947', *Economic Journal*, 58 (1948)
G. J. Walker	'Transport Policy Before and After 1953', *Oxford Economic Papers*, 5 (1953)
G. J. Walker	'Competition in Transport as an Instrument of Policy', *Economic Journal*, 66 (1956)
A. A. Walters	'Subsidies for Transport', *Lloyds Bank Review* (1967)
L. L. Wansbrough-Jones	'Nationalised Transport under the Transport Act of 1962', *Institute of Transport Journal*, 30 (1963)
B. R. Williams	'Transport Act, 1947: Some Benefits and Dangers', *Journal of the Institute of Transport*, 24 (1951)
B. R. Williams	'Nationalisation and After', *Journal of the Institute of Transport*, 25 (1952)
P. M. Williams	'Low Fares and the Urban Transport Problem', *Urban Studies*, 6 (1969)
J. M. Wilson	'The Administrative Problems of the Long-term Planning of Airports', *Public Administration*, 42 (1964)
M. D. N. Wyatt	'British Independent Aviation—Past and Future', *Institute of Transport Journal*, 30 (1963)

OFFICIAL PUBLICATIONS

Report from the Select Committee on Nationalised Industries: The Airways Corporations, HC 213 (1959)

Report of the Committee of Inquiry into the Major Ports of Great Britain, Cmnd, 1824 (1962)

The Financial Problems of the British Overseas Airways Corporation, HC 5 (1963)

The Transport Needs of Great Britain in the Next Twenty Years (1963, HMSO)

Report from the Select Committee on Nationalised Industries: British Overseas Airways Corporation, HC 240 (1964)
Second Report from the Select Committee on Nationalised Industries: British European Airways, HC 673 (1967)
First Report from the Select Committee on Nationalised Industries: Ministerial Control of the Nationalised Industries, HC 371–1 (1968)
Sixth Report from the Estimates Committee: Motorways and Trunk Roads, HC 475 (1969)
Report of the Committee of Inquiry into Civil Air Transport, Cmnd 4018 (1969)
Report of the Committee of Inquiry into Shipping, Cmnd 4337 (1970)
First Report from the Select Committee on Nationalised Industries: British Airports Authority, HC 275 (1971)

KEY STATISTICAL SOURCES

Annual Abstract of Statistics (HMSO)
Basic Road Statistics (British Road Federation)
British Shipping Statistics (Chamber of Shipping)
Development of Civil Air Transport: Traffic Statistics (International Civil Aviation Organisation)
Highway Statistics (HMSO)
Lloyds Register of Shipping
Passenger Transport in Great Britain (HMSO)

Chapter Notes

CHAPTER ONE

1 C. E. Fayle, *The War and the Shipping Industry* (1927), 314.
2 Reports of the Select Committee on Transport, HC, 130/136 (1918).
3 See D. H. Aldcroft, 'The Eclipse of British Coastal Shipping, 1913–21', *The Journal of Transport History*, 6 (1963).
4 Report of the Departmental Committee on Railway Agreements, Cmd 1132 (1921), 31.
5 For the basis of these calculations see D. H. Aldcroft, *British Railways in Transition: The Economic Problems of Britain's Railways Since 1914* (1968), 35.
6 See his comment in the *Railway Gazette*, 22 June 1917.
7 *Second Report of the Select Committee on Transport*, pp. vii, xii.
8 P. J. Cain, 'Railway Combination and Government, 1900–1914', *Economic History Review*, 25 (1972).
9 D. H. Aldcroft, 'The Decontrol of British Shipping and Railways after the First World War', *Journal of Transport History*, 5 (1961), 97–9.
10 For the boom and its consequences see D. H. Aldcroft, 'Port Congestion and the Shipping Boom of 1919–20', *Business History*, 3 (1961).
11 *House of Commons Debates*, 24 June 1920, 130, col 2455.
12 H. Pollins, *Britain's Railways: An Industrial History* (1971), 146–7.
13 £9 million of this sum was to be refunded in tax.
14 *Railways Act*, 1921, 11 and 12 Geo v c55, Section 11 (2).
15 Though in one sense economic criteria featured in this decision since the Scottish companies realised that their financial viability could be threatened if they remained independent.
16 A. A. Harrison, 'Railway Freight Charges', *Journal of the Institute of Transport*, 27 (July 1957).
17 Exceptional fares had to be reported to the Minister who could, under clause 41 Section 2, refer any such fare to the tribunal if he thought it was likely to prejudice the attainment of the standard revenue, whereupon the tribunal could cancel or modify it.

18 It is not altogether clear whether the tribunal had any real power over fares at all. Most of the sections of the Act dealing with charging referred to freight rates, though there is some ambiguity here arising from the fact that the word 'rate' or 'rates' was used frequently to cover both (presumably) freight 'rates' and passenger 'fares'.

CHAPTER TWO

1 C. H. Feinstein, *National Income, Expenditure and Output of the United Kingdom, 1855–1965* (1972), Table 8, T25.
2 This is a very tentative estimate and probably somewhat on the high side.
3 Details of the returns can be found in D. H. Aldcroft, *British Railways in Transition* (1968), 48.
4 W. Smith, *An Economic Geography of Great Britain* (1953, 2nd ed.), 593.
5 Stone and Rowe, op cit, 61.
6 Smith, op cit, 622.
7 G. Walker, *Road and Rail* (1947, 2nd ed.), 20, 127, 129.
8 80 per cent as against 62–63 per cent prewar.
9 E. J. Broster, 'Railway Passenger Receipts and Fares Policy', *Economic Journal*, 47 (1937).
10 On these points see the very valuable discussion in W. G. Scott, 'An Aspect of the British Railways Act 1921', in H. A. Innis (ed.), *Essays in Transportation in Honour of W. T. Jackman* (1941), 131–2.
11 This matter is discussed in D. H. Aldcroft, 'Innovation on the Railways: The Lag in Diesel and Electric Traction', *Journal of Transport Economics and Policy*, 3 (1969).
12 E. J. Broster, 'Variability of Railway Operating Costs', *Economic Journal*, 48 (1938), 677.
13 W. L. Waters, 'Rationalization of British Railways' (paper presented to the American Society of Mechanical Engineers, 11 May 1938, New York), 8–9.
14 Excluding the operations of London Transport. For the complex network of holding arrangements see C. I. Savage, *An Economic History of Transport* (1959), 125–6.
15 J. Hibbs, *Transport for Passengers* (2nd ed. 1971, Hobart Paper 23); P. E. Hart, 'The Restriction of Road Haulage', *Scottish Journal of Political Economy*, 6 (1959).
16 Hibbs, op cit, and G. Walker, *Road and Rail*.

17 R. Brady, *Crisis in Britain* (1950), 264–5.

18 Technical improvement in aircraft performance has been dramatic. Brooks has estimated that for each decade of the period 1919–59 the following improvements have taken place: specific operating costs were reduced on average by one third, vehicle size and carrying capacity doubled, speed rose by about two thirds and there were also big advances in safety, reliability and standards of passenger accommodation. P. Brooks, *The Modern Airliner* (1961), 30.

19 European airlines were much more heavily subsidised than Imperial Airways. See J. Longhurst, *Nationalisation in Practice: The Civil Aviation Experiment* (1950), 14, 34.

20 D. H. Aldcroft, 'Britain's Internal Airways: The Pioneer Stage of the 1930s', *Business History*, 6 (1964), 115–16.

21 Established in March 1934 to provide such air services as the railway companies might require.

22 Altogether 24 of the 40 or so companies established between 1933 and 1939 had either failed or been absorbed.

23 D. H. Aldcroft, 'The Railways and Air Transport in Great Britain, 1933–1939', *Scottish Journal of Political Economy*, 12 (1965), 60–1.

24 P. N. Davies and A. M. Bourn, 'Lord Kylsant and the Royal Mail', *Business History*, 14 (1972).

25 S. G. Sturmey, *British Shipping and World Competition* (1962), 137.

26 Ibid, 127.

27 Ibid, 96.

CHAPTER THREE

1 R. Brady, *Crisis in Britain* (1950), 237.

2 G. L. Wilson, *Nationalisation of Transport in Great Britain* (1949), 24.

3 Railway Clearing House, *Tables of Statistical Returns Relating to the Railways of Great Britain, 1938–1946* (1947); C. I. Savage, *Inland Transport* (1957), 506–7.

4 W. A. Robson (ed.), *Problems of Nationalized Industry* (1952), 281.

5 K. M. Gwilliam, *Transport and Public Policy* (1964), 93.

6 Civil aviation was dealt with separately and most of it had already been taken into public ownership in 1939–40.

7 The BTC also inherited from the railways an equal stake with the British Electric Traction Group in the latter's bus empire. These

interests were managed by BET until 1968 when they were bought out by the Transport Holding Company.

8 That is about 47 per cent of the total vehicles in Britain operated exclusively for hire or reward.

9 B. R. Williams, 'Nationalisation and After', *Journal of the Institute of Transport*, 25 (1952), 15.

10 The Road Transport Executive was subsequently split into two, one each for road haulage and road passenger transport.

11 Gwilliam, op. cit, 102.

12 *Transport Policy*, Cmd 8538 (1952), para 19.

13 The Transport (Disposal of Road Haulage Property) Act of 1956 put a stop to any further denationalisation.

14 Though powers under this clause were never exercised.

15 'Ten Years of Nationalised Transport', *Railway Gazette*, 20 September and 4 October 1957; M. Bonavia, *The Organisation of British Railways* (1971).

16 R. Pryke, *Public Enterprise in Practice: The British Experience of Nationalisation Over Two Decades* (1971), 39.

17 The deficit was even larger when allowance is made for central interest charges.

18 *Report from the Select Committee on Nationalised Industries, British Railways*, HC 254 (1960), para 386.

19 Ibid, para 417.

20 Ibid, para 358.

21 *Reorganisation of the Nationalised Transport Undertakings*, Cmnd 1248 (1960).

22 *The Financial and Economic Obligations of the Nationalised Industries*, Cmnd 1337 (1961). This was followed by a further White Paper in 1967. Cmnd 3437.

23 The Transport Holding Company took over the 16,000 road haulage vehicles belonging to BRS (about 20 per cent of all haulage vehicles operated exclusively for hire or reward) and owned directly one fifth of all buses and coaches, or one third if the interests in British Electric Traction are included. Altogether with its subsidiaries and associates it accounted for some 80 per cent of stage services outside cities., D. L. Munby, 'British Industry Today. 7. Inland Transport', *Journal of the Institute of Bankers*, 85 (Dec 1964), 502.

24 Section 29 (6). The Act did not actually use this phrase but it gav

the THC the power to manage its securities as if it 'were a company engaged in a commercial enterprise'.

25 Transport Holding Company, *Annual Report and Accounts for 1963* p. 8.

26 G. Polanyi, *Contrasts in Nationalised Transport Since 1947* (1968, Institute of Economic Affairs), 49–50.

27 Railway discrimination against coastal shipping might also be prevented by Ministerial intervention.

28 *Transport Policy*, Cmnd 3057 (1966).

29 Ibid, 2.

30 Ibid, par. 15.

31 Ministry of Transport, *British Railways Network for Development* (1967). In all some 11,000 route miles were to be retained as against about 8000 under the original Beeching plan and 13,500 then in existence.

32 See *Railway Policy*, Cmnd 3439 (1967), for full details.

33 Elaborated in *The Transport of Freight*, Cmnd 3470 (1967).

34 Thus removing the liberalisation of 1953 and running counter to the recommendation of the Geddes Report that licensing should be abolished. Ministry of Transport, *Report of the Committee on Carriers' Licensing* (1965, HMSO).

35 Elaborated in a third white paper *Public Transport and Traffic*, Cmnd 3481 (1967). The fourth and final paper (though in fact the first to appear) covered inland waterways. *British Waterways: Recreation and Amenity* Cmnd 3401 (1967).

36 A harkback to the 1947 Act under which the BTC had power to prepare area schemes for the whole country, a power which was rescinded in 1953.

37 Or rather it did by Ministerial Order.

38 Most of which were already in existence under the THC. The structure is complex and reference needs to be made to the details given in the *Annual Reports* of the NFC.

39 This was the original title given in the Act but it subseqently became known as National Carriers Ltd.

40 For Merseyside, South East Lancashire and North East Cheshire, Tyneside, West Midlands and Glasgow.

41 The position at the time of writing remains very fluid and several changes have been made in detail, especially regarding the organisational structures. Further changes in the urban transport structure will no doubt occur with the pending reorganisation of local govern-

ment. A whole series of changes and proposals were announced at the end of 1971.

42 See D. L. Munby, 'Mrs Castle's Transport Policy', *Journal of Transport Economics and Policy*, 2 (1968); N. Lee, 'A Review of the Transport Bill', *District Bank Review*, 165 (March 1968); P. W. Reed, 'The 1968 Transport Act—A New Era for British Railways ?, *The Bankers Magazine*, 209 (April 1970) and 'The 1968 Transport Act—A Triumph for Commonsense ?' Ibid, 209 (March 1970); also the symposium on the Bill in the *Institute of Transport Journal*, 33 (November 1968).

43 Munby, loc cit, 136.

44 Munby, loc cit, 136.

45 Pryke, op cit, 39.

46 Transport Holding Company: *Annual Report and Accounts for 1968*, 9, 39, 43.

47 C. I. Savage, *An Economic History of Transport* (1966 revised edition), 202.

48 *The Economist*, 4 December 1971, 71.

49 See *the Transport Needs of Great Britain in the Next Twenty Years* (1963) (HMSO) and the Buchanan Report on *Traffic in Towns*.

50 Cmnd 1337 (1961).

51 *Nationalised Industries: A Review of Economic and Financial Objectives*, Cmnd, 3437 (1967).

52 *The Economist*, 4 December 1971, 70.

CHAPTER FOUR

1 *National Income and Expenditure*, 1970 18–19, table 15.

2 There are, of course, considerable regional differences in the relative shares of each mode.

3 Department of Employment, *Family Expenditure Survey: Report for 1970* (HMSO, 1971), table 1.

4 Inward movements are almost an identical replica and hence there is no point in repeating the exercise.

5 This paragraph is based on data in the *Annual Abstract of Statistics*.

6 The coastwise distribution of oil from major terminals probably accounts for much of the rise in coastwise activity in recent years.

7 Ministry of Transport, *The Transport of Goods by Road: Report of a Sample Survey made in April 1958*, (1959, HMSO) 24–25.

8 Department of the Environment, *Highway Statistics 1970* (HMSO 1971), Table 41. Though compare S. L. Edwards, 'Transport Costs in British Industry', *Journal of Transport Economics and Policy*, 4 (1970), 274–75.

9 Though see also Chapter 7.

10 In 1949 the maximum number of seats on the Boeing 377 strato-cruiser was 60; twenty years later the Boeing 747 could accommodate 490 passengers.

11 Knut Hammarskjöld, 'The 70s—Challenging Years for the World Air Transport System', *Institute of Transport Journal*, 33 (May 1970), 441.

12 B. T. Bayliss and S. L. Edwards, *Transport for Industry-Summary Report* (HMSO, 1968), iii.

13 Ibid, iii, 19, 31, 68. See also Edwards, loc cit, 268.

14 G. R. Ray, 'Transport: Notes and Comments', *National Institute Economic Review*, 24 (May 1963), 29.

15 Standing charges being assessed for usage of 10,000 miles per annum. D. L. Munby, 'The Economics of City Traffic', in T. E. H. Williams (ed.), *Urban Survival and Traffic* (1962), 217–19.

16 N. Topham, 'Road Passenger Transport in Unremunerative Areas', *Yorkshire Bulletin of Economic and Social Research*, 20 (May 1968), 34–35.

17 Ministry of Transport, *The Transport Needs of Great Britain in the Next Twenty Years* (1963, HMSO), 9.

18 Ray, loc cit, 32.

19 The reverse was the case before about 1950 because of the freezing of public passenger fares.

20 For details of these calculations, see D. H. Aldcroft and P. Bemand. 'A Study of the Changing Expenditure Patterns in Passenger Transport in Great Britain', in D. H. Aldcroft, *Studies in British Transport History 1870–1970* (1974).

21 C. Sharp, *Problems of Urban Passenger Transport* (1967), 57.

22 Aldcroft and Bemand, op cit. Similar calculations by Pryke revealed that a one per cent increase in the relative cost of travelling by rail led to a 1.1 per cent fall in the volume of passenger traffic. R. Pryke, *Public Enterprise in Practice* (1971), 231.

23 See also on this J. C. Tanner, *Factors Affecting the Amount of Travel* (1961, Road Research Laboratory Paper No 51, HMSO).

24 A. D. Evans, 'Intercity Travel and the London Midland Electrification', *Journal of Transport Economics and Policy*, 3 (January 1969), 23; though see Chapter 5.

CHAPTER FIVE

1 In terms of passenger and ton miles the proportions are somewhat higher because of the longer hauls by rail. See chapter 4 page 115.
2 Wartime operation is fully documented in C. Savage, *Inland Transport* (1957).
3 A capital reconstruction was carried out in the early 1960s. See below.
4 Cf *Report of the Committee on Carriers' Licensing* (1965), 28.
5 G. F. Ray 'Transport: Notes and Comments'. *National Institute Economic Review*, 24 (1963), 29.
6 G. L. Reid and K. Allen, *Nationalised Industries* (1970), 111.
7 *Annual Reports of the British Transport Commission*, 1948, 27; 1952, 24.
8 *Report of the Select Committee on Nationalised Industries—British Railways*, HC 254 (1960), para 410.
9 Ibid, para 407.
10 Ibid, para 132.
11 *Annual Report of the British Transport Commission*, 1960, 3.
12 *Annual Report of the British Transport Commission*, 1950, 71.
13 R. Brady, *Crisis in Britain* (1950), 264–5.
14 *The Economist*, 24 January 1959, 335–36.
15 D. L. Munby, 'Economic Problems of British Railways', *Bulletin of the Oxford University Institute of Statistics*, 24 (1962), 25.
16 *Select Committee on British Railways* (1960), para 164.
17 B. M. Deakin and T. Seward, *Productivity in Transport* (1969), 129; D. L. Munby, 'The Productivity of British Railways', *Bulletin of the Oxford University Institute of Statistics*, 24 (1962).
18 D. H. Aldcroft, *British Railways in Transition* (1968), 169–72.
19 Ray, loc cit, 34.
20 See Chapter 3.
21 In actual fact interest charges rose slightly in the 1960s.
22 *Reshaping Report*, 54.
23 D. L. Munby, 'The Reshaping of British Railways', *Journal of Industrial Economics*, 11 (1962–3)
24 C. I. Savage, *An Economic History of Transport* (1966, revised edition), 192.

25 Sir Henry Johnson, 'Twenty Years of Nationalised Railways'. *National Provincial Bank Review*, 83 (August 1968). 5.

26 Deakin and Seward, op cit, 128.

27 C. D. Jones, 'The Performance of British Railways, 1962 to 1968', *Journal of Transport Economics and Policy*, 4 (1970).

28 British Railways Board, *Annual Report and Accounts*, 1965, 2.

29 National Board for Prices and Incomes, *Proposed Increases by British Railways Board in Certain Country-Wide Fares and Charges: Report no 72*, Cmd 3656 (1968), 20.

30 Ibid, 17.

31 For example, many railway freight rates were either lowered or kept stable in the 1960s at a time when road haulage rates were rising rapidly, so that many rates became very competitive with those of road haulage. But the effect on traffic volume was very limited. See R. Pryke, *Public Enterprise in Practice* (1971), 209–12 and Deakin and Seward, op. cit.

32 A. W. J. Thomson and L. C. Hunter, *The Nationalised Transport Industries* (1973), 151, 162–72.

33 First Report from the Select Committee on Nationalised Industries. Ministerial Control of Nationalised Industries, Vol 1, HC, 317–I (1968), paras, 419–56, and Vol III, Appendices 27 and 34.

34 Discussed in Chapter 3.

35 Local authorities and passenger transport authorities can also make payments to the board for keeping rail services open and it was anticipated that they might assume complete financial responsibility in some cases. However, negotiation in this matter has proved difficult. See the *Financial Times*, 13 January 1973.

36 British Railways Board, *Annual Report and Accounts*, 1971, 1.

37 See 'Still off the Rails', *The Economist*, 16 January 1971, 64.

38 *The Economist*, 4 December 1971, 70.

39 See D. W. Wragg, 'Air Versus Rail', *Flight International*, 96 (9 October 1969), 556; *The Times*, 14 May 1971.

CHAPTER SIX

1 Taxis accounted for most of the decline since the number of buses and coaches has remained fairly static in the post-war period.

2 That is if we exclude short distance local journeys.

3 This paragraph is based on tentative estimates of passenger mileage travelled which can be found in my *British Railways in Transition* (1968), 125.

4 W. Plowden, *The Motor Car and Politics, 1896–1970* (1971), 327.

5 J. F. Sleeman, 'A New Look at the Distribution of Private Cars in Britain', *Scottish Journal of Political Economy*, 16 (1969), 314–15.

6 G. E. Cherry, 'Town Planning and the Motor Car in Twentieth Century Britain', *High Speed Ground Transportation Journal*, 4 (January 1970), 70.

7 See chapter 9.

8 These figures include 6400 trams and trolleybuses mainly in local authority hands.

9 In 1968 it acquired the remaining passenger transport interests of the BET group, giving it a monopoly control of inter-urban routes.

10 *Public Transport and Traffic* Cmnd 3481 (1967), para 7.

11 Data from local authority accounts and *Passenger Transport in Great Britain*. For the early years see J. Sleeman, 'The Rise and Decline of Municipal Transport', *Scottish Journal of Political Economy*, 9 (1962).

12 *Passenger Transport Year Books*, 1956, 1968.

13 Though London Transport had a less enviable record in the 1960s with large deficits on its bus services after 1965. By the late 1960s the overall deficit on London Transport was over £10 million per annum and before its transfer to the GLC its capital debt was written down thus relieving it of over £11 million in interest charges.

14 M. E. Beesley and Janet Politi, 'A Study of the Profits of Bus Companies, 1940–1966', *Economica*, 36 (1969).

15 National Bus Company, *Annual Report and Accounts*, 1970, 1971

16 *Report of the Committee on Rural Bus Services* (HMSO 1961).

17 See *The Guardian*, 2 February 1971.

18 See *The Economist*, 4 December 1971, 70.

19 Norman Morton, in *The Guardian*, 17 August 1960.

20 National Bus Company, *Annual Report and Accounts* 1970, p. 23

21 D. A. Quarmby, 'Choice of Travel Mode for Journey to Work', *Journal of Transport Economics and Policy*, 1 (1967). Though a survey of 400 regular London car commuters in 1965 suggested that the response transfer rate given an improvement in service and a reduction in fares on public transport was somewhat greater. But there was an upper limit to the price elasticity; at a zero fare 51 per

318 NOTES

cent of the commuters would be prepared to switch to public transport. Penelope M. Williams, 'Low Fares and the Urban Transport Problem', *Urban Studies*, 6 (1969).

22 H. W. Richardson, *Urban Economics* 1971), 104.

23 T. T. Taber, *Some Information, Observations and Conclusions Concerning the Handling of London's Half-Million Daily Commuters by Railroad in 1961* (1962 New Jersey), 51.

24 Transport Holding Company. *Annual Report and Accounts for 1967*, 25–26.

25 See Liverpool City Transport, *Annual Report of the General Manager for years 1960–61, 1966–67*.

26 See *The Guardian*, 9 November 1970 and *The Observer*, 7 November 1971. Apparently Reading public transport is actually experiencing an increase in traffic.

27 B. M. Deakin and T. Seward, *Productivity in Transport* (1969), 128–29.

28 Though in 1970 the National Bus Company instructed its subsidiaries to withdraw uneconomic rural services unless a subsidy was forthcoming.

29 Manchester City Transport, *Annual Report and Accounts for year ending 31 March 1969*.

30 Aberdeen Transport Department, *Annual Reports and Analysis of Receipts and Expenses*, 1948–1969.

31 Public Transport and Traffic, Cmnd 3481 (1967), para 26.

32 N. Lee and I. Steedman, 'Economies of Scale in Bus Transport: Some British Municipal Results', *Journal of Transport Economics and Policy*, 4 (1970), 27.

33 National Board for Prices and Incomes, *Productivity Agreements in the Bus Industry*, Report no 50 Cmnd 3498 (1967), 5, 31.

34 See J. Hall, 'Problems of One-man Bus Operation', *Institute of Transport Journal*, 33 (May 1969); F. Fishwick, 'One-man Operation in Municipal Transport', Ibid, 33 (May 1970); R. H. Brown and C. A. Nash, 'Cost Savings from One-man Operation of Buses', *Journal of Transport Economics and Policy*, 6 (Sept. 1972), 283–84; Road Research Laboratory Report, 'Bus Boarding and Alighting Times' (LR 521).

35 *Report of the Committee on the Licensing of Road Passenger Services* (1953, HMSO), 39.

36 J. Hibbs, *Transport for Passengers* (1963, 2nd edn 1971, Hobart Paper 23).

37 The public sector refers to road haulage performed for hire and reward and includes vehicles owned by the State.

38 The BTC also had another 15,000 motors and tractors and about 23,000 trailers which were used in connection with the collection and delivery services of the railways. E. Schenker, 'Nationalization and Denationalization of Motor Carriers in Great Britain', *Land Economics*, 39 (August 1963), 223.

39 These vehicles became subject to the licensing system.

40 National Board for Prices and Incomes, *Costs, Charges and Productivity of the National Freight Corporation*. Report no 162, Cmnd 4569 (1971), 27–29.

41 Though not the railways' bulk traffics such as coal and iron and steel.

42 B. R. Williams, 'Nationalisation and After', *Journal of Institute of Transport*, 25 (November 1952), 15; Central Office of Information *Freight Transport* (1971), 8; National Freight Corporation, *Annual Report and Accounts 1970*, 4.

43 The distinction between public and own account vehicles is now outdated in view of the changes made to the licensing system in 1968, though it still has relevance for the division of traffic.

44 In the sense that competition was lessened; on the other hand it could be said that this was counterbalanced by large firms being more adept at acquiring additional licenses.

45 A. W. J. Thomson and L. C. Hunter, *The Nationalised Transport Industries* (1973), 235.

46 A. J. Harrison, 'Economics of Scale and the Structure of the Road Haulage Industry', *Oxford Economic Papers*, 15 (November 1963) and A. A. Walters, *Integration in Freight Transport* (1968), 33. See also S. L. Edwards and B. T. Bayliss, *Operating Costs in Road Freight Transport* (1971, HMSO), 66.

47 Edwards and Bayliss, op cit, 3. The estimate is for 1965.

48 B. M Deakin and T. Seward, *Productivity in Transport* (1969), 160.

49 M. Webb, *Transporting Goods by Road* (1972), 38.

50 C. Sharp, *The Allocation of Freight Traffic—A Survey* (1970, Ministry of Transport), 22.

51 See also chapter 4. Compare K M. Gwilliam, *Transport and Public Policy* (1964), 136–37.

52 Deakin and Seward, op. cit, 128–29.

53 Ibid, 187.

54 Ibid, 60–64; R. Pryke, *Public Enterprise in Practice* (1971), 205–12;

D. M. Dear, 'Some Thoughts on the Comparative Costs of Road and Rail Transport', *Bulletin of the Oxford University Institute of Statistics*, 24 (1962), 68–70.

55 Walters, op cit, 47; see also B. T. Bayliss and S. L. Edwards, *Transport for Industry* (1968, HMSO).

56 G. Walker, *Road and Rail* (2nd edn 1947).

57 National Board for Prices and Incomes, *Road Haulage Rates*, Report No 1 (Interim), Cmnd 2695 (1965), 3–4.

58 Walters, op. cit, 26.

59 National Board for Prices and Incomes, *Charges, Costs and Wages in the Road Haulage Industry*, Report No 48, Cmnd 3482 (1967), para 85. The board re-emphasised this point in a later report, NBPI, *Costs, Charges and Productivity of the National Freight Corporation*, Report No 162, Cmnd 4569 (1971), para 32.

60 There was also a Contract A licence for the exclusive carriage of another person's goods under contract for at least one year.

61 See K. M. Gwilliam, *Transport and Public Policy* (1964), 130–32.

62 Though for a critical assessment of licensing see D. L. Munby, 'The Economics of Road Haulage Licensing', *Oxford Economic Papers*, 17 (March 1965).

63 Ministry of Transport, *Report of the Committee on Carriers' Licensing* (1965, HMSO), 6.

64 *Transport Policy*, Cmnd 3057 (1966), 23 and *The Transport of Freight*, Cmnd 3470 (1967), 10–17.

65 Webb, op cit, 68.

CHAPTER SEVEN

1 Most international freight still goes by sea. See chapter 8.

2 P. W. Brooks, 'The Development of Air Transport', *Journal of Transport Economics and Policy*, 1 (1967), 174.

3 M. R. Straszheim, *The International Airline Industry* (1970), 108.

4 See *Annual Abstract of Statistics 1971*, table 266.

5 Straszheim, op. cit, 129–30; B. A. Schriever and W. Seifert, *Air Transportation 1975 and Beyond: A Systems Approach* (1968), 43.

6 R. Miller and D. Sawers, *The Technical Development of Modern Aviation* (1968) 44; International Civil Aviation Organisation, *A Review of the Economic Situation of Air Transport . . .* (1965), 29, and *A Review of the Economic Situation of Air Transport, 1957–1967* (1968), 2–4.

7 Miller and Sawers, op. cit, 36–42.

8 This measurement of capacity supplied reflects both payload capacity and mileage flown.

9 Actually the North Atlantic route is not typical for various reasons and even on this route it is easy to exaggerate the reduction in fares. Part of the difficulty in assessing movements in fares is that the structure of fares has changed over time so that it is not always possible to compare like with like. If we took charter fares into account the reduction would be even greater but then these were not available earlier and in any case they cannot be compared with scheduled fares because of the difference in quality of service. Moreover, low charter fares are determined by other factors besides technology. But there is no doubt that air fares have fallen considerably since the war though perhaps not by as much as the reduction in operating costs. For a sceptical review of the claim that air fares have fallen substantially see M. H. Cooper and A. K. Maynard, *The Price of Air Travel* (1971), 30–4. But these authors are probably guilty of misinterpretation as well.

10 Control over fares has inevitably led the IATA into the area of service control to the extent that even the size of sandwiches served has been subject to specification!

11 K. G. J. Pillai, *The Air Net: The Case Against the World Aviation Cartel* (1969); see also Cooper and Maynard, op. cit.

12 R. E. G. Davies, *A History of the World's Airlines* (1964), 304–5.

13 *British Air Services*, Cmnd 6712 (1945), para 5.

14 R. W. Spurgeon, 'Subsidy in Air Transport', *Journal of the Institute of Transport*, 27 (1956), 19.

15 BOAC, *Annual Reports and Accounts, 1947/8 to 1949/50*.

16 BSAAC, *Annual Report and Accounts, 1948–49*, 15–16.

17 BSAAC, *Annual Report and Accounts, 1946–47*, 12.

18 J. Pudney, *The Seven Skies: A Study of BOAC and its Forerunners since 1919* (1959), 216.

19 *The Aeroplane*, 30 March 1961, 340.

20 Report of the Committee of Inquiry into Civil Air Transport, Cmnd 4018 (1969), 16.

21 B. M. Deakin and T. Seward, *Productivity on Transport* (1969), 128–9.

22 Cmnd 4018 (1969), 37.

23 Ibid, 20.

24 Report from the Select Committee on Nationalised Industries: The Air Corporations, HC 23 (1959), xxxv–ix.

25 This was before allocating central and interest charges. In that year BEA recorded an overall operating loss of £778,000, the first since the financial year 1953–54. BEA, *Annual Report and Accounts*, 1970–71.

26 Second Report from the Select Committee on Nationalised Industries: British European Airways, HC 673 (1966–67), lix.

27 Third Report of the Air Transport Licensing Board for the Year Ended 31 March 1963, HC 297 (1963), 11–14. 'We endorse the practice of minimising losses by charging what the traffic will bear'.

28 Fifth Report of the Air Transport Licensing Board for the Year Ended 31 March 1965, HC 261 (1964–65), 15.

29 Sixth Report of the Air Transport Licensing Board for the Year Ended 31 March 1966, HC 96 (1966–67), 27.

30 Eighth Report of the Air Transport Licensing Board for the Year Ended 31 March 1968, HC 417 (1967–68), 9.

31 *The Guardian*, 12 December 1970. For a discussion of the work of the board in relation to fares see K. M. Gwilliam, 'Domestic Air Transport Fares', *Journal of Transport Economics and Policy*, 2 (1968).

32 Report of the Committee of Inquiry into the Aircraft Industry, Cmnd 2853 (1965), 6.

33 Report from the Select Committee on Nationalised Industries: The Air Corporations, HC 213 (1959), lix.

34 Ibid, lix.

35 Council of Europe, *Certain Financial and Economic Aspects of Air Transport Operations* (1964, Strasbourg), 8.

36 Report from the Select Committee on Nationalised Industries: British Overseas Airways Corporation, HC 240 (1964), para 316.

37 The Financial Problems of the British Overseas Airways Corporation, HC 5 (1963); also HC 240 (1964).

38 A. W. J. Thomson and L. C. Hunter, *The Nationalised Transport Industries* (1973), 61–6.

39 Even more companies appeared on the scene by the late 1940s; 93 operators are listed in *The Aeroplane Directory* for 1949 and at one point the number is reported to have risen to 120 (see *The Aeroplane*, 14 June 1962, 8). However, estimates of the number vary widely, no doubt partly because many of them were so small and enjoyed such a brief existence.

40 Though very much less in terms of the number of passengers carried.

See British Independent Air Transport Association, *Annual Reports* (Statistical Summary); M. D. N. Wyatt, 'British Independent Aviation—Past and Future', *Institute of Transport Journal*, 3 (1963), 108–9.

41 *The Aeroplane*, 5 February 1960, 156.

42 Cmnd 4018 (1969), 23.

43 This is a rough estimate based on various sources of data including that given in *The Aeroplane*, 18 April 1958, 533.

44 Final Report of the Air Transport Advisory Council for the Year ended 31 March 1961, HC 259 (1961), 11.

45 Changes in the structure and ownership of the private sector are unbelievably complex and it would be quite impossible to detail them in full. Much information can be found in various issues of *The Aeroplane*, see especially the issues 31 July 1953, 146–52 and 5 February 1960, 156–7, and also *Flight*, 16 October 1969, 605–14. There is also a good survey in R. E. G. Davies, *A History of the World's Airlines* (1964), 314–18. The extent of the shipping interest can be found in articles in *The Shipping World*, 13 April 1960, 367–9 and 13 December 1961, 469–70.

46 The list of criteria was a long one; it included the applicant's competence to operate services; his experience, financial resources, equipment etc; the need for the proposed service and the extent of any duplication or diversion from services provided by existing operators; conditions of employment and insurance provisions; and any objections raised by interested parties.

47 Cmnd 4018 (1969), 93–4.

48 This decision was perhaps fortunate since soon afterwards (November 1968) British Eagle folded up. Ninth Report of the Air Transport Licensing Board for the Year ended 31 March 1969, HC 388 (1969), 7.

49 In the 1960s non-scheduled traffic increased much more rapidly than scheduled traffic. Of the total traffic carried by UK airlines one quarter in 1962 and one third in 1967 was on non-scheduled services, and about half of it consisted of inclusive tour traffic. On European routes the proportion of non-scheduled traffic was much higher than the average. The independents accounted for most of the growth in this sector. R. Burns, 'What Are Airlines For?', *Institute of Transport Journal*, 33 (1969), 131.

50 Non-scheduled traffic was by far the most important source of activity of the independents accounting for 80 per cent or more of

the total passenger-miles flown. Inclusive tour traffic was the most important followed by other charter work and trooping, the latter having fallen to less than 30 per cent by 1967. See Cmnd. 4018 (1969), p. 22, 328–9 and Select Committee on Nationalised Industries: Ministerial Control of Nationalised Industries, Vol 3, HC 371–III (1968), 146.

51 Cmnd 4018 (1969), 23, 29.

52 The tally is only approximate and is derived from data in various issues of *The Aeroplane* and *The Aeroplane Directory*. For details of each company in operation at the end of the 1960s see *Flight*, 16 October 1969, 605–14.

53 Third Report of the Air Transport Licensing Board for the Year ended 31 March 1963, HC 297 (1963), 24–5.

54 *The Economist*, 17 March 1963, 604.

55 Eighth Report of the Air Transport Licensing Board for the Year ended 31 March 1968, HC 417 (1968), 9.

56 Cmnd 4018 (1969), 153–61. For further discussion of the work of the ATLB see K. M. Gwilliam, 'The Regulation of Air Transport', *Yorkshire Bulletin of Economic and Social Research*, 18 (1966) and S. Wheatcroft, *Air Transport Policy* (1964), 129–33, 157 et seq.

57 *Civil Aviation Policy*, Cmnd 4213 (1969), para 7.

58 We have resisted debating this controversial issue otherwise this chapter would have become far too long. An able summary of the case for and against a merger can be found in Thomson and Hunter, op. cit, 92–100.

59 Cmnd 4018 (1969), para 1064.

60 BAS was 70 per cent owned by BEA. It would acquire control of the secondary routes of BEA and those of a number of private operators.

61 BEA, *Annual Report and Accounts, 1970–71*, 11; BOAC, *Annual Report and Accounts, 1970–71*, 7.

62 Or more correctly, directives of the Secretary of State; the adjectival form of the latter does not appear very meaningful.

CHAPTER EIGHT

1 Political and Economic Planning, 'The British Shipping Industry', *Planning*, 25 (1959), No 437, 191.

2 C. O'Loughlin, *The Economics of Sea Transport* (1967), 4.

3 OECD, *Maritime Transport 1970*, 110.

4 Ibid, 82–7; United Nations Conference on Trade and Development, *Review of Maritime Transport 1969* (1969, New York), 16–18.

5 Indeed the UK registered fleet would have declined substantially had it not been for the increased operations of merchant companies (own account operations, mainly the oil companies) and overseas owned companies.

6 The main exception being the United States fleet.

7 Chamber of Shipping of the UK, *The Coming Crisis for British Shipping* (1959), 3.

8 S. G. Sturmey, *British Shipping and World Competition* (1962), 403.

9 PEP, 'The British Shipping Industry', op cit, 215–19.

10 Report of the Committee of Inquiry into Shipping, Cmnd 4337 (1970), para. 219.

11 See *Statistical Material presented during the Washington Conference*, Cmnd 6707 (1945) 8; Chamber of Shipping, *Annual Report, 1945–46*, Table 5; *Fairplay*, 7 March 1946, 488.

12 *Fairplay*, 12 January 1956, 32.

13 M. G. Kendall, 'Losses of U.K. Merchant Ships in World War II', *Economica*, 15 (1948), 292.

14 Sturmey, op cit, 148–54.

15 Such as ex-government vessels which had already performed arduous duties, standardised wartime products and vessels built to traditional specifications.

16 For details see W. P. Clegg and J. S. Styring, *British Nationalised Shipping, 1947–1968* (1969), 10–11.

17 F. M. Fisser, *Tramp Shipping* (1957), 53–5.

18 Based on data in the *Annual Reports* of the Liverpool Steam Ship Owners' Association.

19 D. Marx jnr., 'Regulation of International Liner Shipping and 'Freedom of the Seas', *Journal of Industrial Economics*, 16 (1967), 54.

20 Unlike Britain many countries reserve their coastal waters to ships of the national flag.

21 Sturmey, op cit, 189.

22 Chamber of Shipping, *Annual Report, 1958–59*, 58; G. Alexandersson and G. Norström, *World Shipping: An Economic Geography of Ports and Seaborne Trade* (1963), 44.

23 S. G. Sturmey, *A Consideration of the Ends and Means of National Shipping Policy* (1965, Institute of Shipping Research, Bergen), 1.

24 Cmnd 4337 (1970), 45.

25 Ibid, 45.

26 United Nations Conference on Trade and Development, *Liner Shipping in India's Overseas Trade* (1967), 124.

27 Cmnd 4337 (1970), 47–8.

28 For the shipowners' view see H. Hogarth, 'Flags of Convenience and Flag Discrimination', *Institute of Transport Journal*, 30 (1963).

29 D. B. Moloney, 'Trends in Liner Shipping', *Institute of Transport Journal*, 32 (1967), 241.

30 Cmnd 4337 (1970), 333–40.

31 Certainly there were areas in which British owners could have improved their returns.

32 See *Shipping World and Shipbuilder*, November 1969, 1544–45.

33 Much larger vessels are actually in use or on order, the range extending to 500–700,000 deadweight tons. See *Financial Times*, 5 March 1973.

34 G. van den Burg, *Containerisation: A Modern Transport System* (1969), 34.

35 Cmnd 4337 (1970), 155.

36 R. Shone (ed.) *Problems of Investment* (1971), 86; see also S. G. Sturmey, 'The Economics of Running Big Ships', *Shipping World*, 25 June 1964, 1286–87.

37 United Nations Conference on Trade and Development, *Review of Developments in World Shipping* (1967), 10; K. M. Johnson and H. C. Garnett, *The Economics of Containerisation* (1971).

38 Chamber of Shipping, *British Shipping Statistics, 1970–71*, 23.

39 S. G. Sturmey, 'British Industry Today. 6. Merchant Shipping', *Journal of the Institute of Bankers*, 85 (April 1964), 140.

40 The five commodities were iron ore, grain, coal, phosphates and bauxite and alumina. In 1969 these accounted for the major part of the dry bulk commodity trade and for 40 per cent of all dry cargo shipments in terms of weight. A. D. Couper, *The Geography of Sea Transport* (1972), 132; OECD, *Maritime Transport 1970*, 110, 114.

41 S. G. Sturmey, 'British Industry Today . . .', 142; also *British Shipping and World Competition*, 166.

42 B. N. Metaxas, *The Economics of Tramp Shipping* (1971), 76.

43 National Ports Council, *Container and Roll-on Port Statistics, Great Britain 1970: Part 1. Traffic by Type of Unit Service and Overseas Country*, 8–9; *Report of the Working Party on Short Sea Shipping to the Economic Development Committee for the Movement of Shipping* (1970, National Economic Development Office), 46, 55; *Financial Times*, 28 September 1971.

44 Cmnd 4337 (1970), 476.
45 At the end of the 1950s British shipping was in the hands of about 270 companies. But about one half the UK fleet (excluding the oil companies' tanker tonnage) was in the hands of 51 companies within ten major groups: P and O, Furness Withy, British and Commonwealth, Cunard, Ellerman, Blue Funnel, Vestey, Elder Dempster, Inverforth and T. and J. Harrison. All these groups have a long history extending back to the nineteenth century. See PEP, 'The British Shipping Industry', 205–7 and Sturmey, British *Shipping and World Competition*, Ch XIV.
46 Sturmey, op cit, 321; A. S. Svendson, *Sea Transport and Shipping Economics* (1958, 2nd ed Bremen), 171.
47 B. M. Deakin and T. Seward, *Productivity in Transport* (1969), 128. Data collected by the Liverpool Steam Ship Owners Association for the estimated weight of cargo carried per ton of shipping entered and cleared at British ports suggest a similar trend. But this is only a partial productivity measure and the figures include foreign shipping using British ports.
48 Cmnd 4337 (1970), 222.
49 R. O. Goss, 'Some Financial Aspects of Shipping Conferences', *Journal of Transport Economics and Policy*, 5 (1971), 176.
50 For further discussion on conference rate-fixing procedures see E. Bennathan and A. A. Walters, *The Economics of Ocean Freight Rates* (1969); A. G. M. Koch, *Current Pricing Behaviour in Liner Shipping* (1968, Bergen); S. G. Sturmey, 'Economics and International Liner Services', *Journal of Transport Economics and Policy*, 1 (1967).
51 D. L. McLachlan, 'The Pricing Policy of Liner Conferences', *Scottish Journal of Political Economy*, 10 (1963).
52 This conclusion needs to be treated with a certain degree of caution since it may be that British owners were forced to accept lower rates as a result of the pressure of more efficient low cost operators within the conference. But without much more information on comparative costs etc. there is little more that can be added at this point.
53 Cmnd 4337 (1970), 114.
54 Cmnd 4337 (1970), para 1172.

CHAPTER NINE

1 At this point we do not question whether the need or demand for more such facilities can be justified on economic grounds.

2 Though some problems did arise in the past by virtue of the fact that certain terminal facilities, eg at collieries and ports, lay outside the control of the railway companies.

3 British Road Federation, *Basic Road Statistics, 1971,* 36.

4 K. M. Gwilliam, *Transport and Public Policy* (1964), 149. Gwilliam observes that in 1949 total spending on roads was less in real terms than in 1911 despite the fact that during the intervening period the number of vehicles in use had risen more than twenty-fold.

5 A. C. Durie, 'The Road Programme', *National Provincial Bank Review,* 68 (November 1964), 13.

6 *Highway Statistics, 1964.*

7 A. Day, *Roads* (1963), 13.

8 J. Tetlow and A. Goss, *Homes, Towns and Traffic* (1968, 2nd ed), 83.

9 D. J. Reynolds and J. G. Wardrop, 'Economic Losses Due to Traffic Congestion', *5th International Study Week in Traffic Engineering* (1960, Nice), 1–2.

10 D. J. Reynolds, 'The Outlook for Expenditure on Roads', *London and Cambridge Economic Bulletin,* 37 (1961).

11 T. M. Coburn, M. E. Beesley and D. J. Reynolds, *The London–Birmingham Motorway* (1960, Road Research Technical Paper, No 46).

12 A very useful introduction to the subject with illustrations of several case studies is G. H. Peters, *Cost-Benefit Analysis and Public Expenditure* (1968).

13 See *Roads for The Future: The New Inter-Urban Plan for England,* Cmnd 4369 (1970); *Scottish Roads in the 1970s,* Cmnd 3953 (1969); *Basic Road Statistics,* 1972, 30; *The Times* 28 May 1970.

14 W. Plowden, *The Motor Car and Politics, 1896–1970* (1971), 350.

15 R. E. Caves (ed), *Britain's Economic Prospects* (1968), 408.

16 R. J. Smeed, 'Urban Traffic Congestion', Paper to the Annual Conference of Municipal Engineers, June 1968, 2–7.

17 The details of the basis of these calculations can be found in Sixth Report from the Estimates Committee: Motorways and Trunk Roads, HC 475 (1969), 208–15.

18 Though recently the government has recognised that people affected in this way deserve special compensation. But compensation should come not from the general taxpayer but from the road user.

19 *British Air Services,* Cmd 6712 (1945).

20 Quoted in R. S. Doganis, *A National Airport Plan* (1967 Fabian Tract 377), 2.

21 *Civil Aerodromes and Air Navigational Services*, Cmnd 1457 (1961), 3.

22 First Report from the Select Committee on Estimates: Civil Aerodromes and Ground Services, HC 128 (1955–56), x–xi, xiv.

23 Cmnd 1457 (1961), 6, 8.

24 Fifth Report of the Estimates Committee: London Airports, HC 233 (1960–61).

25 In April 1971 the Authority took over Edinburgh (Turnhouse) Airport from the Department of Trade and Industry (formerly the Board of Trade).

26 Report of the Committee of Inquiry into Civil Air Transport, Cmnd 4018 (1969), 40–3.

27 R. S. Doganis, 'Airport Planning and Administration: A Critique', *The Political Quarterly*, 37 (1966), 425.

28 Doganis, A National Airport Plan, op. cit, 4–5.

29 P. G. Masefield, 'Our Future Lies in the Air', *Institute of Transport Journal* 32 (1967), 136; W. J. McKechin, *A Tale of Two Cities* (1967).

30 'Which South Coast Airport?' *The Economist*, 11 February 1967, 502. The situation in the South-west region was even more farcical. At one stage there were no fewer than five airports serving the region (Bristol, Exeter, Gloucester, Plymouth and Newquay) plus a heliport at Penzance, none of which could be said to be properly utilised.

31 In an article written in 1964, J. M. Wilson, the then Deputy Secretary of the Ministry of Aviation, stated that with one exception no town of more than 150,000 inhabitants was more than 30 miles from an aerodrome. It is difficult to see any great virtue in this fact unless the provision of facilities on this scale could be justified on economic grounds, which they cannot. J. M. Wilson, 'The Administrative Problems of the Long-term Planning of Airports', *Public Administration*, 42 (1964), 43.

32 H. J. Dyos and D. H. Aldcroft, *British Transport* (1969), 395.

33 Fifth Report from the Estimates Committee: London's Airports, HC 233 (1960–61), vi and Appendix 2, 26–9.

34 *London's Airports*, Cmd 8902 (1953); *Gatwick Airport*, Cmd 9296 (1954).

35 Fifth Special Report from the Estimates Committee: London's Airports (Observations of the Minister of Aviation), HC 46 (1961–62), 9–10.

34 Ministry of Transport and Civil Aviation, *Report of the London Airport Development Committee* (1957).

37 British Airports Authority, *Annual Report and Accounts*, 1970–71,70.

38 HC 233 (1960–61), xxxi.

39 *The Third London Airport*, Cmnd 3259 (1967).

40 Olive Cook, *The Stansted Affair* (1967), 16.

41 See D. W. Pearce, 'The Roskill Commission and the Location of the Third London Airport', *The Three Banks Review*, 87 (Sept. 1970); E. J. Mishan 'What is Wrong with Roskill?' *Journal of Transport Economics and Policy*, 4 (1970); V. C. Nwaneri, 'Equity in Cost-Benefit Analysis: A Case Study of the Third London Airport', Ibid 4 (1970).

42 *Financial Times*, 27 April 1971. Quite what is likely to happen to Stansted is difficult to say. It will probably be retained as a reserve airport though one sincerely hopes it does not become the subject of controversy over a possible fourth London airport in the future.

43 On this point see R. C. Fordham 'Airport Planning in the Context of the Third London Airport', *Economic Journal*, 80 (1970), 319–20.

44 First Report from the Select Committee on Estimates, HC 128 (1955–56), x–xxiv; Special Report from the Select Committee on Estimates, HC 35 (1956–57), 3–4, 11–12.

45 L. Harris, 'How Profitable is Heathrow', *The Statist*, 18 January 1963, 175.

46 Fifth Report from the Estimates Committee, HC 233 (1960–61), v, xv.

47 Cmnd 4018 (1969), 44–5, 306–7.

48 Doganis, *A National Airport Plan*, (Fabian Tract 377), 7–8. The data relate to the mid 1960s.

49 British Airports Authority, *Annual Report and Accounts, 1970–71*, 18.

50 First Report from the Select Committee on Nationalised Industries: British Airports Authority, HC 275, 1970–71, xxxviii.

51 K. M. Johnson and H. C. Garnett, *The Economics of Containerisation* (1971), 12–15.

52 H. C. Garnett, 'Competition Between Ports and Investment Planning', *Scottish Journal of Political Economy*, 17 (1970), 411.

53 See below.

54 R. B. Oram, *The Story of Our Ports* (1969), 112–15.

55 In addition, there were also 52 minor ports of any commercial significance but these accounted for only 1.5 per cent of all port activity.

56 These were: London (Port of London Authority); Medway (Medway Conservancy Board); Milford Haven (Milford Haven Conservancy Board); Liverpool (Mersey Docks and Harbour Board); the Clyde Port Authority; The Forth Ports Authority; the Port of Tyne Authority; the Tees and Hartlepools Port Authority. The latter four were created estuarial authorities in the 1960s to manage a number of neighbouring ports. Thus in 1966 the Clyde Port Authority took over Glasgow (formerly managed by the Clyde Navigation Trust) as well as Greenock and Ardrossan. The Forth Port Authority became successor to the Leith Dock Commission in 1968 and also embraced Grangemouth, Burntisland, Methil, Granton and Kirkcaldy. In 1967 the Tees and Hartlepools Port Authority acquired the docks formerly belonging to the Tees Conservancy Commission, the Hartlepools Port and Harbour Commissioners as well as the docks at Middlesbrough and Hartlepools formerly owned by the British Transport Docks Board.

57 These were Hull, Immingham, Southampton, Swansea, Newport, Cardiff and Port Talbot. Altogether the British Transport Docks Board owned some 20 ports which accounted for about one third of all traffic. They were formerly owned by the British Transport Commission which had inherited most of them with the railways in 1948.

58 The City Corporation had a financial interest in the Company.

59 See T. G. Gillison, *The Secondary Ports with Special Reference to Unit Load Operations* (1969, Institute of Transport Thesis), 6–7, 141 *et seq.*

60 The packet ports (Folkestone, Heysham, Holyhead, Newhaven and Parkeston) together with Blyth and Poplar were transferred to the British Railways Board after the break-up of the British Transport Commission. These ports cater for short-sea crossings, traffic on which has expanded steadily since the war. Long-distance sea passenger traffic has declined rapidly with the competition from air transport and most of what is left is handled by London, Southampton and Liverpool.

61 Report of the Committee of Inquiry into the Major Ports of Great Britain, Cmnd 1824 (1962), 76–7, 159, 200, 214.

62 A. H. J. Brown, 'Ports and Shipping Turn-Round', *Journal of the Institute of Transport*, 25 (1952), 21.

63 *The Times Port of Liverpool Supplement*, 10 February 1958, iii; British Transport Commission, *Review of Trade Harbours, 1948–50:*

Reports by the Docks and Inland Waterways Executive (1951), 42, 57–8, 81.

64 Cmnd 1824 (1962), 62–5.

65 *Ibid*, Chapter 14; 'U.K. Shipping and Ports', *Financial Times*, 24 June 1957, p. 25; Catherine M. Cunningham, 'The Dock Industry on Merseyside', in R. Lawton and C. M. Cunningham, *Merseyside Social and Economic Studies* (1970), 239.

66 *Financial Times*, 4 November 1963, viii.

67 See G. Hallett and P. Randall, *Maritime Industry and Port Development in South Wales* (1970), 14–16.

68 The committee in fact stressed the need for change in every sphere of activity but only the major recommendations are considered here. For example, it urged that steps be taken to end casual employment among dock workers and to reduce the number of port employers.

69 After reference to the council.

70 Some of the provisions of the 1964 Act were amended or modified slightly by the Docks and Harbours Act 1966.

71 National Ports Council, *Port Development: An Interim Plan* (1965), 1–3.

72 J. M. Gifford, 'Rochdale 1962 and 1967', *Institute of Transport Journal*, 32 (1967), 178.

Index